Study Guide
to accompany

FINANCIAL ACCOUNTING
TOOLS FOR BUSINESS DECISION-MAKING

Fourth Canadian Edition

Paul D. Kimmel Ph.D., C.P.A.
University of Wisconsin–Milwaukee
Milwaukee, Wisconsin

Jerry J. Weygandt Ph.D., C.P.A.
Arthur Andersen Alumni Professor of Accounting
University of Wisconsin–Madison
Madison, Wisconsin

Donald E. Kieso Ph.D., C.P.A.
KPMG Emeritus Professor of Accountancy
North Illinois University
DeKalb, Illinois

Barbara Trenholm M.B.A., F.C.A.
University of New Brunswick
Fredericton, New Brunswick

PREPARED BY:

Cecelia M. Fewox
College of Charleston
Charleston, South Carolina

Gerry Dupont BComm, M.B.A.
Carleton University
Ottawa, Ontario

 John Wiley & Sons Canada, Ltd.

Library and Archives Canada Cataloguing in Publication

Dupont, Gerry
    Study guide to accompany Financial accounting, tools for business decision-making, fourth Canadian edition / Gerry Dupont.

Supplement to: Financial accounting.
ISBN 978-0-470-15573-8

    1. Accounting–Problems, exercises, etc. I. Title.

HF5635.F44 2009 Suppl.   657'.044   C2008-903804-5

Production Credits
Publisher: Veronica Visentin
Acquisitions Editor: Zoë Craig
Editorial Manager: Karen Staudinger
Vice President, Publishing Services: Karen Bryan
Developmental Editor: Daleara Hirjikaka
Editorial Assistant: Rachel Coffey
Marketing Manager: Aida Krneta
Design and Typesetting: Laserwords Private Limited, Chennai, India
Cover Design: Ian Koo
Printing and Binding: EPAC Book Services

Printed and bound in the United States of America
1 2 3 4 5 13 EP 12 11 10 09

John Wiley & Sons Canada, Ltd.
6045 Freemont Blvd.
Mississauga, Ontario L5R 4J3
Visit our website at www.wiley.ca

Contents

chapter 1

The Purpose and Use of Financial Statements

Chapter Overview

Chapter 1 introduces you to a variety of financial accounting topics. You will learn about the primary forms of business organizations and the three principal types of business activity. You will then learn about users of accounting information and how that information is delivered through the basic financial statements.

Review of Specific Study Objectives

Accounting is the information system that identifies and records the economic events of an organization, and then communicates them to a wide variety of interested users. It is very clear that the world's economic systems depend on highly transparent, reliable, and accurate financial reporting. In order for financial information to have value to its users, it must be prepared by individuals with high standards of ethical behaviour. Ethics in accounting is of the utmost importance to accountants and decision-makers who rely on the financial information they produce.

Accountants and other professionals have extensive rules of conduct to guide their behaviour with each other and the public. Business behaviour in general and accounting in particular are guided by improved business practices, corporate governance, public oversight, and accountability requirements.

> **study objective 1**
>
> Identify the users and uses of accounting.

The two broad types of users are internal users and external users:

- **Internal users** are the people who work for the business as well as managers who plan, organize, and run a business. Accounting information helps answer questions such as, "Does the business have enough resources to build a new manufacturing plant?" Internal reports help provide the required information.

- **External users** work outside of the business and include investors, who use accounting information for their share capital decisions; creditors, who evaluate the risk of lending to, and the credit-worthiness of, business borrowers; taxing authorities, which review compliance with tax laws; regulatory agencies, which review compliance with prescribed rules; customers; labour unions; and economic planners.

There are three different types of organizations. They are as follows:

- A **proprietorship** is a business owned by one person. It is simple to set up, and the owner has control over the business. Because they are so simple to organize, there are many thousands of proprietorships operating in the business world.

- A **partnership** is a business owned by more than one person. It provides strength in numbers: Each partner may bring economic resources or unique talents or skills to the combination.

- A **corporation** is a separate legal entity owned by shareholders. Advantages are that shares of ownership are easy to sell and the raising of funds is simple. There are many more proprietorships and partnerships than there are corporations, but corporations produce far more revenue.

study objective 2

Explain the three main types of business activity.

- There are **three types of business activity** that the accounting information system tracks: financing, investing, and operating.

- **Financing activities** deal with the ways a business raises funds for operations. The **two primary sources of outside funds** are borrowing money and issuing shares.

  - A business may **borrow money** by taking out a loan at a bank or borrowing money from other lenders. A **creditor** is a person or entity to whom a business owes money and a **liability** is a debt or other obligation, which represents creditors' claims on the business. There are short-term liabilities such as bank indebtedness and notes payable, resulting from direct borrowing or purchasing on credit. There are also long-term liabilities that can include notes payable, mortgages payable, lease obligations, and other types of debt securities borrowed for longer periods of time. A creditor has a legal right to be paid at an agreed-upon time and must be paid before an owner (shareholder) is paid.

  - A corporation may also **issue shares** to investors. Share capital is the term that describes the total amount paid into the corporation by shareholders for the shares purchased. Common shares are just one type or class of share that a company can issue. A shareholder is an owner of the business and receives payments in the form of dividends. (Please note that there are companies that do not pay dividends to shareholders). As noted above, shareholder claims are secondary to creditor claims.

  - Companies can also use cash for financing activities, such as repaying debt or repurchasing shares from investors.

- **Investing activities** involve the purchase of long-lived resources, called **assets**, which a company needs to operate. Examples of assets are property, plant, and equipment, such as land, buildings, and trucks.

- **Operating activities** are just that: operations of the business. Different businesses have different operations, of course. A paper company produces and sells paper, while a dairy company produces and sells milk. When a company operates, it earns revenues.

  - **Revenues** are increases in economic resources—normally increases in assets but sometimes decreases in liabilities—that result from the operating activities of a business.

  - **Expenses** are the cost of assets consumed, or services used, in the process of generating revenues. If revenues exceed expenses (hopefully!), then a business reports net earnings. If expenses exceed revenues, then a business incurs a net loss.

- Users of financial information are interested in a company's assets, liabilities, shareholders' equity, revenues, and expenses. This financial **information is provided in the form of financial statements**, which form the backbone of financial accounting. There are four financial statements: the statement of earnings, the statement of retained earnings, the balance sheet, and the cash flow statement.

study objective 3

Describe the content and purpose of each of the financial statements.

- The **statement of earnings** reports the success or failure of the company's operations for a period of time. Only **revenues and expenses** appear on the statement of earnings, along with their difference, either net earnings (revenues exceed expenses) or net loss (expenses exceed revenues). New accounting students often want to put the "Cash" account on the statement of earnings, but this is incorrect because cash is an asset (a resource owned by a business). Only revenues and expenses appear on the statement of earnings. Note that the **issue of shares and distribution of dividends do not affect net earnings**.

- The **statement of retained earnings** shows the amounts and causes of changes in the retained earnings balance during the period. Net earnings (or if there is a net loss, that amount is deducted) is added to beginning retained earnings, and then dividends are deducted. (Remember that a business will have either net earnings or net loss; it cannot have both at the same time.) Users of financial statements can find out about management's dividend policy by analyzing this statement. To summarize, the Retained Earnings account is the total of all the net earnings of the company, all the net losses it has incurred, and all the dividends it has paid. The statement of retained earnings documents this activity.

- The **balance sheet** reports assets and claims to those assets at a specific point in time. There are **two types of claims**: claims of creditors (liabilities) and claims of shareholders. The balance sheet is an expanded expression of the **basic accounting equation**, which is as follows:

$$\text{Assets} = \text{Liabilities} + \text{Shareholders' Equity}$$

Please note that this is a mathematical equation and must be in balance at all times. It can be used to answer questions such as: If assets total $100 and liabilities total $20, what is the total of shareholders' equity? (Answer: $80, because $20 plus something must equal $100, and that something must be $80.)

Shareholders' equity consists of **two parts**—share capital (often just one class of shares, common shares, is issued) and retained earnings.

- The **cash flow statement** provides financial information about the cash receipts and cash payments of a business for a specific period of time. Here, a user will find information about the financing, investing, and operating activities of the business.

- Note the **interrelationships between statements**:
    1. Net earnings or net loss from the statement of earnings appears on the statement of retained earnings.
    2. The ending balance of retained earnings is the same number reported on the balance sheet for retained earnings.
    3. The ending balance of cash must be the same, both on the balance sheet and on the cash flow statement.

- Companies usually present **comparative statements**, which are statements reporting information for more than one period, normally two years.

- Please be aware of the following when you **prepare financial statements**:
    1. All statements **must have a heading**. The company name appears on the first line, the name of the document appears on the second line, and the date appears on the third line. With respect to **dates**, the **balance sheet date** is for one point in time (June 30, 2009, or December 31, 2009), while the **date on the statement of earnings, the statement of retained earnings, and the cash flow statement** is for a period of time ("Month ended June 30, 2009" or "Year ended December 31, 2009").
    2. The number at the top of a column should have a dollar sign: this indicates that it is the first number in that column. The final number on a statement, such as Net Earnings or Total Assets, should have a dollar sign and be double-underlined. This indicates that it is the "answer." If there is a negative number, such as Net Loss, then it should be presented in parentheses or brackets. These are parts of a type of shorthand used by people who prepare statements and understood by users of statements.
    3. Numbers are normally reported in thousands of dollars, thus the last three zeroes are omitted.

Chapter Self-Test

As you work through the questions and problems, remember to use the **Decision Toolkit** discussed and used in the text:

1. *Decision Checkpoints*: At this point, you ask a question.
2. *Info Needed for Decision*: You make a choice regarding the information needed to answer the question.
3. *Tool to Use for Decision*: At this point, you review just what the information chosen in step 2 does for the decision-making process.
4. *How to Evaluate Results*: You perform evaluation of information for answering the question.

Note: The notation (SO1) means that the question was drawn from study objective number one.

Multiple Choice

Please circle the correct answer.

(SO1)   1. Which of the following statements is correct?
      a.   A proprietor has no personal liability for debts of his or her business.
      b.   There are far more corporations than there are proprietorships and partnerships.

    c.   Revenue produced by corporations is generally greater than that produced by proprietorships and partnerships.

    d.   It is very difficult for a corporation to raise capital.

2. Which of the following would not be considered an internal user of accounting   (SO1)
data for a particular company?
   a. Marketing manager
   b. Investor
   c. Accounting clerk
   d. Engineering supervisor

3. Which of the following is an example of an external user of accounting   (SO1)
information?
   a. Marketing manager of the business
   b. President of the labour union
   c. Officer of the corporation
   d. Production supervisor of the business

4. The buying of a delivery truck needed to operate a business is an example   (SO2)
of a(n)
   a. financing activity.
   b. delivering activity.
   c. operating activity.
   d. investing activity.

    (SO1)

5. A business organized as a corporation
   a. is not a separate legal entity in most provinces.
   b. requires that shareholders be personally liable for the debts of the
      business.
   c. is not owned by its shareholders.
   d. has tax advantages over a proprietorship or partnership.   (SO1)

6. Which of the following groups uses accounting information to determine
whether the company's net earnings will result in a share price increase?
   a. Investors in common shares
   b. Marketing managers
   c. Creditors
   d. Chief Financial Officer   (SO2)

7. Which of the following activities involves raising the necessary funds to support
the business?
   a. Operating
   b. Investing
   c. Financing
   d. Delivering   (SO2)

8. Which activities involve putting the resources of the business into action to
generate a profit?
   a. Delivering
   b. Financing

        c.   Investing
        d.   Operating

(SO2)   9. Which of the following is an investing activity?
        a.   Borrowing money from a bank
        b.   Earning revenue from the sale of products
        c.   Incurring salaries expense
        d.   The purchase of a delivery truck

(SO2)   10. A business's earning of revenues is considered to be a(n)
        a.   operating activity.
        b.   investing activity.
        c.   financing activity.
        d.   balance sheet activity.

(SO2)   11. Borrowing money from a bank is considered to be a(n)
        a.   operating activity.
        b.   investing activity.
        c.   financing activity.
        d.   balance sheet activity.

(SO3)   12. Which of the following accounts will be found on a statement of earnings?
        a.   Revenues, expenses, and dividends
        b.   Revenues and expenses
        c.   Revenues, expenses, and cash
        d.   Expenses, dividends, and cash

(SO3)   13. If revenues are $20,000 and expenses are $5,000, then the business
        a.   incurred a net loss of $25,000.
        b.   had net earnings of $20,000.
        c.   had net earnings of $15,000.
        d.   incurred a net loss of $15,000.

(SO3)   14. If beginning retained earnings is $10,000, net loss is $3,000, and dividends are $1,000, then the ending retained earnings shown on the statement of retained earnings is
        a. $14,000.
        b. $12,000.
        c. $8,000.
        d. $6,000.

(SO3)   15. Which of the following is an appropriate date for a balance sheet?
        a.   December 31, 2009
        b.   Month ending December 31, 2009
        c.   Quarter ending December 31, 2009
        d.   Year ending December 31, 2009

16. Which of the following is the correct expression of the basic accounting equation?   (SO3)
    a.   Liabilities = Assets + Shareholders' Equity
    b.   Shareholders' Equity = Assets + Liabilities
    c.   Assets = Liabilities + Shareholders' Equity
    d.   Assets = Liabilities – Shareholders' Equity

17. Assets total $20,000, common shares total $9,000, and retained earnings total   (SO3)
    $6,000. What is the dollar amount of liabilities?
    a. $23,000
    b. $17,000
    c. $11,000
    d. $5,000

18. The statement that shows the operating, investing, and financing activities of a   (SO3)
    business is the
    a.   statement of retained earnings.
    b.   cash flow statement.
    c.   statement of earnings.
    d.   balance sheet.

19. At the end of year 2008, a company had total assets of $100,000 and total   (SO3)
    shareholders' equity of $60,000. During year 2009, this same company had net
    earnings of $15,000 and at the end of year 2009 had total assets of $120,000.
    As a result of this activity, total liabilities at the end of 2009
    a.   increased by $5,000.
    b.   had an ending balance of $60,000 at the end of year 2009.
    c.   decreased by $15,000.
    d.   had an ending balance of $75,000 at the end of year 2009.

Problems

1. From the appropriate accounts given below, please prepare a balance sheet for   (SO3)
   Jerome Corporation on September 30, 2009:

Common shares	15,000
Service revenue	20,000
Notes payable	5,000
Salaries expense	10,000
Accounts receivable	7,000
Dividends	2,000
Unearned revenue	6,000
Retained earnings	24,000
Supplies	2,000
Insurance expense	1,500
Prepaid insurance	3,000
Utilities expense	4,000
Office equipment	17,000
Accounts payable	1,000
Cash	22,000

(SO3)   2. Use the following accounts and information to prepare, in good form, a statement of earnings, a statement of retained earnings, and a balance sheet for Azro Corporation for the month ended September 30, 2009.

Maintenance expense	2,400
Accounts receivable	1,400
Office buildings	60,000
Supplies	400
Revenues	16,100
Common shares	52,000
Retained earnings (beginning)	18,900
Dividends	1,000
Insurance expense	2,200
Cash	15,600
Notes payable	3,300
Accounts payable	3,100
Salaries expense	10,000
Income tax expense	400

(SO3)   3. Classify each of the following items first as a financing, investing, or operating activity, and then indicate whether the transaction increases or decreases cash.

a. Inventory is purchased for cash.
b. A company sells services for cash.
c. A company buys equipment for cash.
d. Dividends are paid to shareholders.
e. A company sells equipment for cash.
f. Employees are paid.
g. A company borrows money from the bank.
h. A company issues shares.
i. A company pays back a loan.

4. Please refer to the Domtar Corporation and Cascades Inc. financial statements found in the appendices at the end of this study guide for information for answering the following questions. Do not forget to use the **Decision Toolkit** approach for help in the problem solving.

(SO3)   a. For Domtar and Cascades, what is the total dollar amount of each of the company's classes of assets in 2007?

(SO3)   b. For Domtar and Cascades, which class of liabilities has the largest total dollar amount in 2007?

(SO3)   c. Were the companies profitable in 2007? What has been the trend for each of the company's net earnings over the three years shown?

(SO3)   d. What was the biggest expense in 2007, for each of the companies?

Solutions to Self-Test

Multiple Choice

1. c   Proprietors are liable for debts of their businesses, there are more proprietorships and partnerships than there are corporations, and corporations can raise capital through selling of shares and bonds.

2. b   The investor **would not** be considered an internal user.

3. b   The marketing manager, corporation officer, and production supervisor all work for the business and are therefore internal users.

4. d   The buying of a long-lived asset, such as a delivery truck, is an investing activity.

5. c   Corporations are legal entities and do not require shareholders to be personally responsible for debts of the business and are owned by shareholders.

6. a   Accounting information will be the major source that investors use to assess whether earnings will result in a share price increase.

7. c   The raising of funds is a financing activity.

8. d   The day-to-day operations where revenue is generated and expenses are incurred to generate a profit are called operating activities.

9. d   Borrowing money is a financing activity, and earning revenue and incurring expense are operating activities.

10. a   Investing activities deal with the purchase of assets, and financing activities deal with the borrowing of money and selling of shares.

11. c   Borrowing money is a financing activity.

12. b   Dividends appear on the statement of retained earnings, and cash is an asset on the balance sheet.

13. c $20,000 - $5,000 = $15,000

14. d $10,000 - $3,000 - $1,000 = $6,000

15. a   The balance sheet shows balances on a specific date, not for a period of time.

16. c   Answer c is the correct expression of the accounting equation.

17. d   Assets = Liabilities + Shareholders' Equity

    Total Shareholders' Equity = Common Shares + Retained Earnings. ($9,000 + $6,000 = $15,000). Therefore, Assets - Shareholders' Equity = Liabilities ($20,000 - $15,000 = $5,000)

18. b   The statement of retained earnings shows changes in the retained earnings account over the period, the statement of earnings summarizes revenue and expense activity, and the balance sheet shows assets, liabilities, and shareholders' equity items.

19. a   Using the accounting equation A = L + SE, at the end of 2009, A of $100,000 - SE of $60,000 = L of $40,000. During 2009, net earnings would increase SE from $60,000 to $75,000 because net earnings is a subdivision of SE. At the end of 2009, A of $120,000 - SE of $75,000 = L of $45,000. Therefore liabilities increased from $40,000 at the end of 2008 to $45,000 at the end of 2009, or a $5,000 increase.

Problems

1.

JEROME CORPORATION
Balance Sheet
September 30, 2009

Assets

Cash	$22,000
Accounts receivable	7,000
Supplies	2,000
Prepaid insurance	3,000
Office equipment	17,000
Total assets	$51,000

Liabilities and Shareholders' Equity

Liabilities

Notes payable	$5,000	
Accounts payable	1,000	
Unearned revenue	6,000	
Total liabilities		$12,000

Shareholders' equity

Common shares	$15,000	
Retained earnings	24,000	
Total shareholders' equity		39,000
Total liabilities and shareholders' equity		$51,000

2.

AZRO CORPORATION
Statement of Earnings
Month Ended September 30, 2009

Revenues		
Revenues		$16,100
Expenses		
Salaries expense	$10,000	
Maintenance expense	2,400	
Insurance expense	2,200	
Total expenses		14,600
Earnings before income taxes		1,500
Income tax expense		400
Net earnings		$ 1,100

AZRO CORPORATION
Statement of Retained Earnings
Month Ended September 30, 2009

Retained earnings, September 1	$18,900
Add: Net earnings	1,100
	20,000
Less: Dividends	1,000
Retained earnings, September 30	$19,000

AZRO CORPORATION
Balance Sheet
September 30, 2009

Assets

Cash	$15,600
Accounts receivable	1,400
Supplies	400
Office buildings	60,000
Total assets	$77,400

Liabilities and Shareholders' Equity

Liabilities		
Accounts payable	$3,100	
Notes payable	3,300	
Total liabilities		$ 6,400
Shareholders' equity		
Common shares	$52,000	
Retained earnings	19,000	
Total shareholders' equity		71,000
Total liabilities and shareholders' equity		$77,400

3.

a.   Operating activity; cash is decreased.
b.   Operating activity; cash is increased.
c.   Investing activity; cash is decreased.
d.   Financing activity; cash is decreased.
e.   Investing activity; cash is increased.
f.   Operating activity; cash is decreased.
g.   Financing activity; cash is increased.
h.   Financing activity; cash is increased.
i.   Financing activity; cash is decreased.

4. Please note that all dollars shown on the financial statements and below are stated in millions of Canadian dollars for Cascades and millions of U.S. dollars for Domtar.

a.

	Domtar	Cascades
Current assets	$1,798	$1,204
Property, plant, and equipment (net)	5,362	1,886
Intangible assets	111	130
Goodwill	372	312
Other assets	105	237
Total assets	$7,748	$3,769

b. Long-term debt was the largest class of liabilities for each company, in the amounts of $2,213 for Domtar and $1,570 for Cascades.

c. Domtar was profitable in 2007. It incurred net earnings of $70 in 2007, which compares with a net loss of $609 in 2006 and a net loss of $478 in 2005. Cascades was profitable in 2007 reporting net earnings of $95, which compares with net earnings of $3 in 2006, and a net loss of $97 in 2005.

d. Cost of sales was the largest expense for both companies: $4,757 for Domtar and $3,201 for Cascades.

chapter 2

Financial Statements— Framework, Presentation, and Usage

Chapter Overview

Chapter 2 explains the conceptual framework of accounting, which provides a general guide for financial reporting. You will take a further look at the balance sheet and learn how to evaluate information provided by a company's financial statements.

Review of Specific Study Objectives

Conceptual Framework of Accounting

study objective 1

Describe the conceptual framework of accounting, including the objective, qualitative characteristics, and elements of financial reporting.

- The **conceptual framework** of accounting guides decisions of what to present in financial statements and has four main sections:

  1. The objective of financial reporting
  2. The qualitative characteristics of accounting information
  3. The elements of financial statements
  4. Recognition and measurement criteria (assumptions, principles, and constraints)

The Objective of Financial Reporting

- The main objective of financial **reporting** is to provide useful information for decision-making. More specifically, the conceptual framework states that the

objective of financial reporting is to communicate information that is useful to current and potential investors, creditors, and other users when they are making their resource allocation decisions.

Qualitative Characteristics of Accounting Information

- To be useful, information should have the following **qualitative characteristics**: relevance, faithful representation, comparability, and understandability.

- Accounting information has **relevance** if it influences a business decision. Relevant information helps users make predictions about the potential effects of past, present, or future transactions or other events. It is therefore said to have predictive value. Relevant information also helps users confirm or correct their previous expectations. It is said to have feedback value. For accounting information to be relevant, it must also be timely.

- For information to be useful, it must be a **faithful representation** of what really exists or happened. Faithful representation also means that the information must be verifiable, neutral, and complete. Verifiability means that two or more people reviewing the same information and using the same methods would reach the same results or similar conclusions. Neutrality means the absence of bias. That is, accounting information cannot be selected, prepared, or presented to favour one set of interested users over another. Completeness means that all the information that is needed to faithfully represent economic reality must be included. Factual, unbiased, and complete information is critical in financial reporting.

- **Comparability** enables users to identify the similarities and differences from period to period, or across companies. Accounting information is comparable when different companies use the same accounting principles or when one company uses the same accounting principles from year to year. Accounting information should also be consistent, which means that a company should use the same accounting treatment for similar events from year to year. However, this does not mean that a company must use the same principles forever after making the initial selection. If the company makes changes in order to produce more meaningful information, then it must disclose the change in the notes to the financial statements.

- Accounting information is **understandable** if the average user has an understanding of accounting concepts and procedures, as well as an understanding of general business and economic conditions, so that the financial statements can be intelligently studied.

Elements of Financial Statements

study objective 2

Identify and apply assumptions, principles, and constraints of the conceptual framework.

- The elements of financial statements include terms such as assets, liabilities, equity, revenue, and expenses. These terms are discussed later in this chapter.

Recognition and Measurement Criteria

- Recognition and measurement criteria are classified as **assumptions**, **principles**, and **constraints**.

Assumptions

- Four assumptions guide when to recognize events and how to measure them:

    1. The **monetary unit** assumption, which requires that only those things that can be expressed in money are included in the accounting records. Customer satisfaction and a loyal, competent workforce are extremely important, but these do not appear on a financial statement.

    2. The **economic entity assumption**, which states that every economic entity can be separately identified and accounted for. If an individual owns a business, that individual must have two sets of records: one for that individual's transactions and one for the business.

    3. **Time period assumption**, which states that the life of a business can be divided into artificial time periods, and that useful reports covering those periods can be prepared for the business.

    4. The **going concern assumption**, which states that the business will remain in operation for the foreseeable future. This principle underlies much of what we do in accounting. If it seems likely that a company will go out of business in the near future, then different assumptions will govern the preparation of the financial statements.

Accounting Principles

- **Generally accepted accounting principles** (GAAP) are a recognized set of principles used in financial reporting. These principles are widely recognized and have authoritative support through the Canadian and provincial business corporations acts and securities legislation. Canada is in the process of moving from Canadian generally accepted accounting principles to International Financial Reporting Standards. The changeover will be fully effective by January 1, 2011.

- Four accounting **principles** are covered in the textbook, of which the following two are covered in this chapter:

    1. The **cost principle**, which dictates that assets are recorded at their cost, not only at the time of their acquisition but also for the entire time that they are held. There is much discussion about the relevance of this principle, especially for predicting the value of an asset. Over time, the fair value (amount it could be sold for) of an asset can be substantially different than its historical cost. Therefore, some argue that fair value is more representative of the value of the asset than its historical cost. Supporters of the cost principle say that cost is the more faithful representation because it can be easily verified and is neutral. Fair value, on the other hand, is more subjective. The movement to international financial reporting standards is expected to result in even more of a mixed cost and fair valuation model. We will learn more about this in later chapters, but for now we will concentrate on using cost to record transactions.

    2. The **full disclosure principle**, which requires that all circumstances and events that would make a difference to the users of the financial statements be disclosed, either in the statements themselves or in the notes and supporting schedules that accompany the statements and are an integral part of them.

Constraints in Accounting

- **Constraints** permit a company to modify GAAP without jeopardizing the usefulness of the reported information. Two of these constraints are materiality and cost-benefit.

    1. An item is **material** if it influences the decision of an investor or creditor. It is important to note that what is material for one company may be immaterial for another. Assume that companies A and B each have a $1,000 error in the financial statements. Company A's net earnings is $10,000, while company B's net earnings is $100,000. The $1,000 error most likely will be material for A because it is 10 percent of net earnings, while it most likely will be immaterial for B because it is only 1 percent of net earnings.

    2. The **cost-benefit** constraint ensures that the value of the information exceeds the cost of providing it.

The Classified Balance Sheet

study objective 3

Identify the sections of a classified balance sheet.

- The **balance sheet** of a company presents a snapshot of its financial position at any point in time. A **classified balance sheet** breaks the statement components into several classifications, usually having four asset categories, two liability categories, and two shareholders' equity categories.

- The following are the **four common asset categories**:

    1. **Current assets** are those expected to be converted into cash or used in the business within a relatively short period of time, usually within one year. Current assets are listed in the order in which they are expected to be converted into cash and include **cash, short-term investments, receivables, inventories, and prepaid expenses**.

    2. **Long-term investments** are investments in shares and bonds of other corporations that are normally held for many years.

    3. **Property, plant, and equipment** are assets with physical substance that have relatively long useful lives and are used in the operations of the business. Examples include **land, buildings, equipment,** and **furniture**. These long-lived assets, except land, have estimated useful lives over which they are expected to generate revenues. Because property, plant, and equipment benefit future periods, their cost is matched to revenues over their estimated useful life through a process called **depreciation**. The sum of all past depreciation is called **accumulated depreciation**. It is a contra asset that is subtracted from the asset itself. The difference between the cost and accumulated depreciation is referred to as the **carrying amount** of the asset.

    4. **Intangible assets** are assets that have no physical substance. They are essentially long-lived rights. Examples include **goodwill, patents, copyrights, trademarks, trade names, and licences that give the company exclusive right of use**. Similar to buildings and equipment, intangible assets with estimated useful lives are also amortized over their useful lives. Similar to land, intangible assets with indefinite lives are not amortized. Note that the term used with respect to intangibles is *amortized*, while *depreciated* is the term used with respect to property, plant, and equipment.

- The following are the **two common liability categories**:

    1. **Current liabilities** are obligations that are to be paid within one year. Examples include **accounts payable, short-term notes payable, salaries payable, interest payable, taxes payable, and current maturities of long-term obligations**. Notes payable are usually listed first, followed by accounts payable and other current liabilities.

2. **Long-term liabilities** are expected to be paid after one year from the balance sheet date. If the balance sheet date is December 31, 2009, and an obligation is due on June 30, 2012, then the obligation is long term. Examples include **bonds payable, mortgages payable, long-term notes payable, lease liabilities, and pension liabilities**. There is no particular guidance for listing these long-term obligations, and companies simply choose a way of disclosing them that is most useful to the users of their financial statements.

● **Shareholders' equity** has two components: share capital and retained earnings. Share capital consists of shareholders' **investments** of assets in the business, while retained earnings is just that: earnings retained for use in the business.

Using the Statement of Earnings

● Financial statements are used to gauge the strength or weakness of a company. To make the numbers in the statements more useful and meaningful, users conduct **ratio analysis**, a technique for expressing relationships among selected financial statement data.

| study objective 4 |
| Identify and calculate ratios for analyzing a company's profitability. |

● **Profitability ratios** measure the earnings or operating success of a company for a given period of time. Two such ratios are the **earnings per share** and the **price-earnings ratio**.

● The **earnings per share** measures the net earnings for each common share. It is calculated by dividing net earnings available to the common shareholders by the weighted average number of common shares issued during the year.

● The **price-earnings ratio** measures the ratio of the market price of each share to its earnings per share. It is calculated by dividing the market price per share by earnings per share. The price-earnings ratio reflects the investors' assessment of a company's future earnings.

● Please note that one ratio by itself does not convey very much. The ratio must be compared with something—with the ratios from prior years of the company, the ratios of other companies in the same industry, or the particular industry's averages.

Using the Balance Sheet

● **Liquidity** refers to a company's ability to pay obligations expected to fall due within the next year or operating cycle.

● One measure of liquidity is **working capital**, which is the difference between current assets and current liabilities. It is certainly preferable to have a positive number (current assets exceed current liabilities) because this indicates that a company has a good likelihood of being able to pay its liabilities. If current assets are $300 and current liabilities are $100, then the working capital is $200.

| study objective 5 |
| Identify and calculate ratios for analyzing a company's liquidity and solvency. |

● Another measure of liquidity is the **current ratio**, which is calculated by dividing current assets by current liabilities. Referring to the numbers just above, dividing $300 by $100 yields a current ratio of 3:1, meaning that the company has $3 of current assets for every $1 of current liabilities. Remember that a ratio by itself does not convey very much information. The current ratio is impacted by the liquidity of the accounts receivable and inventory, which must also be reviewed before evaluating the current ratio. Each of these effects is considered in later chapters.

● **Solvency** deals with a company's ability to survive over a long period of time, with its ability to pay its long-term obligations and the interest due on them.

- The **debt to total assets ratio** is one source of information about a company's solvency and measures the percentage of assets financed by creditors rather than invested by shareholders. It is calculated by dividing total debt (both current and long term) by total assets. The higher the percentage of debt financing, the greater is the risk that the company may be unable to pay its debts as they mature. If total debt is $3 million and total assets are $5 million, then the ratio is 60 percent, meaning that for every dollar invested in company assets, creditors have provided $0.60. A creditor does not like to see a high debt to total assets ratio for a company.

Using the Cash Flow Statement

- The cash flow statement reports the cash effects of a company's operating activities, investing activities, and financing activities. Cash provided by operating activities is often adjusted to take into account that a company must invest in new assets to maintain its current level of operations. In addition, companies must also keep paying dividends to satisfy investors. The result is known as **free cash flow**, which is a solvency-based measure. It is calculated by subtracting the sum of net capital expenditures and dividends paid from cash provided by operating activities. It indicates the cash available for paying dividends or expanding operations.

Chapter Self-Test

As you work through the questions and problems, remember to use the **Decision Toolkit** discussed and used in the text:

1. *Decision Checkpoints*: At this point, you ask a question.
2. *Info Needed for Decision*: You make a choice regarding the information needed to answer the question.
3. *Tool to Use for Decision*: At this point, you review just what the information chosen in step 2 does for the decision-making process.
4. *How to Evaluate Results*: You conduct an evaluation of information for answering the question.

Note: The notation (SO1) means that the question is drawn from study objective number one.

Multiple Choice

Please circle the correct answer.

(SO1)   1. If accounting information has relevance, it is useful in making predictions about
    a.   future government audits.
    b.   new accounting principles.
    c.   foreign currency exchange rates.
    d.   the future events of a company.

(SO1)   2. Accounting information should be neutral in order to enhance
    a.   faithful representation.
    b.   materiality.

    c.   comparability.
    d.   timeliness.

3. Accounting information is _____ if it makes a difference in a user's decision. (SO1)
    a.   material
    b.   relevant
    c.   comparable
    d.   understandable

4. _____ results when different companies use the same accounting (SO1)
principles.
    a.   Relevance
    b.   Understandability
    c.   Comparability
    d.   Reliability

5. Accounting assumptions include (SO1)
    a.   materiality.
    b.   monetary unit.
    c.   historical cost.
    d.   neutrality.

6. Accounting rules having substantial authoritative support and recognized as a (SO2)
general guide for financial reporting purposes are called
    a.   general accounting principles.
    b.   generally accepted auditing principles.
    c.   generally accepted accounting standards.
    d.   generally accepted accounting principles (GAAP).

7. Which of the following assumptions states that every business must be separately (SO2)
identified and accounted for?
    a.   Monetary unit assumption
    b.   Economic entity assumption
    c.   Time period assumption
    d.   Going concern assumption

8. Which of the following assumes that a business will remain in operation for the (SO2)
foreseeable future?
    a.   Monetary unit assumption
    b.   Economic entity assumption
    c.   Time period assumption
    d.   Going concern assumption

9. Which of the following requires that all circumstances and events that would (SO2)
make a difference to users of financial statements, should be disclosed?
    a.   Full disclosure principle
    b.   Economic entity assumption
    c.   Time period assumption
    d.   Cost principle

(SO2)   10. The _____ assumption states that the life of a business can be
          divided into artificial time periods and that useful reports covering those periods
          can be prepared for the business.
          a.   monetary unit
          b.   going concern
          c.   time period
          d.   economic entity

(SO2)   11. An item is _____ if it is likely to influence the decision of an investor or
          creditor.
          a.   consistent
          b.   reliable
          c.   conservative
          d.   material

(SO2)   12. The constraint that says "Make sure the information is worth it," is
          a.   cost-benefit.
          b.   materiality.
          c.   relevance.
          d.   reliability.

(SO3)   13. Which of the following statements report the ending balance of the retained
          earnings account?
          a.   Statement of retained earnings and balance sheet
          b.   Statement of retained earnings only
          c.   Balance sheet only
          d.   Cash flow statement

(SO3)   14. Which of the following is considered a current asset on a classified balance
          sheet?
          a.   Short-term investments
          b.   Land
          c.   Building
          d.   Patent

(SO3)   15. Which of the following is classified as property, plant, or equipment on a balance
          sheet?
          a.   Supplies
          b.   Investment in Intel Corporation shares
          c.   Land
          d.   Copyright

(SO3)   16. Current liabilities are $10,000, long-term liabilities are $20,000, common
          shares are $50,000, and retained earnings totals $70,000. Total shareholders'
          equity is
          a. $150,000.
          b. $140,000.

    c. $120,000.
    d. $ 70,000.

17. Net earnings available to common shareholders is $90,000 and the weighted   (SO4)
average number of common shares during the year is 50,000. The earnings
per share is
    a. $2.00.
    b. $1.80.
    c. $1.50.
    d. $1.60.

18. Net earnings available to common shareholders is $140,000 and the weighted   (SO4)
average number of common shares during the year is 80,000. The market price of
each common share is $8.75. The price-earnings ratio is
    a.   5.
    b.   4.
    c.   4.375.
    d.   16.

19. The ability to pay obligations that are expected to become due within the next   (SO5)
year is called
    a.   working capital.
    b.   profitability.
    c.   solvency.
    d.   liquidity.

20. Current assets are $60,000, total assets are $180,000, current liabilities are   (SO5)
$30,000, and total liabilities are $50,000. The current ratio is
    a.   2:1.
    b.   1.2:1.
    c.   0.5:1.
    d.   0.3:1.

21. Which ratio measures the percentage of assets financed by creditors rather than   (SO5)
by shareholders?
    a.   Current ratio
    b.   Debt to total assets ratio
    c.   Free cash flow ratio
    d.   Price-earnings ratio

22. Which of the following statements provides information about the operating,   (SO5)
investing, and financing activities of a company?
    a.   Cash flow statement
    b.   Balance sheet
    c.   Statement of earnings
    d.   Statement of retained earnings

23. Free cash flow: (SO5)
    a.   Is a liquidity-based measure.
    b.   Is calculated by using information shown on the balance sheet.

    c.   Measures a company's ability to pay its short-term debts.
    d.   Helps investors assess how much money a company has to pay additional dividends.

(SO4)   24. Net earnings is $7,500, total assets are $500,000, weighted average number of shares is 5,000, market price per share is $20, sales are $100,000, total liabilities are $357,140. Based on this information, the price-earnings ratio is

    a.   1.4.
    b.   13.3.
    c.   1.0.
    d.   10.0.

Problems

(SO1, 2)   1.   Qualitative characteristics of accounting information, assumptions, principles, and constraints are shown below.

1. Going concern	7. Faithful representation
2. Predictive value	8. Comparability
3. Neutrality	9. Feedback value
4. Understandability	10. Cost-benefit
5. Economic entity	11. Consistency
6. Timeliness	12. Full disclosure

Match each of the following statements with one of the items on the above list.

_____ a.   You need to have one set of books for each business activity.

_____ b.   Accounting information cannot be presented to favour one set of users over another.

_____ c.   Information that is presented must portray what really happened.

_____ d.   The average user of accounting information is expected to have a reasonable understanding of accounting concepts and procedures, as well as a general understanding of business and economic conditions.

_____ e.   A company uses the same accounting treatment for similar events from year to year.

_____ f.   Relevant information helps users make predictions about the potential effects of past, present, or future transactions or other events.

_____ g.   Accounting information must be available to decision-makers before it loses its ability to influence their decisions.

_____ h.   The business will remain in operation for the foreseeable future.

_____ i.   Companies with similar circumstances use the same accounting standards.

_____ j.   Financial statements are expected to confirm and not correct expectations.

_____ k.   The benefits of financial reporting information should justify the costs of providing and using it.

_____ l.   This requires that all circumstances and events, which would make a difference to users of financial statement, be disclosed.

2. The following presents December 31, 2009, year-end balances for the Variety   (SO3)
   Corporation:

Cash	$5,900
Accounts payable	3,300
Accumulated depreciation–equipment	13,500
Prepaid insurance	1,400
Common shares	25,000
Intangible assets	5,500
Accounts receivable	13,600
Retained earnings	49,300
Equipment	63,000
Land	10,500
Inventory	14,400
Long-term notes payable	20,000
Wages payable	3,200

Prepare a classified balance sheet.

3. Consider the following data from Meadows Corporation:

	2009	2008
Current assets	$61,000	$50,000
Total assets	108,000	85,000
Current liabilities	47,000	39,000
Total liabilities	80,000	62,000
Net sales	200,000	180,000
Net earnings available to common shareholders	30,000	20,000
Market price per common share	9	6.4
Weighted average number of common shares	30,000	25,000

Calculate the following and explain what the results mean:
   a. Working capital for 2009 and 2008.   (SO5)
   b. Current ratio for 2009 and 2008.   (SO5)
   c. Debt to total assets for 2009 and 2008.   (SO5)
   d. Earnings per share for 2009 and 2008.   (SO4)
   e. Price-earnings ratio for 2009 and 2008.   (SO4)

4. Please refer to the Domtar and Cascades financial statements found in the   (SO3, 5)
   appendices at the end of this study guide for information for answering the following questions. Do not forget to use the **Decision Toolkit** approach for help in
   the problem solving.

   a. The balance sheet for Domtar shows property, plant, and equipment of
       U.S. $5,362 million at the end of 2007. What does this amount represent?
   b. Can Cascades meet its near-term obligations in 2007 and 2006? Please
       comment on the trend that you see.
   c. Calculate the debt to total assets ratio for both companies for 2007.

Solutions to Self-Test

Multiple Choice

1. d   Future events of a company influences business decisions.

2. a   Faithful representation means information must be verifiable, neutral, and complete.

3. a   Accounting information that is relevant helps users make proper decisions.

4. c   It makes it easier to compare companies who use the same accounting principles.

5. b   Four assumptions guide when to recognize and how to measure events: monetary unit, economic entity, time period, and going concern.

6. d   Generally accepted accounting principles are a recognized set of principles used in financial reporting.

7. b   The monetary unit assumption requires that only those things that can be expressed in money are included in the accounting records; the time period assumption states that the life of a business can be divided into artificial time periods; and the going concern assumption assumes that a business will remain in operation for the foreseeable future.

8. d   The going concern assumption states that a business will remain in operation for the foreseeable future.

9. a   The economic entity assumption states that every business must be separately identified and accounted for; the time period assumption states that the life of a business can be divided into artificial time periods; and the cost principle dictates that assets are recorded at their cost.

10. c   The time period assumption states that the life of a business can be divided into artificial time periods.

11. d   An item is material when it is likely to influence the decision of an investor or creditor.

12. a   The cost-benefit constraint ensures that the value of the information exceeds the cost of providing it.

13. a   The statement of retained earnings reports the ending balance of the retained earnings account. So, too, does the balance sheet, in its shareholders' equity section.

14. a   Land, Building, and Patent are all long-term assets.

15. c   Supplies is a current asset, investment is not a property, plant, or equipment item, and copyright is an intangible asset.

16. c $50,000 + $70,000 = $120,000.

17. b $900,000 ÷ 50,000 common shares = $1.80.

18. a   Earnings per share = $140,000 ÷ 80,000 common shares = $1.75. Price-earnings ratio = $8.75 ÷ $1.75 = 5.

19. d   Working capital is the difference between current assets and current liabilities. Profitability refers to the operating success of a company during a period. Solvency is the ability of a company to pay interest as it comes due and to repay the face value of the debt at maturity.

20. a $60,000 \div \$30,000 = 2:1$.

21. b The debt to total assets ratio is the percentage of assets financed by creditors rather than invested by shareholders.

22. a The balance sheet reports assets, liabilities, and shareholders' equity items. The statement of earnings reports revenues and expenses. The statement of retained earnings reports changes in the retained earnings account.

23. d Free cash flow indicates the cash available for paying additional dividends or expanding operations.

24. b EPS = $7,500 \div 5,000 = \$1.50$.

   P-E Ratio = $20 \div \$1.50 = 13.3$ times.

Problems

1.

a.	5	g.	6
b.	3	h.	1
c.	7	i.	8
d.	4	j.	9
e.	11	k.	10
f.	2	l.	12

2.

VARIETY CORPORATION
Balance Sheet
December 31, 2009

Assets

Current assets

Cash	$5,900	
Accounts receivable	13,600	
Inventory	14,400	
Prepaid insurance	1,400	
Total current assets		$35,300

Property, plant, and equipment

Land		$10,500	
Equipment	$63,000		
Less: accumulated depreciation—equipment	13,500	49,500	
Total property, plant, and equipment			60,000

Intangible assets		5,500
Total assets		$100,800

Liabilities and Shareholders' Equity

Current liabilities

Accounts payable	$ 3,300	
Wages payable	3,200	
Total current liabilities		$ 6,500
Long-term liabilities		
Notes payable		20,000
Total liabilities		26,500
Shareholders' equity		
Common shares	$ 25,000	
Retained earnings	49,300	
Total shareholders' equity		74,300
Total liabilities and shareholders' equity		$100,800

3.

a. Current Assets – Current Liabilities = Working Capital
2009: $61,000 – $47,000 = $14,000
2008: $50,000 – $39,000 = $11,000
Working capital is a measure of liquidity. Since this company's working capital is positive, there is a greater likelihood that it will pay its liabilities.

b. Current Assets ÷ Current Liabilities = Current Ratio
2009: $61,000 ÷ $47,000 = 1.30:1
2008: $50,000 ÷ $39,000 = 1.28:1
The current ratio is another measure of liquidity. In 2009, the company had $1.30 of current assets for every dollar of current liabilities. In 2008, it had $1.28 of current assets for every dollar of current liabilities.

c. Total Debt ÷ Total Assets = Debt to Total Assets
2009: $80,000 ÷ $108,000 = 74%
2008: $62,000 ÷ $85,000 = 73%
This ratio measures the percentage of assets financed by creditors rather than by shareholders. In 2009, $0.74 of every dollar invested in assets was provided by creditors. In 2008, $0.73 of every dollar was provided by creditors. The higher the percentage of debt financing, the riskier the company.

d. Net Earnings Available to Common Shareholders ÷ Weighted Average Number of Common Shares = Earnings per Share
2009: $30,000 ÷ 30,000 = $1.00
2008: $20,000 ÷ 25,000 = $0.80
This ratio is a measure of profitability. It measures the amount of net earnings for each common share. It provides a useful perspective for determining the return for the investment provided by the common shareholder.

e.   Market Price per Share ÷ Earnings per Share = Price-Earnings Ratio
      2009: $9.00 ÷ $1.00 = 9 times
      2008: $6.40 ÷ $0.80 = 8 times
      This ratio reflects the investors' assessment of a company's future earnings. The
      ratio will be higher if the investor thinks that the company's current earnings
      level will persist or increase in the future.

4.   (Domtar $ in USD millions; Cascades $ in CAD millions)

a.   The $5,362 represents the carrying amount of Domtar's property, plant, and
      equipment. The notes to Domtar's financial statements would include a detailed
      breakdown of this amount.

b.   Yes, working capital (current assets less current liabilities) is $1,204 – $623 =
      $581 in 2007 and $1,232 – $658 = $574 in 2006. The trend shows that working
      capital has increased slightly from 2006 to 2007.

      Furthermore, the current ratio also showed a small increase in 2007 as follows:
      For year 2007, it was $1,204 ÷ $623 = 1.93:1, and for 2006 it was $1,232 ÷ $658 =
      1.87:1.

c.

Ratio	Domtar	Cascades
Debt to total assets	($895 + $2,213 + $1,003 + $440) ÷ $7,748 = 58.7%	$2,570 ÷ $3,769 = 68.2%

chapter 3

The Accounting Information System

Chapter Overview

Chapter 3 shows you how to analyze transactions and their effect on the accounting equation. You will learn about accounts, debits, and credits and how to perform the basic steps in the recording process: journalizing, posting transactions to the ledger, and preparing a trial balance.

Accounting Transactions

- The system of collecting and processing transaction data and communicating financial information to decision-makers is known as the **accounting information system**.

- An accounting information system begins with determining what transaction data should be collected and processed.

- An **accounting** transaction occurs when assets, liabilities, or shareholders' equity items change as a result of some economic event.

Analyzing Transactions

The accounting equation is stated as follows:

Assets = Liabilities + Shareholders' Equity

study objective 1

Analyze the effects of transactions on the accounting equation.

- Transactions will affect the components of the accounting equation in various ways, and it is important to remember that the **accounting equation** must **always be in balance** after a transaction is recorded. It is a mathematical equation. For example, if an individual asset is increased, there must be a corresponding decrease in another asset, or increase in a specific liability, or shareholders' equity. It is also possible that two or more items could be affected. For example, supplies may have been purchased by paying some cash and a promise to pay the remainder some time later. In that case, supplies, an asset account would increase; cash, another asset account would decrease; and a liability called accounts payable would increase.

- You should also remember the following with respect to specific aspects of the accounting equation:

  1. If a company receives cash for work to be performed in the future, then it should not record this cash as a revenue. It records an increase in cash on the left side of the equation and an increase in liabilities on the right side of the equation. It owes performance of that work in the future.
  2. Revenues increase shareholders' equity.
  3. Expenses decrease shareholders' equity.
  4. Some events in the life of a corporation are not transactions and are not to be recorded. The hiring of an employee and the beginning of an employees' strike are two such events.

- **An accounting** information **system uses accounts** that are individual accounting records of increases and decreases in a specific asset, liability, or shareholders' equity item.

- The simplest form of an account is the **T account**, so named because of its shape. T accounts have **account** titles, a left side (called the debit side), and a right side (called the credit side).

study objective 2

Define debits and credits and explain how they are used to record transactions.

- **Debit (DR) means left, while credit (CR) means right.** These terms simply denote position. They do not mean good or bad, increase or decrease. The important thing is to know what a debit does to a particular account and what a credit does to that same account.

- **To debit an account** means to enter an amount on the left side of the account. **To credit an account** means to enter an amount on the right side of the account. If an account has $300 on the debit side and $100 on the credit side, then that account has an overall debit balance of $200. If an account has $500 on the credit side and $200 on the debit side, then that account has an overall credit balance of $300. **Debits are always added together, and credits are always added together, but a debit and a credit are subtracted one from the other**.

- The **dollar amount of the debits and the dollar amount of the credits must be equal in each** transaction. The equality of debits and credits is the basis of the double-entry accounting system.

- The following is a summary of the **debit/credit rules for the accounts that you know** ("+" means increase, while "–" means decrease). For example, assets are increased by debits and decreased by credits, and so on. Note that the normal balance of each account is on the increase (plus) side.

	Debit	Credit
Assets	+	−
Dividends	+	−
Expenses	+	−
Liabilities	−	+
Shareholders' Equity	−	+
Revenues	−	+

- Remember that **shareholders' equity has two components: common shares** (or share capital if there is more than one class of shares) **and retained earnings**. Both follow the procedures for Shareholders' Equity indicated above.

- **Retained earnings** can be further divided into three components: revenues and expenses that determine net earnings and dividends. **Dividends and expenses both reduce shareholders' equity**; therefore, they follow procedures contrary to those followed by equity. **Common shares, retained earnings, and revenues all increase shareholders' equity.**

- Since assets are on the left side of the accounting equation and liabilities and shareholders' equity are on the right side, the procedures for assets are contrary to the procedures for liabilities and equity items.

- The **normal balance** is the balance expected to be in an account. Please note that the normal balance is found on the side that increases a particular account. Dividends are increased by debits, so the normal balance is a debit. Revenues are increased by credits, so the normal balance is a credit. Occasionally, an account may have a balance other than its normal balance. As your text points out, the Cash account will have a credit balance when it is overdrawn at the bank.

- The **recording process begins with a source document**.

- Each **transaction is** analyzed **and entered in a journal**. Then, the **journal information is transferred to** the appropriate accounts in **the ledger**.

study objective 3

Identify the basic steps in the recording process.

- A **journal** is a place where a transaction is initially recorded before it is transferred to the accounts. It may be recorded on paper or stored as an electronic file on a computer. **Transactions are entered in chronological order**.

- **Journalizing** is the process of entering transaction data in the journal. A **complete journal entry** consists of the following:

1. The date of the transaction.
2. The accounts and amounts to be debited and credited.
3. An explanation of the transaction.

- A typical journal entry has the following format:

May 12	Supplies	500	
	Cash		500
	(Purchased supplies for cash)		

Please note that the **credit account title is indented**. This decreases the possibility of switching the debit and credit amounts. It also makes it easy to see that the Cash account is credited without having to glance right to see in which column the Cash amount is residing. It is tiring to have your eyes continually scan back and forth across a page.

- The **ledger** is the entire group of accounts maintained by a company. It keeps all the information about changes in specific account balances, in one place. A **general ledger** contains all the assets, liabilities, and shareholders' equity accounts.

- As is true for the journal, a general ledger may be recorded on paper or may be stored as an electronic file on a computer.

- The chart of accounts is the framework for the accounting database. It lists all of the accounts anticipated to be used by the business. These accounts would be put in order of the accounting equation with Assets listed first, followed by Liabilities, and then Shareholders' Equity items.

- **Posting** is the procedure of transferring journal entries to ledger accounts. Posting accumulates the effects of journalized transactions in the individual accounts.

- To **illustrate posting**, consider the entry above in which Supplies was debited and Cash was credited for $500 on May 12. In the ledger account Supplies, the date is recorded, and $500 is written in the debit column. In the ledger account Cash, the date is again recorded, and $500 is written in the credit column.

<table>
<tr><td>

study objective 4

Prepare a trial balance.

</td></tr>
</table>

- A **trial balance** is a list of general ledger accounts and their balances at a given time. A trial balance is usually prepared at the end of an accounting period. Accounts are listed in their ledger order with the balances listed in the appropriate debit or credit column. The **dollar amount of the debits must equal the dollar amount of the credits**; otherwise, there is an error that must be corrected. The **primary purpose** of a trial balance is to prove the mathematical equality of debits and credits in the ledger. It also helps uncover errors in journalizing and posting and is useful in the preparation of financial statements.

- It is, of course, preferable that **a trial balance has equal debits and credits, but mistakes can still be present**. If a journal entry has not been posted, then an error has occurred, but the trial balance will be in balance. If a journal entry is posted twice, then the same is true. If a journal entry is recorded as $500 instead of $5,000 on both the debit and the credit sides, then an error has occurred, but, once again, the trial balance will be in balance. If a $200 debit is posted to Cash instead of to another asset account, then an error is present, but the trial balance will be in balance.

Chapter Self-Test

As you work through the questions and problems, remember to use the **Decision Toolkit** discussed and used in the text:

1. *Decision Checkpoints*: At this point, you ask a question.
2. *Info Needed for Decision*: You make a choice regarding the information needed to answer the question.

3. *Tool to Use for Decision*: At this point, you review just what the information chosen in step 2 does for the decision-making process.
4. *How to Evaluate Results*: You conduct an evaluation of information for answering the question.

Note: The notation (SO1) means that the question was drawn from study objective 1.

Multiple Choice

Please circle the correct answer.

1. If a company receives cash from a customer before performing services for the customer, then   (SO1)
   a.   assets increase, and liabilities decrease.
   b.   assets increase, and shareholders' equity increases.
   c.   assets decrease, and liabilities increase.
   d.   assets increase, and liabilities increase.

2. If a company performs services for a customer and receives cash for the services, then   (SO1)
   a.   assets increase, and liabilities decrease.
   b.   assets increase, and shareholders' equity increases.
   c.   assets decrease, and liabilities increase.
   d.   assets increase, and liabilities increase.

3. When collection is made on an accounts receivable balance, then   (SO1)
   a.   total assets will remain the same.
   b.   total assets will decrease.
   c.   total assets will increase.
   d.   shareholders' equity will increase.

4. Which of the following items has no effect on retained earnings?   (SO1)
   a.   Expense
   b.   Dividends
   c.   Land
   d.   Revenue

5. A payment of a portion of accounts payable will   (SO1)
   a.   not affect total assets.
   b.   increase liabilities.
   c.   not affect shareholders' equity.
   d.   decrease net earnings.

6. An accountant has debited an asset account for $1,000 and credited a liability account for $400. What can be done to complete the recording of the transaction?   (SO2)
   a.   Credit a different asset account for $400.
   b.   Debit a shareholders' equity account for $400.
   c.   Debit another asset account for $600.
   d.   Credit a different asset account for $600.

(SO2)   7. An account will have a credit balance if the
   a.   credits exceed the debits.
   b.   first transaction entered was a credit.
   c.   debits exceed the credits.
   d.   last transaction entered was a credit.

(SO2)   8. An account has $600 on the debit side and $400 on the credit side. The overall balance in the account is a
   a.   debit of $200.
   b.   credit of $200.
   c.   debit of $600.
   d.   credit of $400.

(SO2)   9. Which of the following statements is correct?
   a.   A debit decreases an asset account.
   b.   A credit decreases a liability account.
   c.   A credit increases shareholders' equity.
   d.   A credit decreases a revenue account.

(SO2)   10. Which of the following statements is incorrect?
   a.   A debit increases the Dividends account.
   b.   A debit increases an expense account.
   c.   A credit increases a revenue account.
   d.   A credit increases the Dividends account.

(SO3)   11. Which of the following is the correct sequence of events?
   a.   Analyze a transaction; post it in the ledger; record it in the journal.
   b.   Analyze a transaction; record it in the journal; post it in the ledger.
   c.   Record a transaction in the journal; analyze the transaction; post it in the ledger.
   d.   None of the above is in the correct sequence.

(SO3)   12. Transactions are initially recorded in chronological order in a _____ before they are transferred to the accounts.
   a.   journal
   b.   register
   c.   ledger
   d.   T account

(SO3)   13. If a corporation borrows money and issues a 3-month note in exchange, then the journal entry requires a
   a.   debit to Notes Payable and a credit to Cash.
   b.   debit to Notes Payable and a credit to Unearned Revenue.
   c.   debit to Cash and a credit to Notes Payable.
   d.   debit to Cash and a credit to Unearned Revenue.

(SO3)   14. If a company pays its employees their weekly salaries, then the journal entry requires a
   a.   debit to Unearned Revenue and a credit to Cash.
   b.   debit to Retained Earnings and a credit to Cash.
   c.   debit to Cash and a credit to Salaries Expense.
   d.   debit to Salaries Expense and a credit to Cash.

15. A general ledger of a company contains   (SO3)
    a.   only Asset and Liability accounts.
    b.   all the Asset, Liability, and Shareholders' Equity accounts.
    c.   only Shareholders' Equity accounts.
    d.   only Asset and Shareholders' Equity accounts.

16. The entire group of accounts maintained by a company is referred to collectively   (SO3)
    as the
    a.   ledger.
    b.   journal.
    c.   register.
    d.   T accounts.

17. If an accountant wants to know the balance in the company's cash account, then   (SO3)
    he/she would look in
    a.   the journal.
    b.   the ledger.
    c.   both the journal and the ledger.
    d.   neither the journal nor the ledger.

18. When an accountant posts, he/she is transferring amounts from   (SO3)
    a.   the ledger to the journal.
    b.   T accounts to the ledger.
    c.   the journal to the ledger.
    d.   the ledger to T accounts.

19. If an account is debited in the journal entry, then   (SO3)
    a.   that account will be debited in the ledger.
    b.   that account will be credited in the ledger.
    c.   that account will be both debited and credited in the ledger.
    d.   none of the above is correct.

20. Which of the following is the correct sequence of events?   (SO3)
    a.   Prepare a trial balance; journalize; post.
    b.   Journalize; post; prepare a trial balance.
    c.   Post; journalize; prepare a trial balance.
    d.   Prepare a trial balance; post; journalize.

21. The primary purpose of a trial balance is to   (SO4)
    a.   get a total of all accounts with a debit balance.
    b.   get a total of all accounts with a credit balance.
    c.   prove the mathematical equality of debits and credits after posting.
    d.   get a list of all accounts used by a company.

22. Which of the following errors, each considered individually, would cause the trial   (SO4)
    balance to be out of balance?
    a.   A payment of $75 to a creditor was posted as a debit to Accounts Payable
        and a debit of $75 to Cash.
    b.   Cash received from a customer on account was posted as a debit of $350 to
        Cash and as a credit of $350 to Revenue.

    c.   A payment of $59 for supplies was posted as a debit of $95 to Supplies and a credit of $95 to Cash.

    d.   A transaction was not posted.

(SO4)   23. If the totals of a trial balance are not equal, it could be due to

    a.   a failure to record or post a transaction.

    b.   recording the same erroneous amount for both the debit and the credit parts of a transaction.

    c.   an error in calculating the account balances.

    d.   recording the transaction more than once.

Problems

(SO1, 2)   1.   A company has started a business of doing repairs to small engines on June 1, 2009, and had the following transactions.

June 1	The company issued common shares for cash.
2	Paid cash for a 1-year insurance policy.
3	Paid landlord for June rent.
4	Purchased equipment paying cash for part of the amount due and signing a note for the remainder.
5	Paid for advertising used during June.
6	Purchased office supplies on account.
7	Completed repair services for a customer who paid in cash.
8	Purchased repair supplies on account. These supplies will be used during June.
9	Billed customer for repair services done.
10	Received cash from a customer for repair services to be performed next month.
19	Paid for office supplies purchased on June 6.
22	Paid employee salaries.
23	Paid for repair supplies purchased on June 8.
25	Received payment from customer for repair services provided on June 9.
26	Paid dividends.

Examine the above transactions in an answer sheet like the one shown below:

    a.   Name the accounts affected in each transaction.

    b.   Categorize the accounts that you named in (a) above as either Assets (A), Liabilities (L), Common Shares (CS), Revenue (Rev), Expense (Exp), or Dividends (Div). To do this step, use the accounts in the expanded accounting equation where Shareholders' Equity is divided into Common Shares and Retained Earnings and Retained Earnings is further divided into Revenues, Expenses, and Dividends as shown below:

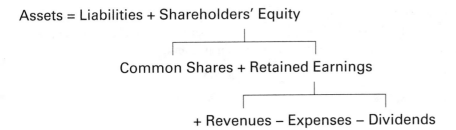

Assets = Liabilities + Shareholders' Equity

Common Shares + Retained Earnings

+ Revenues – Expenses – Dividends

    c.   Identify whether the accounts increase or decrease.
    d.   Signify the increase or decrease with a debit (Dr) or credit (Cr).

The first one has been done for you as an example.

Date	Account Names	Category of Account	Increase or Decrease	Dr or Cr
June 1	Common Shares	CS	Increase	Cr
	Cash	A	Increase	Dr

2.   Journalize the following business transactions. Identify each transaction by letter.   (SO3)
    You may omit explanations for the transactions.

    a.   Shareholders invest $40,000 in cash to start an interior decorating business.
    b.   Purchased office equipment for $5,500, paying $2,000 in cash, and signed a 30-day, $3,500 note payable.
    c.   Purchased $350 of office supplies on credit.
    d.   Billed $3,000 to clients for services provided during the past month.
    e.   Paid $750 in cash for the current month's rent.
    f.   Paid $225 cash on account for office supplies purchased in transaction c.
    g.   Received a bill for $500 for advertising for the current month.
    h.   Paid $2,300 cash for office salaries.
    i.   Paid $1,000 cash dividends to shareholders.
    j.   Received a cheque for $2,000 from a client in payment on account for amount owed in transaction d.

(SO4)   3.   The following is an alphabetical listing of accounts for Davis Corporation. Please prepare a trial balance on September 30, 2009, assuming that all accounts have their normal balance. List the accounts in their proper order.

Accounts payable	$ 4,000
Advertising expense	5,000
Cash	35,000
Common shares	20,000
Dividends	2,000
Equipment	15,000
Prepaid insurance	3,000
Rent expense	6,000
Retained earnings	30,000
Salaries expense	8,000
Service revenue	15,000
Unearned revenue	5,000

(SO3)   4.   For each of the following accounts, indicate whether the account is an Asset, Liability, or Shareholders' Equity account and whether the account normally possesses a debit (DR) or credit (CR) balance.

	Type of Account: Asset, Liability, or Shareholders' Equity	Normal Balance: Debit or Credit
a. Cash		
b. Accounts payable		
c. Unearned revenue		
d. Land		
e. Service revenue		
f. Accounts receivable		
g. Rent expense		
h. Common shares		
i. Loan payable		
j. Dividends		
k. Prepaid rent		
l. Notes payable		

5.   Please refer to the Domtar and Cascades financial statements found in the appendices at the end of this study guide for information for answering the following questions. Do not forget to use the **Decision Toolkit** approach for help in the problem solving.

(SO2)   a.   Did the companies pay dividends in 2007? What were the amounts for each company, and where do you find this information?

(SO2)   b.   What were the total assets, liabilities, and shareholders' equity for Cascades in 2007?

Solutions to Self-Test

Multiple Choice

1. d   Cash (an asset) increases, and unearned revenue (a liability) increases.
2. b   Cash (an asset) increases, and shareholders' equity increases because one of its components, revenue, increases.
3. a   Cash (an asset) increases, and accounts receivable (an asset) decreases; therefore, total assets remain the same.
4. c   Land is an asset.
5. c   The asset Cash is decreased, the liability Accounts Payable is decreased, and Shareholders' Equity is not affected.
6. d   An example would be:

Office Supplies	1,000	
Accounts Payable		400
Cash		600

7. a   If total credits exceed total debits, the account will have a credit balance regardless of the type of account.
8. a $600 DR − $400 CR = $200 DR
9. c   A debit increases an asset, a credit increases a liability, and a credit increases a revenue account.
10. d   A debit increases the dividends account.
11. b   It reflects the correct sequence of events.
12. a   The ledger is a collection of accounts, and a T account is a form of account.
13. c   The company receives an asset (Cash is increased by the debit), and its liabilities increase (Notes Payable is increased by the credit).
14. d   Expenses increase with a debit, and cash decreases with a credit to Cash.
15. b   All elements of the accounting equation (assets, liabilities, and shareholders' equity items) are contained in the general ledger.
16. a   The journal is the book of original entry, and T accounts are simply a form of account.
17. b   The easiest place to find the information is in the ledger. Anyone can find it in the journal, but would have to add and subtract all the entries to cash, which would be very time-consuming.
18. c   Posting involves transferring information from the journal to the ledger.
19. a   Whatever is done to an account in the journal entry is done to that account in the ledger.
20. b   It reflects the correct sequence.
21. c   While the trial balance may give a list of all accounts (an account with a zero balance may not be listed) and certainly lists debit and credit balances, these are not the primary purpose of the document.
22. a   Two debits will cause the trial balance to be out of balance.
23. c   Answers a, b, and d, reflect errors but those errors would not cause the trial balance to be out of balance.

Problems

1.

Date	Account Names	Category of Account	Increase or Decrease	Dr. or Cr.
June 1	Common Shares	CS	Increase	Cr
	Cash	A	Increase	Dr

Note: Common Shares is part of Shareholders' Equity (SE) and the account increases because the company has issued shares. Refer to the textbook for the reasons why Debits and Credits increase or decrease various accounts.

Date	Account Names	Category	Increase/Decrease	Dr/Cr
June 2	Prepaid Insurance	A	Increase	Dr
	Cash	A	Decrease	Cr

Note: The insurance policy will last 1 year; therefore it has value beyond the month of June, therefore it is an asset. The common name for this account is Prepaid Insurance.

Date	Account Names	Category	Increase/Decrease	Dr/Cr
June 3	Rent Expense	Exp	Increase	Dr
	Cash	A	Decrease	Cr

Note: This rent will be used up in the current month, therefore it is an expense incurred for the purpose of generating revenues. Rent Expense is part of Retained Earnings, which is part of SE. Management would assign the name "Rent Expense" when it begins business. That would be done in the chart of accounts where all of the accounts anticipated to be used by the business would be identified. These accounts would be put in order of the accounting equation with Assets listed first, then Liabilities, then Shareholders' Equity items.

Date	Account Names	Category	Increase/Decrease	Dr/Cr
June 4	Equipment	A	Increase	Dr
	Cash	A	Decrease	Cr
	Note Payable	L	Increase	Cr

Note: Three accounts are affected. The name Equipment is assigned by management as explained in the June 3 note. Management could have assigned "Office Equipment" instead. The key point is that this item is an asset whatever name is assigned. When the name of the account is not provided, as in this problem, you are free to use a name that is descriptive of the nature of the transaction as long as you recognize that the item is, in this case, an asset. Note Payable is used when there is a formal agreement that money is owed; in this case, the transaction states that a note was signed.

Date	Account Names	Category	Increase/Decrease	Dr/Cr
June 5	Advertising Expense	Exp	Increase	Dr
	Cash	A	Decrease	Cr

Note: Advertising is used in the current month for the purpose of generating revenues, which makes it an expense.

June 6	Office Supplies	A	Increase	Dr
	Accounts Payable	L	Increase	Cr

Note: There is no indication that the supplies were used up in June, therefore it has future value, which makes it an asset. The name "Supplies" as opposed to "Office Supplies" could have been used. Again, see the note for June 3, which explains how naming of accounts is done. The key point is to recognize that this item is an asset whatever the name of the account that is used. Accounts Payable is the account used to reflect the fact that the company incurred a liability by promising to pay cash in the future.

June 7	Cash	A	Increase	Dr
	Repair Revenue	Rev	Increase	Cr

Note: The company has performed work, therefore it has earned revenue. The name "Repair Revenue" was used to describe the type of revenue that this company is engaged in. Other names such as "Revenue" or "Service Revenue" could have been used as well. The key point is to recognize that this is a revenue account. Revenue is part of Retained Earnings, which is part of SE.

June 8	Repair Supplies Expense	Exp	Increase	Dr
	Accounts Payable	L	Increase	Cr

Note: The repair supplies are expensed because they will be used in the current month and have been incurred for the purpose of generating revenues. The name "Repair Supplies Expense" was used to reflect the nature of supplies and to differentiate between the office supplies. These supplies were purchased on account, meaning that the company incurred a liability and will pay cash later.

June 9	Accounts Receivable	A	Increase	Dr
	Repair Revenue	Rev	Increase	Cr

Note: The company has billed the customer for repair work done, therefore it has earned revenue regardless of the fact that the customer has not paid for this work. The customer owes money to the company. Accounts Receivable is an asset and is the account used to reflect that the customer owes money. The use of the Repair Revenue account was explained in the June 7 transaction. It should also be noted that once the name of the revenue account has been decided upon, it must be used for all subsequent similar revenue transactions. For example, if the account had been named "Service Revenue" in the June 7 transaction, then "Service Revenue" would have been used in this transaction as well.

June 10	Cash	A	Increase	Dr
	Unearned Repair Revenue	L	Increase	Cr

Note: The company has received cash for repair work to be done later. This transaction must be recognized even though the work has not been done because cash has been received. The company owes the customer some repair work to be done later, therefore the company must recognize a liability because it owes this work. As previously explained, there is flexibility in deciding upon names for this account. For example, "Unearned Revenue" could have been used.

| June 19 | Accounts Payable | L | Decrease | Dr |
| | Cash | A | Decrease | Cr |

Note: The company is now paying cash for the office supplies that it purchased on June 6. It is therefore discharging or eliminating the liability. Accordingly, the accounts payable is now decreased.

| June 22 | Salary Expense | Exp | Increase | Dr |
| | Cash | A | Decrease | Cr |

Note: Employees are being for paid for the work they have done in June. It is an expense incurred for the purpose of generating revenues.

| June 23 | Accounts Payable | L | Decrease | Dr |
| | Cash | A | Decrease | Cr |

Note: The company is now paying cash for the repair supplies that it purchased on June 8. It is therefore discharging or eliminating the liability. Accordingly, the accounts payable is now decreased.

| June 25 | Accounts Receivable | A | Decrease | Cr |
| | Cash | A | Increase | Dr |

Note: The company is now receiving cash for the work done for a customer on June 9. The customer has now paid the debt owing to the company, therefore the accounts receivable account must be decreased. You should note that the revenue was already recognized on June 9, therefore it should not be recognized again in this transaction.

| June 26 | Dividends | Div | Increase | Dr |
| | Cash | A | Decrease | Cr |

Note: Dividends are a distribution of retained earnings rather than an expense—they are not incurred for generating revenues.

2.

a. Cash   40,000
        Common Shares   40,000

b. Office Equipment   5,500
        Cash   2,000
        Notes Payable   3,500

c.	Office Supplies	350	
	Accounts Payable		350
d.	Accounts Receivable	3,000	
	Decorating Revenue		3,000
e.	Rent Expense	750	
	Cash		750
f.	Accounts Payable	225	
	Cash		225
g.	Advertising Expense	500	
	Accounts Payable		500
h.	Office Salaries Expense	2,300	
	Cash		2,300
i.	Dividends	1,000	
	Cash		1,000
j.	Cash	2,000	
	Accounts Receivable		2,000

3.

DAVIS CORPORATION
Trial Balance
September 30, 2009

	Debit	**Credit**
Cash	$35,000	
Prepaid insurance	3,000	
Equipment	15,000	
Accounts payable		$ 4,000
Unearned revenue		5,000
Common shares		20,000
Retained earnings		30,000
Dividends	2,000	
Service revenue		15,000
Advertising expense	5,000	
Salaries expense	8,000	
Rent expense	6,000	
	$74,000	$74,000

4.

	Type of Account: Asset, Liability, or Shareholders' Equity	Normal Balance: Debit or Credit
a. Cash	Asset	Debit
b. Accounts payable	Liability	Credit
c. Unearned revenue	Liability	Credit
d. Land	Asset	Debit
e. Service revenue	Shareholders' Equity	Credit
f. Accounts receivable	Asset	Debit
g. Rent expense	Shareholders' Equity	Debit
h. Common shares	Shareholders' Equity	Credit
i. Loan payable	Liability	Credit
j. Dividends	Shareholders' Equity	Debit
k. Prepaid rent	Asset	Debit
l. Notes payable	Liability	Credit

5.   (Domtar $ in USD millions; Cascades $ in CAD millions)

a.   Cascades paid dividends in 2007 but Domtar did not. Cascades paid dividends of $16 to its common shareholders. The information was found in the Retained Earnings section of the Statement of Shareholders' Equity. We will learn more about this statement in Chapter 11.

b.   Total assets were $3,769; total liabilities were $2,570; and total shareholders' equity was $1,199. The total liabilities and total shareholders' equity total $3,769, which equals total assets.

chapter 4

Accrual Accounting Concepts

Chapter Overview

In Chapter 4, you will learn about two generally accepted accounting principles: the revenue recognition principle and the matching principle. This chapter will explain what adjusting journal entries are, why adjustments are needed, and how to prepare them. You will learn how to prepare an adjusted trial balance and closing journal entries.

Timing Issues

- **Accounting divides the economic life of a business into artificial time periods**, such as a month, a quarter, or a year. Some business transactions affect more than one accounting period, and it is necessary to consider a transaction's impact on the affected periods. This is known as the **time period assumption**.

- The **revenue recognition principle** states that revenue must be recognized in the accounting period in which it is earned. (To "recognize" means to record in a journal entry.) For a service firm, revenue is earned at the time that the service is performed, which may or may not be the time at which cash is received. A company may perform services for a client and receive in return the client's promise to pay the firm in the future. In this case, unearned revenue, a liability account, would be recognized.

- The **matching principle** states that (efforts) expenses must be matched with (accomplishments) revenues. This means the following: If a company performs services and, thus, earns revenue in a given accounting period, then any expenses that helped the company earn the revenue must be recorded in that same accounting period. The **critical issue** is determining when the expense makes its contribution to revenue. The principle is easy to state, but sometimes difficult to implement.

- **Accrual basis accounting**, resulting from application of the revenue recognition and matching principles, means that transactions that change a company's financial statements are recorded in the periods in which the events occur, rather than in the periods in which the company receives or pays cash.

- With **cash basis accounting**, revenue is recorded only when cash is received, and an expense is recorded only when cash is paid. The cash basis can lead to misleading financial statements because, most of the time, it fails to recognize revenue when it is earned and fails to match expenses incurred to generate those revenues.

<table>
<tr><td>

study objective 2

Prepare adjusting entries for prepayments.

</td><td>

- **Adjusting entries** are needed to ensure that the revenue recognition and matching principles are followed. Before adjusting entries are recorded, some accounts may have incorrect balances because some events are not journalized daily. Some events are not journalized during the accounting period because these costs expire with the passage of time, and some items may simply be unrecorded for a variety of reasons.

</td></tr>
</table>

- **Adjusting entries** are required every time financial statements are prepared. Sometimes, students will comment that adjusting entries are simply "cooking the books," but the opposite is actually true. Because of the reasons noted above, some accounts may have incorrect balances, and adjusting entries will correct them.

- There are **two broad groups of adjusting entries: prepayments and accruals. Prepayments** include prepaid expenses (expenses paid in cash and recorded as assets before they are used) and unearned revenues (cash received and recorded as liabilities before revenue is earned). **Accruals** include accrued revenues (revenues earned but not yet received in cash or recorded) and accrued expenses (expenses incurred but not yet paid in cash or recorded).

- There are **two important items** to note before we look at the specifics of adjusting entries:

  1. The adjusting entries that you will learn will always involve one statement of earnings account and one balance sheet account. Please note that this does not say that the statement of earnings account is always increased and the balance sheet account is always decreased, or vice versa. The usefulness of this fact lies in the following: If you prepare an adjusting entry and know that the debit to an expense (a statement of earnings account) is correct, then the credit must be to a balance sheet account.
  2. The account Cash is never used in an adjusting entry. If cash is involved, then the event is simply a transaction, not an adjustment to the accounts.

- **Prepaid expenses** (or prepayments) are payments of expenses that will benefit more than one accounting period. They are initially recorded as assets and expire either with the passage of time or through use. An adjusting entry for a prepaid expense results in an increase (debit) to an expense account and a decrease (credit) to an asset account. A good general rule to remember is that as an asset is used up or consumed, its cost becomes an expense.

- **Supplies** are one example of a prepaid expense. A company purchases $800 of supplies at the beginning of the accounting period. At the end of the period, a physical count shows that only $200 of supplies are left. Therefore, $600 of supplies were used up. The asset account Supplies still has the $800 balance and, if that number is recorded on the balance sheet, then the statement will not be conveying the truth. An accountant may not record $200, the correct number, on the balance sheet if the ledger account for Supplies shows an amount of $800. So, an adjusting entry to adjust the Supplies account by $600 ($800 − $200) is required:

Supplies Expense	600	
Supplies		600
(To record supplies used)		

After the entry is recorded and posted, the Supplies account will show the correct balance, $200 ($800 − $600), and that number will then correctly be shown on the balance sheet. **If the entry had not been made**, expenses would have been understated, net earnings would have been overstated, and assets and shareholders' equity would have each been overstated by $600.

- **Insurance** and **rent** are two more examples of a prepaid expense. A company pays 6 months' rent, $2,400, at the beginning of March and wants to prepare financial statements at the end of March. The asset account Prepaid Rent shows a balance of $2,400, but this is no longer correct because the company has used up 1 month's rent. The balance sheet should show Prepaid Rent of $2,000, but the amount of $2,000 should not be recorded in the adjusting entry if the ledger account for Prepaid Rent shows a balance of $2,400. Again, an adjusting entry is required for the amount of $400 ($2,400 − $2,000) to adjust the Prepaid Rent account to its correct balance:

Rent Expense	400	
Prepaid Rent		400
(To record expired rent)		

After the entry is recorded and posted, the Prepaid Rent account will show the correct balance, $2,000 ($2,400 − $400), and that number will then correctly be shown on the balance sheet. **If the entry had not been made**, expenses would have been understated, net earnings would have been overstated, and assets and shareholders' equity would have been overstated by $400.

- The adjusting entry for **depreciation** is another example of a prepayment. Long-lived assets, such as vehicles, equipment, and buildings, are recorded at cost. Their acquisition is basically a long-term prepayment for services. As the useful life of those long-lived assets with limited useful lives progresses, part of the cost should be recorded as an expense. **Depreciation** is the process of allocating the cost of an asset to expense over its useful life in a rational and systematic manner. It is important to remember that **depreciation is an allocation concept, and not a valuation concept**. It does not attempt to reflect the actual change in the value of the asset.

A common practice for calculating depreciation expense is to divide the cost of the asset by its estimated useful life. This is known as the straight-line method of depreciation. Assume that a vehicle costs $18,000 and has an estimated useful life of 5 years. The depreciation on that vehicle is $3,600 per year, or $300 per month. The following entry records 1 month of depreciation:

Depreciation Expense	300	
Accumulated Depreciation—Vehicle		300
(To record monthly depreciation)		

Accumulated Depreciation is a contra asset account, offset against, or subtracted from, the Vehicle account on the balance sheet. Its normal balance is a credit. The use of this account allows the user to see the original cost of the asset as well as the total cost that has expired to date. The balance sheet presentation of this vehicle after adjustment is:

Vehicle	$18,000
Less: Accumulated depreciation—Vehicle	300
Carrying amount	17,700

The $17,700 is the **carrying amount** or book value of the asset. The carrying amount is calculated by subtracting the accumulated depreciation from the cost of the asset. Depreciation is also commonly known as amortization and the carrying amount is also commonly known as book value.

As was true with Supplies and Prepaid Rent, **failure to record this adjusting entry** for depreciation would have meant that expenses would have been understated, net earnings would have been overstated, and assets and shareholders' equity would have each been overstated by $300.

- **Unearned revenues** occur when cash is received before revenue is earned. Magazine subscriptions and rent are two examples. Unearned revenues are the opposite of prepaid expenses—an unearned revenue on one company's books is a prepaid expense on another company's books. If my company pays your company $6,000 toward 6 months' rent in advance, then my company will have Prepaid Rent of $6,000, while your company will have Unearned Rent of $6,000. After 1 month has elapsed, your company must write the following adjusting entry to show that it has earned 1 month's rent revenue, or $1,000 ($6,000 ÷ 6):

Unearned Rent	1,000	
Rent Revenue		1,000
(To record revenue earned)		

Please note that the entry involves a decrease (debit) to the liability account and an increase (credit) to the revenue account. **If the entry is not recorded**, then revenues, net earnings, and shareholders' equity will be understated by $1,000, while liabilities will be overstated by $1,000. Most liabilities are discharged by the payment of money. Note that **an unearned revenue, a liability, is discharged by the performance of a service.**

study objective 3

Prepare adjusting entries for accruals.

- Adjusting entries for **accruals** are required in order to record revenues earned and expenses incurred in the current accounting period that have not been recognized through daily entries and, thus, are not yet reflected in the accounts. Accruals occur in the form of **accrued revenues** and **accrued expenses**.

The adjusting entry for accruals will **increase** both **the balance sheet and the statement of earnings account**.

- **Accrued revenues** are revenues earned but not yet received in cash or recorded, as on the date of the financial statement. Examples are interest, rent, and services. They may accrue with the passage of time or may result from services performed, but they may be neither billed nor collected. The adjusting entry for an accrued revenue will always involve an **increase in a receivable (debit) and an increase in a revenue (credit)**. A company has earned $300 in interest revenue, but has not received that amount in cash. If financial statements are to be prepared, then an adjusting entry to recognize that revenue is required:

Interest Receivable	300	
Interest Revenue		300
(To record interest revenue)		

If **this entry is not made**, then assets and shareholders' equity on the balance sheet, as well as revenues and net earnings on the statement of earnings, will be understated. When the company receives that interest in cash, it will record a debit to Cash and a credit to Interest Receivable, not to Interest Revenue.

- **Accrued expenses** are expenses incurred but not yet paid or recorded on the statement date. Examples include interest, rent, taxes, and salaries. The company, which owes the $300 of interest in the above example has an accrued expense of $300. The adjusting entry for an accrued expense will always involve **an increase (debit) to an expense account and an increase (credit) to a liability account**.

Assume that a company borrows $12,000 at 6 percent interest for 6 months on November 1. The principal and all the interest are due on May 1. If financial statements are prepared on December 31, then the company must record an adjusting entry for the interest owed but not yet paid. Interest is calculated by multiplying the face value of the note by the interest rate, which is always expressed as an annual rate. In our example, $12,000 \times 0.06 \times 2/12$ or $120, the entry is:

Interest Expense	120	
Interest Payable		120
(To record accrued interest)		

It is **important to note** that the account Notes Payable is not used in the entry. Notes Payable was credited when the money was borrowed and will be debited when the note principal of $12,000 is repaid. **If this adjusting entry is not made**, then liabilities and interest expense will be understated and net earnings and shareholders' equity will be overstated.

- Regarding **accrued income taxes**, for accounting purposes, corporate income taxes must be accrued on the basis of the current period's earnings. Corporations pay corporate income taxes in monthly instalments. The payment is based on the income tax that was actually payable in the preceding year. If there was no preceding year or if there was no tax payable in the preceding year, then no income tax instalments are required to be paid. However, the tax liability must still be accrued if there are earnings in the current year. In that case, the following adjusting entry would be required to record the estimate of corporate taxes owed on the earnings (assume that the amount is $500):

Income Tax Expense	500	
Income Tax Payable		500
(To record income tax expense)		

<table>
<tr><td>

study objective 4

Describe the nature and purpose of the adjusted trial balance.

</td><td>

• A **trial balance is prepared after the journal entries have been journalized and posted**. Just as a trial balance is prepared after journalizing and posting regular transactions, so is an **adjusted trial balance** prepared after adjusting entries have been journalized and posted. The purpose of an adjusted trial balance is to prove the equality of debits and credits in the general ledger.

</td></tr>
</table>

• Since all account balances have been brought up to date, the adjusted trial balance can be used in the preparation of financial statements. The **statement of earnings** is prepared from the revenue and expense accounts. The **statement of retained earnings** is derived from the retained earnings account, the dividends account, and the net earnings (or net loss) shown on the statement of earnings. The **balance sheet** is then prepared from the asset, liability, and shareholders' equity accounts, which include the ending retained earnings as reported in the statement of retained earnings.

• **Temporary accounts** relate to only a given accounting period and include revenues, expenses, and dividends. **Permanent accounts** have balances that carry forward into future accounting periods and include assets, liabilities, and shareholders' equity—the balance sheet accounts.

<table>
<tr><td>

study objective 5

Explain the purposes of closing entries.

</td><td>

• At the end of the accounting period, **temporary account balances are closed or zeroed out**. Their balances are transferred to the permanent shareholders' equity account, Retained Earnings. **Closing entries** transfer net earnings or net loss and dividends to Retained Earnings. Revenues and expenses are transferred to another temporary account, Income Summary, and the resulting net earnings or net loss is then transferred to Retained Earnings.

</td></tr>
</table>

• **Closing entries accomplish two things**. They update the retained earnings account and they zero out the balance in the temporary accounts, making them ready to accumulate data in the next accounting period.

• **After closing entries have been journalized and posted, a post-closing trial balance is prepared**. Once again, the purpose is to prove the equality of debits and credits in the ledger. It also helps show all temporary accounts that have been closed. If, for example, the accountant prepares a post-closing trial balance and finds a balance of $5,000 in Salaries Expense, then he/she will know that a temporary account was improperly excluded when closing entries were prepared. Only permanent accounts should appear on the post-closing trial balance.

• The accounting cycle was first introduced in Chapter 3. The cycle begins with the analysis of business transactions and ends with the preparation of a post-closing trial balance. The steps are done in sequence and are repeated in each accounting period.

Steps 1–3 may occur daily during the accounting period, as we learned in Chapter 3. Steps 4–7 are done on a periodic basis, such as monthly, quarterly, or annually.

Steps 8 and 9, closing entries and a post-closing trial balance, are usually prepared only at the end of a company's annual accounting period.

The following are the steps in the **accounting cycle**:

1. Analyze business transactions.
2. Journalize the transactions.
3. Post to general ledger accounts.
4. Prepare a trial balance.
5. Journalize and post adjusting entries.
6. Prepare an adjusted trial balance.
7. Prepare financial statements.
8. Journalize and post closing entries.
9. Prepare a post-closing trial balance.

These steps are repeated in each accounting period.

Chapter Self-Test

As you work through the questions and problems, remember to use the **Decision Toolkit** discussed and used in the text:

1. *Decision Checkpoints:* At this point, you ask a question.
2. *Info Needed for Decision:* You make a choice regarding the information needed to answer the question.
3. *Tool to Use for Decision:* At this point, you review just what the information chosen in Step 2 does for the decision-making process.
4. *How to Evaluate Results:* You conduct an evaluation of information for answering the question.

Note: The notation (SO1) means that the question was drawn from study objective number one.

Multiple Choice

Please circle the correct answer.

1. The generally accepted accounting principle that dictates that revenue be recognized in the accounting period in which it is earned is the   (SO1)
   a. time period principle.
   b. matching principle.
   c. revenue recognition principle.
   d. accrued revenues principle.

2. In 2009, the Abbott Corporation performs work for a customer and bills the customer $10,000; it also pays expenses of $3,000. The customer pays Abbott in 2010. If Abbott uses the cash basis of accounting, then Abbott will report   (SO1)
   a. revenue of $10,000 in 2009.
   b. revenue of $10,000 in 2010.
   c. expenses of $3,000 in 2010.
   d. net earnings of $7,000 in 2009.

(SO1)   3.   In 2009, the Abbott Corporation performs work for a customer and bills the customer $10,000; it also pays expenses of $3,000. The customer pays Abbott in 2010. If Abbott uses the accrual basis of accounting, then Abbott will report
    a.   revenue of $10,000 in 2009.
    b.   revenue of $10,000 in 2010.
    c.   expenses of $3,000 in 2010.
    d.   net earnings of $7,000 in 2010.

(SO1)   4.   Adjusting journal entries must be prepared
    a.   at the end of every calendar year.
    b.   at the end of every month.
    c.   when the accountant has time to write them.
    d.   whenever financial statements are to be prepared.

(SO1)   5.   The generally accepted accounting principle that dictates that efforts be matched with accomplishments is the
    a.   accrued expenses principle.
    b.   matching principle.
    c.   revenue recognition principle.
    d.   time period principle.

(SO2)   6.   A company has the following results for the year ended December 31, 2009:

Revenues	$160,000
Depreciation expense	50,000
Rent expense	10,000
Wages expense	25,000
Advertising expense	30,000
Dividends	10,000
Utilities expense	15,000

The corporate income tax rate is 40 percent, and no instalment payments were made during 2009. The corporate income taxes for 2009 will be paid on March 31, 2010. What adjusting entry, if any, is required on December 31, 2009, with respect to corporate income tax?

    a.   Income Tax Expense   8,000
           Income Tax Payable   8,000
    b.   Income Tax Expense   12,000
           Income Tax Payable   12,000
    c.   Income Tax Payable   8,000
           Income Tax Expense   8,000
    d.   No entry is required.

(SO2)   7.   Cash received and recorded as a liability before revenue is earned is called
    a.   an accrued revenue.
    b.   an unearned revenue.

   c.   an unrecorded revenue.
   d.   none of the above.

8. On October 1, a company paid $6,000 for a 1-year insurance policy, debiting   (SO2)
     Prepaid Insurance and crediting Cash. The adjusting entry on December 31 will
     require a
    a.   debit to Insurance Expense for $1,500.
    b.   debit to Insurance Expense for $4,500.
    c.   credit to Prepaid Insurance for $4,500.
    d.   credit to Cash for $1,500.

9. At the beginning of an accounting period, a company purchased $800 of   (SO2)
     supplies, debiting Supplies and crediting Cash. At the end of the accounting
     period, a physical count of supplies showed that only $100 of supplies were still
     on hand. The adjusting entry will require a
    a.   credit to Supplies Expense for $700.
    b.   debit to Supplies Expense for $100.
    c.   debit to Supplies for $700.
    d.   credit to Supplies for $700.

10. Little Corporation received $5,000 from a customer for whom it is to perform   (SO2)
     work in the future, debiting Cash and crediting Unearned Revenue. At the end
     of the accounting period, Little has earned $2,000 of the revenue. The adjusting
     entry will require a
    a.   debit to Cash for $2,000.
    b.   debit to Service Revenue for $2,000.
    c.   credit to Service Revenue for $2,000.
    d.   credit to Service Revenue for $3,000.

11. At the end of its accounting period, Pooky Corporation has not billed a customer   (SO3)
     for $400 rent. The adjusting entry will require a
    a.   debit to Cash for $400.
    b.   credit to Accounts Receivable for $400.
    c.   credit to Unearned Revenue for $400.
    d.   credit to Rent Revenue for $400.

12. If the adjusting entry for an accrued expense is not recorded, then   (SO3)
    a.   liabilities and expenses will be understated.
    b.   liabilities and expenses will be overstated.
    c.   net earnings will be understated.
    d.   liabilities and shareholders' equity will be overstated.

13. Buddy Corporation pays its employees $1,000 per 5-day week. The last day of the   (SO3)
     month falls on a Thursday, and financial statements will be prepared that day.
     The adjusting entry for salaries will require a
    a.   debit to Salaries Payable for $200.
    b.   credit to Salaries Expense for $200.
    c.   debit to Salaries Expense for $200.
    d.   debit to Salaries Expense for $800.

(SO3)   14. Failure to record accrued interest expense at the end of the period would cause
     a.   net earnings to be understated.
     b.   an overstatement of assets and an overstatement of liabilities.
     c.   an understatement of expenses and an understatement of liabilities.
     d.   an overstatement of expenses and an overstatement of liabilities.

(SO3)   15. Failure to prepare an adjusting entry at the end of a period to record an accrued revenue would cause
     a.   net earnings to be overstated.
     b.   an understatement of assets and an understatement of revenues.
     c.   an understatement of revenues and an understatement of liabilities.
     d.   an understatement of revenues and an overstatement of liabilities.

(SO4)   16. Which of the statements below is not true?
     a.   An adjusted trial balance should show ledger account balances.
     b.   An adjusted trial balance can be used to prepare financial statements.
     c.   An adjusted trial balance proves the mathematical equality of debits and credits in the ledger.
     d.   An adjusted trial balance is prepared before all transactions have been journalized.

(SO5)   17. Financial statements can be prepared directly from the
     a.   trial balance.
     b.   adjusted trial balance.
     c.   post-closing trial balance.
     d.   reversing trial balance.

(SO5)   18. Which of the following is a temporary account?
     a.   The dividends account
     b.   An asset account
     c.   A liability account
     d.   A shareholders' equity account

(SO5)   19. Which of the following is true?
     a.   Only permanent accounts are closed.
     b.   Both permanent and temporary accounts are closed.
     c.   Neither permanent nor temporary accounts are closed.
     d.   Only temporary accounts are closed.

(SO5)   20. Which of the following correctly describes the closing process?
     a.   Net earnings or net loss is transferred to the Cash account.
     b.   Net earnings or net loss is transferred to Retained Earnings.
     c.   Permanent accounts become ready to accumulate data in the next accounting period.
     d.   Each revenue and each expense account is closed individually to Retained Earnings.

(SO5)   21. Which is the correct order of selected steps in the accounting cycle?
     a.   Post transactions, journalize transactions, prepare a trial balance, prepare financial statements.
     b.   Journalize and post transactions, journalize and post closing entries, journalize and post adjusting entries.

c.   Journalize and post transactions, journalize and post adjusting entries, journalize and post closing entries. ~

d.   Prepare financial statements, prepare adjusting entries, prepare closing entries, prepare a post-closing trial balance.

Problems

1.   (SO2, 3)

a.   Prepare the annual adjusting entries for the following situations for Cassie Corporation, as of June 30:

    i.   The Supplies account shows a balance of $1,500, but a physical count on June 30 shows only $300 of supplies.

    ii.   The corporation purchased a 1-year insurance policy for $3,600 on May 1, debiting Prepaid Insurance.

    iii.   On June 1, the corporation received $1,200 from another corporation, which is renting a small building from Cassie for 6 months. Cassie credited Unearned Rent Revenue.

    iv.   Cassie's accountant discovered that Cassie had performed services for a client totalling $900, but has not yet billed the client or recorded the transaction.

    v.   Cassie pays employees $2,000 per 5-day work week, and June 30 falls on a Wednesday.

    vi.   The corporation owns a van that cost $18,000 and has a useful life of 6 years. The corporation purchased the van in early April this year.

1500
- 300
1200

Date	Account Titles	Debit	Credit
June 30	Supplies Expense	1200	
	Supplies		1200
	Insurance Expense	600	
	Prepaid Insurance		600
	Unearned Rent	200	
	Rent		200
	A/R	900	
	Revenue		900

b.   What type of an account is the account that you credited in (vi) above? Please show the balance sheet presentation for the van after you have recorded the depreciation entry.

2.   For each of the following transactions, identify whether assets, liabilities, share-holders' equity (SE) or net earnings were overstated (O), understated (U), or had no effect (NE). Assume that the company's year end is June 30.

a.   The company did not do an adjusting entry for a utility bill received in July but represented consumption for June.

b.   During June, $700 of supplies were purchased and debited to the Supplies account. At the end of June, an inventory count showed that $300 was left. The following adjusting entry was made:

Supplies Expense	300	
Supplies		300

c.   The company completed work for a customer on June 30 but a bill for the work was not prepared until July.

d.   The company did not do an adjusting entry for depreciation for its equipment.

e.   At the beginning of June, Unearned Revenue had a balance of $1,000. During the month of June, $700 of that unearned revenue had been earned.

(SO2, 3)   3.   The Upshaw Park Corporation prepares monthly financial statements. Presented below is a statement of earnings for the month of June:

UPSHAW PARK CORPORATION
Statement of Earnings
Month Ended June 30

Revenues		
Admission revenues		$30,000
Expenses		
Salary expense	$4,000	
Advertising expense	700	
Insurance expense	4,200	
Depreciation expense	2,200	
Total expenses		11,100
Earnings before income tax		18,900
Income tax expense		0
Net earnings		$18,900

Additional Data: When the statement of earnings was prepared, the company accountant neglected to take into consideration the following information:

a.   An electricity bill for $1,500 was received on the last day of the month for electricity used in the month of June.

b.   An advance payment of $1,000 was received in June for a park rental space to be used in July. That amount was included in the admission revenues for June.

c.   Supplies on hand at the beginning of the month were $2,000. The corpora-
tion purchased additional supplies during the month for $1,500 in cash and
$1,100 of supplies were on hand at June 30.

d.   At the beginning of the month, the corporation purchased a new truck,
with an estimated useful life of 8 years, for $38,400 cash. That amount was
not included in the depreciation expense for June.

e.   Salaries owed to employees at the end of the month total $4,400. The sala-
ries will be paid on July 3.

f.   Income tax expense not yet paid is estimated to be at the rate of 40 percent
of net earnings before income taxes.

Prepare a corrected statement of earnings.

4.   Please refer to the Domtar and Cascades financial statements found in the appen-   (SO2, 3)
dices at the end of this study guide for information for answering the following
questions. Do not forget to use the **Decision Toolkit** approach for help in the
problem solving.

a.   Using Domtar's balance sheet and statement of earnings, identify items that
may result in adjusting entries for prepayments.

b.   Using Cascades' balance sheet and statement of earnings, identify accounts
that may be involved in adjusting entries for accruals.

Solutions to Self-Test

Multiple Choice

1. c   The time period assumption says that the economic life of a business can
be divided into artificial time periods, the matching principle dictates that
expenses be matched with revenues, and the accrued revenues principle is
a nonexistent principle.

2. b   Under the cash method, revenue cannot be reported in 2009 because
Abbott did not receive cash. It paid the expenses in 2009 and must report
them in that year. Since it recorded no revenue in 2009, it had a net loss of
$3,000 (the expenses it paid) in 2009.

3. a   It reports revenue in the year when the work is performed (2009, not
2010). Expenses are reported in 2009, when incurred, and net earnings of
$7,000 is reported in 2009, not 2010.

4. d   Adjusting entries are prepared whenever financial statements are prepared.

5. b   "Accrued expenses principle" is a nonexistent term. The revenue recognition principle states that revenue must be recognized when it is earned,
and the time period assumption says that the economic life of a business
can be divided into artificial time periods.

6. b   Earnings before income taxes = $30,000. So, income tax expense =
$30,000 × 40% = 12,000. Remember that Dividends is not an expense
and, therefore, does not enter into the calculation of earnings before
(or after) income taxes.

7. b   An accrued revenue arises when money is owed to a company, not when it owes money. "Unrecorded revenue" is an accounting term, but it is not appropriate in this instance.

8. a   The journal entry is:

Insurance Expense	1,500	
Prepaid Insurance		1,500
$6,000 \times 3/12 = $1,500		

9. d   The journal entry is:

Supplies Expense	700	
Supplies		700

10. c   The journal entry is:

Unearned Revenue	2,000	
Service Revenue		2,000

11. d   The journal entry is:

Accounts Receivable	400	
Rent Revenue		400

12. a   The journal entry debits an expense and credits a liability, thereby increasing both accounts. If an expense is not recorded, then net earnings will be overstated (as will shareholders' equity) and, if a liability is not recorded, then liabilities will be understated.

13. d   The journal entry is:

Salaries Expense	800	
Salaries Payable		800

14. c   An adjusting entry for an accrued expense involves an expense account and a liability account. Failure to record such an entry would result in an understatement of expenses, understatement of a liability, and an overstatement of net earnings because expenses are less than what they should be.

15. b   An adjusting entry for an accrued revenue involves a revenue account and an asset account. Failure to record such an entry would result in an understatement of revenue, understatement of an asset, and an understatement of net earnings because revenues are less than what they should be.

16. d   The adjusted trial balance is prepared after all adjusting entries have been journalized and posted. It shows the balance of all accounts at the end of the accounting period. The purpose of the adjusted trial balance is to prove the equality of total debits and total credits of the accounts in the general ledger after adjustments have been made.

17. b   The trial balance does not have the adjustments updates, the post-closing trial balance has no temporary accounts, and there is no such thing as a reversing trial balance.

18. a   The other three types of accounts are all permanent accounts.

19. d   Permanent accounts are not closed.

20. b   Net earnings and loss are not transferred to the Cash account, permanent accounts are not closed, and revenue and expense accounts are closed first to Income Summary (which is itself closed to Retained Earnings).

21. c   All of the other answers are incorrect.

Problems

1. a.

i.   Supplies Expense   1,200
         Supplies   1,200
         (To record supplies used. $1,500 − $300)

ii. Insurance Expense   600
         Prepaid Insurance   600
         (To record insurance expired)
         $3,600 ÷ 12 months = $300 per month × 2 months

iii. Unearned Rent Revenue   200
         Rent Revenue   200
         (To record rent earned)
         $1,200 ÷ 6 months = $200 per month

iv. Accounts Receivable   900
         Service Revenue   900
         (To record revenue earned)

v.   Salaries Expense   1,200
         Salaries Payable   1,200
         (To record accrued salaries)
         $2,000 ÷ 5 days = $400 per day × 3 days

vi. Depreciation Expense   750
         Accumulated Depreciation—Van   750
         (To record depreciation)
         $18,000 ÷ 6 years = $3,000 per year × 3/12

b.   Accumulated Depreciation is a contra asset account, which is offset against,
     or subtracted from, the asset account. The advantage of this presentation is
     that the user sees both the original cost of the asset and the total cost that
     has expired to date.

Van	$18,000
Less: Accumulated depreciation—van	750
Carrying amount	17,250

     The $17,250 is the carrying amount of the asset and has no relationship to
     the market value (what a willing buyer would pay a willing seller) of the
     asset. Remember that depreciation is an allocation concept, not a valuation
     concept.

2.

Item	Assets	Liabilities	Net Earnings	SE	Reason
a.	NE	U	O	O	Utility expense was incurred in June. Net earnings is a part of shareholders' equity, therefore if net earnings are overstated then SE will also be overstated and vice versa if understated.
b.	O	NE	O	O	The adjusting entry should have been: Supplies Expense 400 Supplies 400 Therefore, supplies expense was understated and supplies overstated
c.	U	NE	U	U	The work was done in June so revenue should be recognized in June by making the following adjusting entry: Accounts Receivable Revenue
d.	O	NE	O	O	The adjusting entry should have been: Depreciation Expense Accumulated Depreciation – Equipment Accumulated depreciation is a contra asset account, therefore it reduces assets
e.	NE	O	U	U	The adjusting entry should have been: Unearned Revenue 700 Revenue 700

3.

UPSHAW PARK CORPORATION
Statement of Earnings
Month Ended June 30

Revenues

Admission revenues ($30,000 – $1,000)		$29,000
Expenses		
Salary expense ($4,000 + $4,400)	$8,400	
Advertising expense	700	
Insurance expense	4,200	
Depreciation expense ($2,200 + $400)	2,600	
Electricity expense ($0 + $1,500)	1,500	
Supplies expense ($0 + $2,400)	2,400	
Total expenses		19,800

Earnings before income tax	9,200
Income tax expense ($9,200 × 40%)	3,680
Net earnings	$ 5,520

(*Note:* Depreciation on new truck is $38,400 ÷ 8 years = $4,800 ÷ 12 months = $400)

4.

a.   Examples of prepayments found on Domtar's balance sheet would include prepaid expenses and property, plant, and equipment. Expenses such as insurance expense and property tax expense, likely included in the selling, general, and administrative expense category shown on the statement of earnings, would result in an adjusting entry for their prepaid portions. Depreciation and amortization expense, related to the long-term prepayment for property, plant, and equipment, is reported on the statement of earnings.

b.   Examples of accruals found on Cascades' balance sheet include accounts receivable and accounts payable and accrued liabilities. Accounts receivable would be used to record sales made but not yet collected. Accounts payable and accrued liabilities would include accruals for some of the selling and administrative expenses, such as salaries and utilities. In addition, some of the interest expense reported on the statement of earnings would likely have resulted from accruing the interest incurred on the long-term debt reported on the balance sheet.

chapter 5

Merchandising Operations

Chapter Overview

Chapter 5 discusses the differences between service companies and merchandising companies. You will learn the basics of accounting for merchandising transactions. You will also learn how to prepare and analyze the statement of earnings for a merchandising company.

Review of Specific Study Objectives

- The **operating cycle** of a merchandising company is longer than that of a service company because of the purchase and sale of merchandise inventory.

- The primary source of revenue for a merchandising company is the sale of merchandise, called **sales revenue**. Expenses are divided into two categories: cost of goods sold (the total cost of merchandise sold during the period) and operating expenses. Net earnings is determined as follows:

	Sales revenue
−	Cost of goods sold
=	Gross profit
−	Operating expenses
	Earnings before income tax
−	Income tax expense
=	Net earnings (loss)

study objective 1

Identify the differences between service and merchandising companies.

- There are two systems of inventory available to a merchandising company: the **perpetual inventory system** and the **periodic inventory system**.

  With a perpetual system, detailed records of the cost of each inventory purchase and sale are maintained. These records show at all times the inventory that should be on hand for every item. Cost of goods sold is determined each time a sale occurs. The use of calculator systems, bar codes, and optical scanners makes such a system practicable.

  With a periodic system, detailed records are not kept throughout the period. Cost of goods sold is **determined only at the end of the accounting period** when a physical count of goods is taken. The calculation is as follows:

	Beginning inventory
+	Cost of goods purchased
=	Cost of goods available for sale
–	Ending inventory
=	Cost of goods sold

study objective 2

Prepare entries for purchases under a perpetual inventory system.

- A perpetual system provides better inventory control. Goods can be counted at any time to see whether they exist, and shortages can be immediately investigated. The quantity of inventory can be managed so that neither too much nor too little is on hand at a given time.

- **Purchases**, either for cash or on account (credit), are normally recorded when the goods are received from the seller. A business document (a cancelled cheque or a cash register receipt for a cash purchase or a purchase invoice for a credit purchase) will provide written evidence of the purchase.

- A purchase is recorded by a debit to Merchandise Inventory and a credit to Cash or Accounts Payable. The Merchandise Inventory account is used for purchases of goods that will be resold only. If the company buys another type of asset (such as equipment), then the debit will be to the individual asset account (e.g., Equipment).

- The purchase invoice should indicate whether the seller or buyer must pay the cost of transporting the goods to the buyer's place of business. Freight terms generally say who pays the freight and who is responsible for the risk of damage to the merchandise during transit. Terms are often expressed as **F.O.B. shipping point** or **F.O.B. destination**. F.O.B. means "free on board."

  F.O.B. shipping point means that the goods are delivered to the point of shipping (normally the seller's place of business) by the seller. The buyer pays the freight costs to get the goods from the point of shipping to the destination (normally the buyer's place of business). In this situation, the shipping is considered to be part of the cost of purchasing the inventory. The cost of the shipping is recorded by a debit to Merchandise Inventory and a credit to Cash or Accounts Payable.

  F.O.B. destination means that the goods are delivered by the seller to their destination. The seller pays the freight to get the goods to their destination.

- Purchased goods might be unsuitable because they are damaged or defective, are of inferior quality, or do not meet the purchaser's specifications. A **purchase return** occurs when goods are returned to the seller. A **purchase allowance** occurs when the purchaser keeps the merchandise but is granted an allowance (deduction) by the seller. A purchase return or allowance is recorded by debiting Cash or Accounts Payable and crediting Merchandise Inventory.

- The terms of a purchase may include a **quantity discount** for a bulk purchase. Quantity discounts are not recorded or accounted for separately. The net amount of the invoice is simply recorded as the purchase cost. On the other hand, a purchase discount may be offered to the buyer of merchandise to induce early payment for the goods. Purchase discounts are noted on the invoice through credit terms. For example, credit terms of 1/10, *n*/30 means that the purchaser will receive a one percent cash discount on the invoice price (net of any purchase returns or allowances) if the invoice is paid within 10 days; otherwise, the net amount is due in 30 days. Assume that on May 1, a buyer purchased $5,000 of merchandise on account with terms of 2/10, *n*/30.

Merchandise Inventory	5,000	
Accounts Payable		5,000
(To record purchase on account)		

If the invoice is paid by May 11, then the following entry is required:

Accounts Payable	5,000	
Cash		4,900
Merchandise Inventory		100
(To record goods purchased on account, terms 2/10, *n*/30)		

If the buyer pays after May 11, then the entry will be:

Accounts Payable	5,000	
Cash		5,000
(To record payment—no discount)		

It is usually advantageous for the buyer to take all cash discounts. Passing up a 2/10, *n*/30 discount is the equivalent of paying an annual interest rate of 36.5 percent (2% × 365 ÷ 20)! Some companies even borrow money at 8 to 12 percent to take the discount because that is cheaper than paying 36.5 percent.

- Sales revenues are recorded when earned, in accordance with the revenue recognition principle. As is true for purchases, sales may be for cash or on account (credit) and should be supported by a business document (a cash register tape for cash sales and a sales invoice for credit sales).

study objective 3

Prepare entries for sales under a perpetual inventory system.

- Two entries are made for each sale in the perpetual inventory system. One records the sale and the other records the cost of merchandise sold. If goods costing $200 are sold for cash of $400, then the following entries are required:

Cash	400	
Sales		400
(To record a cash sale)		
Cost of Goods Sold	200	
Merchandise Inventory		200
(To record the cost of merchandise sold)		

Note carefully that the selling price of the goods is used for the amount recorded in the first entry, while the cost is used for the amount recorded in the second entry. If the goods had been sold on account, then the only thing that would have changed in either entry is that the debit in the first entry would have been to Accounts Receivable instead of Cash.

- The **Sales** account is used only for sales of merchandise inventory. If an asset is sold, then the credit is to the asset account. A company may choose to have several Sales accounts, each one dedicated to a type of product. This helps to give management information needed to manage its inventory. Such a company will report only one sales figure on the statement of earnings. To report many sales accounts would lengthen the statement of earnings and perhaps give too much detail on operating results to competitors. There are many users of a company's financial statements, and one such group of users is a company's competitors.

- As discussed earlier, freight terms on the sales invoice—F.O.B. destination or F.O.B. shipping point—indicate who is responsible for shipping costs. If the term is F.O.B. destination, the seller assumes responsibility for getting the goods to their destination. Freight costs incurred by the seller on the outgoing merchandise are an operating expense. These costs are debited to Freight Out or Delivery Expense and credited to Cash or Accounts Payable.

- If sold goods are returned to the company, then two entries are required. Assume that the goods sold above are all returned in good working order to the company. The required entries are

Sales Returns and Allowances	400	
Cash		400
(To record return of goods)		
Merchandise Inventory	200	
Cost of Goods Sold		200
(To record cost of goods returned)		

Once again, note that the first entry records the selling price of the returned goods while the second entry records the cost of the goods.

Sales Returns and Allowances is a **contra revenue account** to Sales. If the debit had been to Sales, then the return would have been buried in that account. Management needs to monitor the amount of returned goods so that it may correct an unsatisfactory situation. The goods the company is selling may be of poor quality or defective, and management will have to deal with the supplier of the goods. If the company itself is making mistakes in delivery or shipment of goods, then management will have to deal with this internal problem. Consequently, it is important to use the Sales Returns and Allowances account, rather than the Sales account, for merchandise returns.

- Like a purchase discount, the seller may offer the buyer a cash discount to induce early payment of the balance due. Using the previous example, on May 1, a buyer purchased $5,000 of merchandise on account with terms of 2/10, *n*/30. The buyer then sells this merchandise on account for $6,000. The entry to record the sale on the books of the buyer is as follows:

Accounts Receivable	6,000	
Sales		6,000
(To record sales on account)		
Cost of Goods Sold	5,000	
Merchandise Inventory		5,000
(To record the cost of merchandise sold)		

If the buyer pays by May 11, then the selling company records the following entry:

Cash	5,880	
Sales Discounts	120	
Accounts Receivable		6,000
(To record collection within the 2/10, *n*/30 discount period)		

If the buyer pays after May 11, then the entry is

Cash	6,000	
Accounts Receivable		6,000
(To record collection—no discount allowed)		

Sales Discounts is another contra revenue account to Sales.

- The following provides a summary of the revenue and contra revenue accounts used in merchandising companies:

Account Name	Account Type	Normal Balance
Sales	Revenue	Credit
Sales Returns and Allowances	Contra Revenue	Debit
Sales Discounts	Contra Revenue	Debit

- A **single-step** statement of earnings works in the following way: all revenues are totalled, all expenses are totalled, and expenses are then subtracted from revenues to determine earnings or net loss before income tax. (The subtraction gives the name "single step" to this statement of earnings.) Income tax expense is normally separated and shown separately, making it a modified single-step statement of earnings. This form is simple and easy to read and understand.

> **study objective 4**
>
> Prepare a single-step and a multiple-step statement of earnings.

- A **multiple-step** statement of earnings breaks net earnings (or loss) into several components that financial statement users find useful.

1. Net Sales: sales returns and allowances and sales discounts are subtracted from gross sales to determine net sales.
2. Gross Profit: cost of goods sold is subtracted from net sales to determine gross profit.
3. Earnings from Operations: operating expenses are deducted from gross profit to determine earnings from operations.

4. Non-Operating Activities: the results of activities that are not related to operations are added (as other revenue) or subtracted (as other expenses) to determine earnings before income tax.

5. Net Earnings: income tax expense is subtracted from earnings before income tax is deducted to determine net earnings (loss).

- Earnings from operating activities are considered sustainable and long term, while those from non-operating activities are considered non-recurring and short term. It is obviously important for a company to derive the bulk of its income from its main line of operations and not from peripheral activities, such as the sale of factories and equipment.

To recap, if there are no non-operating activities, then the statement appears as follows:

	Sales revenue
–	Cost of goods sold
=	Gross profit
–	Operating expenses
=	Earnings before income tax
–	Income tax expense
=	Net earnings (loss)

If there are non-operating activities, then the statement appears as follows:

	Sales revenue
–	Cost of goods sold
=	Gross profit
–	Operating expenses
=	Earnings from operations
+	Other revenues
–	Other expenses
=	Earnings before income tax
–	Income tax expense
=	Net earnings (loss)

study objective 5
Calculate the gross profit margin and profit margin.

- A company's **gross profit** can be expressed as a percentage. The gross profit margin is calculated by dividing gross profit by net sales. The gross profit margin is closely monitored. A decline in the margin may result from selling items with lower markup, from having to lower selling prices due to increased competition, or from having to pay higher prices for merchandise without being able to pass those higher costs onto customers.

- The **profit margin** measures the percentage of each dollar of sales that results in net earnings. It is calculated by dividing net earnings by net sales for the period. High-volume stores usually have low profit margins, while low-volume stores have high profit margins.

study objective 6
Prepare entries for purchases and sales under a periodic inventory system and calculate cost of goods sold (Appendix 5A).

- A **periodic inventory system** differs from a perpetual inventory system in various ways, one of which is the time at which cost of goods sold is calculated. With a periodic system, cost of goods sold is calculated only at the end of an accounting period, while with a perpetual system, cost of goods sold is calculated each time the inventory is sold.

- With a periodic system, a physical count of inventory is taken at the end of the accounting period to determine the cost of merchandise on hand. This figure is then used to calculate the cost of goods sold during the period. Purchases of inventory are recorded in a Purchases account, not in Merchandise Inventory, and there are separate accounts for purchase returns and allowances, purchase discounts, and freight costs on purchases.

- Consider the following data. On April 4, Orion Corporation purchased $5,000 of inventory on account with credit terms of 2/10, *n*/30. It paid shipping costs of $200 on April 5 and, on April 7, it returned $500 of merchandise. It paid the amount due on April 13. The journal entries for these transactions are as follows:

April 4	Purchases	5,000	
	Accounts Payable		5,000
	(To record purchases on account)		
5	Freight In	200	
	Cash		200
	(To record freight payment)		
7	Accounts Payable	500	
	Purchase Returns and Allowances		500
	(To record return of merchandise)		
13	Accounts Payable	4,500	
	Purchase Discounts		90
	Cash		4,410
	(To record payment of account within discount period)		

Please note the following:

a. Purchases is a temporary expense account with a normal debit balance that is reported on the statement of earnings.
b. Purchase Returns and Allowances and Purchase Discounts are temporary accounts with a normal credit balance.
c. Discounts do not apply to freight in charges. Freight in is part of the cost of goods purchased and is a temporary account with a normal debit balance.

- Sales of merchandise are recorded in the same way as they are recorded in a perpetual system. Sales has a normal credit balance, while the contra revenue accounts—Sales Returns and Allowances and Sales Discounts—have normal debit balances.

- Under a periodic inventory system, the cost of goods sold is **calculated**. The following provides an example of the calculation:

Cost of goods sold:			
Inventory, January 1			$ 30,000
Purchases		$90,000	
Less: Purchase returns and allowances	$15,000		
Purchase discounts	5,000	20,000	
Net purchases		70,000	
Add: Freight in		10,000	
Cost of goods purchased			80,000
Cost of goods available for sale			110,000
Inventory, December 31			70,000
Cost of goods sold			$ 40,000

Chapter Self-Test

As you work through the questions and problems, remember to use the **Decision Toolkit** discussed and used in the text:

1. *Decision Checkpoints:* At this point, you ask a question.
2. *Info Needed for Decision:* You make a choice regarding the information needed to answer the question.
3. *Tool to Use for Decision:* At this point, you review just what the information chosen in step 2 does for the decision-making process.
4. *How to Evaluate Results:* You conduct an evaluation of information for answering the question.

Note: The notation (SO1) means that the question was drawn from study objective number one. All questions marked with an asterisk (*) relate to material in Appendix 5A.

Multiple Choice

Please circle the correct answer.

(SO1)   1. The operating cycle of a merchandising company is ordinarily _____ that of a service firm.
    a.   the same as
    b.   shorter than
    c.   longer than
    d.   four times as long as

(SO1)   2. Which of the following statements is correct?
    a.   A periodic inventory system gives better control over inventories than does a perpetual inventory system.
    b.   A perpetual inventory system gives better control over inventories than does a periodic inventory system.
    c.   A periodic inventory system calculates cost of goods sold each time a sale occurs.
    d.   A perpetual inventory system calculates cost of goods sold only at the end of the accounting period.

(SO2)   3. Poobah Corporation, which uses a perpetual inventory system, purchased $3,000 of merchandise on account on June 4. What entry is required on June 8, when it returned $500 of the merchandise to the seller?

a.	Accounts Payable	500	
	Merchandise Inventory		500
b.	Merchandise Inventory	500	
	Accounts Payable		500
c.	Accounts Payable	500	
	Purchases Returns		500
d.	Cash	500	
	Merchandise Inventory		500

4. Cassie Corporation, which uses a perpetual inventory system, purchased $2,000   (SO2)
   of merchandise on account on July 5. Credit terms were 2/10, *n*/30. It returned
   $400 of the merchandise on July 9. When the company pays its bill on July 11, the
   journal entry will require a
   a. debit to Accounts Payable for $2,000.
   b. debit to Accounts Payable for $1,600.
   c. credit to Cash for $1,600.
   d. debit to Merchandise Inventory for $32.

5. Cosmos Corporation, which uses a perpetual inventory system, purchased $2,000   (SO2)
   of merchandise on account on July 5. Credit terms were 2/10, *n*/30. It returned
   $400 of the merchandise on July 9. When the company pays its bill on July 21, the
   journal entry will require a
   a. debit to Accounts Payable for $2,000.
   b. credit to Accounts Payable for $1,600.
   c. credit to Cash for $1,600.
   d. debit to Cash for $1,600.

6. Elizabeth Corporation uses a perpetual inventory system and purchased merchan-   (SO2)
   dise on November 30 for which it must pay the shipping charges. When the company pays the shipping charges of $200, the journal entry will require a debit to
   a. Delivery Expense.
   b. Cash.
   c. Freight In.
   d. Merchandise Inventory.

7. Which of the following statements is correct?   (SO3)
   a. A company that uses a perpetual inventory system needs only one journal
       entry when it sells merchandise.
   b. A company that uses a perpetual inventory system needs two journal entries
       when it sells merchandise.
   c. A company that uses a perpetual inventory system debits Merchandise
       Inventory and credits Cost of Goods Sold when it sells merchandise.
   d. None of the above is correct.

8. Cynthia Corporation, which uses a perpetual inventory system, received $500   (SO3)
   of returned merchandise, which it had sold a week earlier for $750 on account.
   Assuming the merchandise is not damaged, when Cynthia records the return, the
   journal entries will require a
   a. debit to Sales Returns and Allowances for $750.
   b. debit to Cost of Goods Sold for $500.
   c. debit to Accounts Receivable for $750.
   d. credit to Merchandise Inventory for $500.

9. Sales Returns and Allowances and Sales Discounts are   (SO3)
   a. revenue accounts.
   b. expense accounts.
   c. contra revenue accounts.
   d. contra expense accounts.

(SO3)   10. A company that uses a perpetual inventory system sold $400 of merchandise on July 23 with credit terms of 1/10, *n*/30. The purchaser paid the amount due on July 30. Which journal entry will the selling company record on July 30?

a.	Cash	400	
	Accounts Receivable		400
b.	Cash	400	
	Sales Discounts		4
	Accounts Receivable		396
c.	Accounts Receivable	400	
	Sales Discounts		4
	Cash		396
d.	Cash	396	
	Sales Discounts	4	
	Accounts Receivable		400

(SO4)   11. Sales revenues are $10,000, sales returns and allowances are $500, and sales discounts are $1,000. What is the dollar amount of net sales?
   a. $11,500
   b. $10,500
   c. $10,000
   d. $8,500

(SO4)   12. Gross profit is $50,000, operating expenses are $15,000, income tax expense is $9,000, and net sales total $75,000. What is the cost of goods sold?
   a. $10,000
   b. $25,000
   c. $26,000
   d. $35,000

(SO4)   13. Gross profit is $50,000, operating expenses are $15,000, income tax expense is $9,000, and net sales total $75,000. What is the net earnings?
   a. $10,000
   b. $25,000
   c. $26,000
   d. $35,000

(SO4)   14. Net earnings is $15,000, operating expenses are $20,000, income tax expense is $3,000, and net sales total $75,000. What is the gross profit?
   a. $35,000
   b. $37,000
   c. $38,000
   d. $55,000

(SO4)   15. Net earnings is $15,000, operating expenses are $20,000, income tax expense is $3,000, and net sales total $75,000. What is the cost of goods sold?
   a. $35,000
   b. $37,000
   c. $38,000
   d. $55,000

16. Which of the following is not true about a multiple-step statement of earnings?   (SO4)
    a.   Operating expenses are often classified as selling and administrative expenses.
    b.   There may be a section for non-operating activities.
    c.   There may be a section for operating assets.
    d.   There is a section for cost of goods sold.

17. Net earnings is $15,000; operating expenses are $20,000; income tax expense is   (SO5)
    $3,000; and net sales total $75,000. What is the gross profit margin?
    a.   47 percent
    b.   49 percent
    c.   51 percent
    d.   73 percent

18. After gross profit is calculated, operating expenses are deducted to determine   (SO5)
    a.   gross margin.
    b.   earnings from operations.
    c.   cost of goods sold.
    d.   profit margin.

19. A decline in a company's gross profit could be caused by all of the following, except   (SO5)
    a.   selling products with a lower markup.
    b.   clearance of discontinued inventory.
    c.   paying lower prices to its suppliers.
    d.   increased competition resulting in a lower selling price.

*20. Frank Corporation has the following account balances: (SO6)

Purchases	$28,000
Sales returns and allowances	4,000
Purchase discounts	2,500
Freight in	1,875
Freight out	2,500

The cost of goods purchased for the period is
    a. $30,500.
    b. $27,375.
    c. $29,875.
    d. $25,875.

*21. The Wales Corporation has a beginning merchandise inventory of $15,000. Dur-   (SO6)
    ing the period, purchases were $70,000; purchase returns, $2,000; and freight in
    was $5,000. A physical count of inventory at the end of the period revealed that
    $10,000 was still on hand. The cost of goods available for sale was
    a. $82,000.
    b. $78,000.
    c. $88,000.
    d. $92,000.

*22. The calculation of the cost of goods sold under the periodic system is   (SO6)
    a.   Beginning Inventory + Ending Inventory – Purchases.
    b.   Beginning Inventory + Ending Inventory + Purchases.

    c. Beginning Inventory + Purchases − Ending Inventory.
    d. Ending Inventory + Purchases − Beginning Inventory.

(SO6) *23. Under a periodic inventory system, acquisition of merchandise is debited to the
    a. Merchandise Inventory account.
    b. Cost of Goods Sold account.
    c. Purchases account.
    d. Accounts Payable account.

Problems

(SO4) 1. From the appropriate accounts below, prepare a multiple-step statement of earnings for Buff Corporation for the year ended January 31, 2009.

Cash	$ 13,000
Rental revenue	5,000
Interest revenue	1,000
Utilities expense	15,000
Cost of goods sold	24,000
Insurance expense	2,000
Accounts receivable	12,000
Sales returns and allowances	4,000
Advertising expense	7,000
Merchandise inventory	35,000
Depreciation expense	8,000
Sales revenues	118,000
Freight out	3,000
Loss on sale of equipment	1,500
Sales discounts	5,000
Salaries expense	23,000
Rent expense	10,000
Interest expense	2,000
Income tax expense	7,800

  2. Hiller Corporation is a merchandising company, and the following accounting transactions occurred during the month of January.

Jan. 5 Purchased goods costing $10,000. The goods were shipped F.O.B. shipping point with terms of 2/10, *n*/30

  7 Hiller paid freight costs of $100 on the January 5 purchase

  10 Hiller returned $2,000 of the goods purchased on January 5 to its supplier. (Ignore freight on this return.)

  12 Hiller sold $2,000 of merchandise to Ms. Jones with terms 2/10, *n*/30 and F.O.B. destination. The cost of the goods sold was $1,600

  14 Hiller paid the amount due to its supplier

  16 Hiller paid $50 in freight costs on the goods sold and shipped them to Ms. Jones

20   Ms. Jones returned $100 of goods sold on January 12. The returned goods cost $80 and were put back on Hiller's store shelf for resale, as they were in good condition. (Ignore freight on this return.)

21   Ms. Jones paid her account in full

25   Hiller purchased $500 of general office supplies on account

a.   Record the above transactions for Hiller Corporation using the perpetual inventory system.   (SO3, 4)

*b.   Record the above transactions for Hiller Corporation using the periodic inventory system.   (SO6)

*3.   The Willis Merchandising Corporation employs the periodic inventory system   (SO6)
and prepares monthly financial statements. All accounts have been adjusted except for merchandise inventory. A physical count of merchandise inventory on September 30, 2009, indicates that $3,300 was on hand. A partial listing of account balances is as follows:

Accounts receivable	$5,000
Cash	9,000
Accounts payable	7,000
Merchandise inventory, September 1	2,500
Freight in	1,000
Purchase returns and allowances	900
Sales discounts	700
Purchases	26,000
Sales	49,000

Prepare a statement of earnings through gross profit for Willis Merchandising Corporation for the month ended September 30, 2009.

4.   The following information is presented in summarized form, and has been selec-   (SO2)
ted from the Merchandise Inventory account of a company for the most recent 2 years. The company uses the perpetual inventory system.

	Year 1	Year 2
Balance in account, beginning of period	$400	$(d)
Purchases of merchandise	1,000	900
Returns of merchandise purchased	100	(e)
Net purchases	870	690
Purchase discounts on merchandise	(a)	60
Freight costs incurred on merchandise purchased	(b)	100
Cost of goods purchased	1,000	790
Cost of goods sold	750	(f)
Balance in account, end of period	(c)	400

From the above information, reconstruct the company's Merchandise Inventory account. You might find it helpful to refer to Illustration 5-5 in your textbook when completing this assignment.

(SO6)   5.   The following table represents the cost of goods sold section of a company for the most recent 2 years. The company uses a periodic inventory system.

	Year 1	Year 2
Beginning inventory	$ 400	$ (e)
Purchases	1,000	900
Purchase returns and allowances	100	(f)
Purchase discounts	(a)	60
Net purchases	870	690
Freight in	(b)	100
Cost of goods purchased	1,000	(g)
Cost of goods available for sale	(c)	(h)
Ending inventory	(d)	400
Cost of goods sold	750	(i)

Fill in the lettered blanks to complete the cost of goods sold sections.

6.   Please refer to the Domtar and Cascades financial statements found in the appendices at the end of this study guide for information for answering the following questions. Do not forget to use the **Decision Toolkit** approach for help in the problem solving.

(SO5)   a.   Compare the gross profit and gross profit margin for both companies for 2007. Assume that the industry average for the gross profit margin was 17.7 percent in 2007.

(SO4)   b.   What are the operating expenses and earnings from operations for each company for 2007?

(SO5)   c.   Calculate and compare the profit margin for both companies for 2007. Assume that the industry average for the profit margin was 1.7 percent for 2007.

Solutions to Self-Test

Multiple Choice

1.   c   The purchase of merchandise inventory and the lapse of time until it is sold and collected lengthens the cycle.

2.   b   Periodic systems do not show the quantity of goods that should be on hand, making control more difficult. Cost of goods sold is calculated each time a sale occurs under the perpetual system.

3.   a   Since the sale was on account, the return entry requires a decrease in the liability, and Accounts Payable is debited. Since the company uses a perpetual system, all merchandise dollar amounts are recorded in the Merchandise Inventory account. A decrease due to the returned merchandise requires a credit to Merchandise Inventory. Purchases Returns would have been used if the company had used a periodic system.

4. b   The journal entry is:

Accounts Payable	1,600	
Merchandise Inventory		32
Cash		1,568

5. c   The journal entry is:

Accounts Payable	1,600	
Cash		1,600

6. d   The journal entry is:

Merchandise Inventory	200	
Cash		200

7. b   A perpetual inventory system requires two entries when merchandise is sold. One of the entries is to record the sale (debit Cash or Accounts Receivable and credit Sales). The second entry records the cost of the sale with a debit to Cost of Goods Sold and the a credit to Merchandise Inventory.

8. a   The journal entries are:

Sales Returns and Allowances	750	
Accounts Receivable		750
Merchandise Inventory	500	
Cost of Goods Sold		500

9. c   While these accounts have a normal debit balance, they are not expenses, nor are they revenue accounts. They are subtracted from a revenue account, making them contra revenue accounts.

10. d   The entry requires a debit to Cash, but not for $400, since the purchaser receives a $4 discount. Accounts Receivable must be credited for $400, the full amount owed. The $4 difference between the amount owed and the amount of cash received is the debit to Sales Discounts.

11. d $10,000 − $500 − $1,000 = $8,500

12. b $75,000 − $50,000 = $25,000

13. c $50,000 − $15,000 − $9,000 = $26,000

14. c $15,000 + $3,000 + $20,000 = $38,000

15. b $15,000 + $3,000 + $20,000 = $38,000 of gross profit; $75,000 − $38,000 = $37,000

16. c   Assets are not included in any statement of earnings.

17. c $15,000 + $3,000 + $20,000 = $38,000 of gross profit; $38,000 ÷ $75,000 = 51 percent (rounded)

18. b   Sales less cost of goods sold equals gross margin less operating expenses equals earnings from operations.

19. c   Lower prices from suppliers would result in an increase in gross profit.

20. b $28,000 − $2,500 + $1,875 = $27,375

21. c $15,000 + $70,000 − $2,000 + $5,000 = $88,000

22. c   Beginning Inventory + Purchases = Cost of Goods Available for Sale − Ending Inventory = Cost of Goods Sold

23. c   Under a periodic inventory system, the acquisition of merchandise would be debited to the Purchases account.

Problems

1.

BUFF CORPORATION
Statement of Earnings
Year Ended January 31, 2009

Sales revenues		
Sales		$118,000
Less: Sales returns and allowances	$4,000	
Sales discounts	5,000	9,000
Net sales		109,000
Cost of goods sold		24,000
Gross profit		85,000
Operating expenses		
Salaries expense	$23,000	
Utilities expense	15,000	
Rent expense	10,000	
Depreciation expense	8,000	
Advertising expense	7,000	
Freight out	3,000	
Insurance expense	2,000	
Total operating expenses		68,000
Earnings from operations		17,000
Other revenues		
Rental revenue	$5,000	
Interest revenue	1,000	
Total non-operating revenues	6,000	
Other expenses		
Interest expense	$2,000	
Loss on sale of equipment	1,500	
Total non-operating expenses	3,500	
Net non-operating revenue		2,500
Earnings before income tax		19,500
Income tax expense		7,800
Net earnings		$ 11,700

2.

Perpetual Inventory System

a. Jan. 5   Merchandise Inventory   10,000
                    Accounts Payable   10,000
            (To record purchase of goods, with terms 2/10, n/30, F.O.B.
            shipping point)

      7   Merchandise Inventory   100
                    Cash   100
            (To record freight on purchases)

            [The terms of F.O.B. shipping point means Hiller, the buyer, is
            responsible for picking up the goods from the supplier's warehouse or
            shipping point.]

      10   Accounts Payable   2,000
                    Merchandise Inventory   2,000
            (To record return of goods to supplier)

      12   Accounts Receivable   2,000
                    Sales   2,000
            (To record sales with terms 2/10, n/30 and F.O.B. destination)
            Cost of Goods Sold   1,600
                    Merchandise Inventory   1,600
            (To record cost of merchandise sold)

      14   Accounts Payable   8,000
                    Merchandise Inventory   160
                    Cash   7,840
            (To record payment, net of purchase return within the discount
            period)
            Discount = ($10,000 − $2,000) × 0.02 = $160
            [Discount does not apply to freight.]

      16   Freight Out   50
                    Cash   50
            (To record freight on sales)

            [F.O.B. destination means that it is Hiller's responsibility to pay the
            freight.]

20	Sales Returns and Allowances	100	
	Accounts Receivable		100

(To record return of goods by Ms. Jones)

	Merchandise Inventory	80	
	Cost of Goods Sold		80

(To record the cost of merchandise return)

21	Cash	1,862	
	Sales Discounts	38	
	Accounts Receivable		1,900

(To record collection of account within the discount period)

Discount = ($2,000 − $100) × 0.02 = $38

25	Office Supplies (or expense)	500	
	Accounts Payable		500

(To record purchase of office supplies)

[Note that the amount is not debited to merchandise inventory because these are not goods for resale.]

Periodic Inventory System

b.	Jan. 5	Purchases	10,000	
		Accounts Payable		10,000

(To record purchase of goods with terms 2/10, n/30, F.O.B. shipping point)

	7	Freight In	100	
		Cash		100

(To record freight on purchases)

[The terms of F.O.B. shipping point means Hiller, the buyer, is responsible for picking up the goods from the supplier's warehouse or shipping point.]

	10	Accounts Payable	2,000	
		Purchase Returns and Allowances		2,000

(To record return of goods to supplier)

	12	Accounts Receivable	2,000	
		Sales		2,000

(To record sales with terms 2/10, n/30 and F.O.B. destination)

14	Accounts Payable	8,000	
	Purchase Discounts		160
	Cash		7,840

(To record payment, net of purchase return within the discount period)

Discount = ($10,000 − $2,000) × 0.02 = $160

[Discount does not apply to freight.]

16	Freight Out	50	
	Cash		50

(To record freight on sales)

[F.O.B. destination means that it is Hiller's responsibility to pay the freight.]

20	Sales Returns and Allowances	100	
	Accounts Receivable		100

(To record return of goods by Ms. Jones)

21	Cash	1,862	
	Sales Discounts	38	
	Accounts Receivable		1,900

(To record collection of account within the discount period)

Discount = ($2,000 − $100) × 0.02 = $38

25	Office Supplies (or expense)	500	
	Accounts Payable		500

(To record purchase of office supplies)

[Note that the amount is not debited to purchases because these are not goods for resale.]

3.

WILLIS MERCHANDISING CORPORATION
Statement of Earnings
Month Ended September 30, 2009

Sales revenues		
Sales	$49,000	
Less: Sales discounts	700	
Net sales		$48,300

Cost of goods sold

Merchandise inventory, September 1		$ 2,500
Purchases	$26,000	
Less: Purchase returns and allowances	900	
Net purchases	25,100	
Add: Freight in	1,000	
Cost of goods purchased		26,100
Cost of goods available for sale		28,600
Merchandise inventory, September 30		3,300
Cost of goods sold		25,300
Gross profit		$ 23,000

4.

Merchandise Inventory

Beg. of Year 1	Bal.	400		
(Purchase)		1,000	100	(Purchase return)
(Freight)		(b) 130	(a) 30	(Purchase discount)
			750	(Cost of goods sold)
End of Year 1; Beg. of Year 2				
	Bal. (c), (d)	650		
(Purchase)		900		
			(e) 150	(Purchase return)
(Freight)		100	60	(Purchase discount)
			(f) 1,040	(Cost of goods sold)
End of Year 2	Bal.	400		

The missing data can then be calculated as follows:

a. Purchases – purchase returns – purchases discounts = net purchases

   $1,000 – $100 – purchase discount = $870
   Purchase discount = $30

b. Net purchases + freight = Cost of goods purchased

   $870 + freight = $1,000
        Freight = $130

c. Ending inventory = $400+ $1,000 + $130 – $100 – $30 – $750
                    = $650

d. Opening inventory Year 2 = ending inventory Year 1
     = $650

e. Purchases – purchase returns – purchases discounts = net purchases
    $900 – purchase returns – $60 = $690
    Purchase returns = $150

f. Beginning inventory + cost of goods purchased – cost of goods sold = ending inventory
    $650 + $790 – cost of goods sold = $400
    Therefore cost of goods sold equals $650 + $790 – $400 = $1,040

Note: Other calculations could have been used to arrive at the answers shown above.

5.

a. $ 30 ($1,000 - $100 - $870)
b. $ 130 ($1,000 - $870)
c. $ 1,400 ($400 + $1,000)
d. $ 650 ($1,400 (from c) - $750)
e. $ 650 (from d)
f. $ 150 ($900 - $60 - $690)
g. $ 790 ($690 + $100)
h. $ 1,440 ($650 (from e) + $790 (from g))
i. $ 1,040 ($1,440 (from h) - $400)

6. (Domtar $ in USD millions; Cascades $ in CAD millions)

a.

	Domtar	Cascades
Net sales	$5,947	$3,929
Cost of sales	4,757	3,201
Gross profit	1,190	728
Gross profit margin	$\frac{\$1,190}{\$5,947} = 20.0\%$	$\frac{\$728}{\$3,929} = 18.5\%$

b. Each of the companies uses slightly different terminology that has the same meaning as earnings from operations, as follows:

	Domtar	Cascades
Gross profit (from above)	$1,190	$728
Less operating expenses:		
Domtar: ($471 + $408 + $92 + $4 + $14 – $69) =	920	
Cascades: ($208 + $390 – $17 +$9 – $6) =		584
Operating income	$270	$144

c.

	Domtar	Cascades
Domtar: $70 ÷ $5,947 =	1.2%	
Cascades: $95 ÷ $3,929 =		2.4%

As we saw in (a), Domtar reported the best gross profit margin of both companies, at 20 percent. However, Domtar reports the worst profit margin, at 1.2 percent, lower than both Cascades and the industry. This is primarily because Cascades reported additional earnings from companies it owns shares in (significantly influences).

chapter 6

Reporting and Analyzing Inventory

Chapter Overview

Chapter 6 explains the procedures for determining inventory quantities and the methods for determining the cost of goods sold and the cost of inventory on hand, their specific identification method, and the two cost formulas: first-in, first-out (FIFO) and average. You will also see the effects of inventory errors on the statement of earnings and the balance sheet. Finally, we will discuss how to report and analyze inventory.

Review of Specific Study Objectives

- All companies need to determine inventory quantities at the end of the accounting period, regardless of whether a company uses **a periodic inventory system or a perpetual inventory system**.

study objective 1

Describe the steps in determining inventory quantities.

- If a **perpetual** inventory system is used, a company takes a physical inventory at the end of the year for two purposes:

  1. to check the accuracy of its perpetual inventory records, and
  2. to determine the amount of inventory lost due to shrinkage or theft.

- If a **periodic** inventory system is used, a company takes a physical inventory at the end of the year for two different purposes:

  1. to determine the inventory on hand on the balance sheet date, and
  2. to determine the cost of goods sold for the period.

- Taking a physical inventory count involves actually counting, weighing, or measuring each kind of inventory on hand. To minimize errors, a company should ensure that it has a good system of internal control in place. **Internal control** consists of all the related methods and measures adopted within an organization to help it achieve reliable financial reporting, effective and efficient operations, and compliance with relevant laws and regulations. Some internal control measures include the following:

  1. The counting should be done by employees who do not have responsibility for the custody or recordkeeping of the inventory.
  2. Each counter should establish the validity of each inventory item: this means checking if the items actually exist, how many of them are there, and what condition they are in.
  3. There should be a second count by another employee or auditor. Counting should take place in teams of two.
  4. Prenumbered inventory tags should be used to ensure that all inventory items are counted and that none are counted more than once.

- Before the counting process begins, the ownership of the goods must be determined. There is one rule to follow. **Goods in transit should be included in the inventory of the company that has legal title to the goods.** The terms of sale determines ownership as follows:

  1. When terms are **free on board (F.O.B.) shipping point**, ownership of the goods passes to the buyer when the public carrier accepts the goods from the seller.
  2. When terms are **F.O.B. destination**, ownership of the goods remains with the seller until the goods reach the buyer.

- In some lines of businesses, it is customary to hold goods belonging to other parties and sell them, for a fee, without ever taking ownership of the goods. These are called **consigned goods**. These goods must be included in the inventory count of the other party and not the dealer. For example, Charlie takes goods that he wishes to sell to Barb's place of business. Barb agrees to try to sell them for Charlie, for a commission, of course. Charlie is at all times the owner of the goods until they are sold. Even though the goods are physically at Barb's place of business, Barb never has title to the goods. So, at the time of the physical count of the inventory, Charlie must remember to count those consigned goods as part of the inventory.

study objective 2

Apply the methods of cost determination— specific identification, FIFO, and average—under a perpetual inventory system.

- After the quantity of units of inventory has been determined, unit costs are applied to those quantities to determine the total cost of goods sold and cost of ending inventory. The cost of goods sold and of ending inventory will differ depending on which cost method is selected.

- The first method that can be used to determine cost of goods sold and ending inventory is specific identification, which requires that records be kept of the original cost of each individual inventory item. **Specific identification is appropriate and required for goods that are not ordinarily interchangeable, and for goods that are produced and segregated for specific projects.** This method is most practical to use when a company sells a limited number of items, such as cars or antiques, that have high unit costs and can easily be traced from purchase through to sale. While specific identification works well when a company sells high-unit-cost items that can be clearly identified from purchase through to sale, there are also disadvantages to using this method. For example, management may manipulate earnings by choosing to sell units with higher or lower purchase costs and therefore affecting cost of goods sold, which then affects earnings.

- Because the specific identification method is only suitable for certain kinds of inventories, other methods of cost determination, known as "cost formulas," are available.

  1. FIFO
  2. Average

  These two cost formulas can be used in both the perpetual and periodic inventory systems.

  We will first examine these under a perpetual inventory system.

- **First-in, first-out (FIFO)** assumes that the earliest (oldest) goods purchased are the first ones to be sold. FIFO parallels the actual physical flow of goods. Although a cost formula chosen by a company does not have to match the actual physical flow of goods, it should correspond as closely as possible. FIFO achieves that because it makes good business sense to sell the oldest units first.

- **Average cost** recognizes that it is not possible to measure a specific physical flow of inventory when the goods available for sale are homogeneous or indistinguishable. Under this cost formula, the allocation of the cost of goods available for sale between cost of goods sold and ending inventory is made based on the weighted average unit cost of the merchandise.

- To illustrate how the FIFO and average cost formulas work in a perpetual inventory system, assume that the following purchases are made:

Oct. 10	100 units @ $2
Nov. 11	200 units @ $3
Dec. 15	300 units @ $4

If 400 units are finally sold on December 20, FIFO yields the following:

	Purchases			Cost of Goods Sold			Balance		
Date	Units	Cost	Total	Units	Cost	Total	Units	Cost	Total
Oct. 10	100	$2	$200				100	$2	$200
Nov. 11	200	$3	600				100 200	$2 $3	} 800
Dec. 15	300	$4	1,200				100 200 300	$2 $3 $4	} 2,000
Dec. 20				100 200 100	$2 $3 $4	} $1,200	200	$4	800

Please note that FIFO always yields the same results whether a perpetual or periodic inventory system is used.

Under the average cost formula, a new average cost is calculated after each purchase is made. Assume that the same purchases made under FIFO are also made in this example. When the 400 units are sold under the average cost formula, the following results:

	Purchases			Cost of Goods Sold			Balance		
Date	Units	Cost	Total	Units	Cost	Total	Units	Cost	Total
Oct. 10	100	$2	$200				100	$2.00	$200
Nov. 11	200	$3	600				300	$2.67[1]	800
Dec. 15	300	$4	1,200				600	$3.33[2]	2,000
Dec. 20				400	$3.33	$1,333[3]	200	$3.33	667

[1] $800 \div 300 = $2.67
[2] $2,000 \div 600 = $3.33
[3] Adjusted for the effects of rounding.

In contrast to FIFO, the average cost formula will yield different results in a perpetual and periodic inventory system.

- Inventory affects both the balance sheet and statement of earnings since ending inventory is included as a current asset on the balance sheet and cost of goods sold is included on the statement of earnings.

- Companies that have goods that are not ordinarily interchangeable, or goods that have been produced and segregated for specific projects, must use the specific identification method to determine the cost of their inventory. Otherwise, they can choose to use either FIFO or average. It should consider the following objectives in making its choice:

  1. Choose a method that corresponds as closely as possible to the physical flow of goods.
  2. Report an inventory cost on the balance sheet that is close to the inventory's recent cost.
  3. Use the same method for all inventories having a similar nature and usage in the company.

study objective 3

Explain the financial statement effects of the inventory cost determination methods and of inventory errors.

- The following table summarizes the financial statement effects of the three cost determination methods, assuming that prices are rising:

	Specific Identification	FIFO	Average
Statement of earnings			
Cost of goods sold	Variable	Lowest	Highest
Gross profit	Variable	Highest	Lowest
Net earnings	Variable	Highest	Lowest
Balance sheet			
Cash (pre-tax)	Same	Same	Same
Ending inventory	Variable	Highest	Lowest
Retained earnings	Variable	Highest	Lowest

These effects will be the inverse if prices are falling, and the same for all three methods if prices are constant. In all cases, it does not matter whether a company uses the perpetual or periodic inventory system. Also, all three inventory cost determination methods will result in the same cash flow because sales and purchases are not affected.

- Inventory errors affect the determination of cost of goods sold and net earnings in two periods because the ending inventory of one period becomes the beginning inventory of the next period.

- An error in beginning inventory will have a reverse effect on net earnings of the same accounting period (if beginning inventory is understated, then net earnings will be overstated). An error in ending inventory will have the same effect on net earnings of the same accounting period (if ending inventory is understated, then net earnings will be understated, too).

- An error in ending inventory of the current period will have a reverse effect on net earnings of the next accounting period. Even though there is an error, total net earnings will be correct over the two periods because the errors offset each other.

- An error in beginning inventory does not result in a corresponding error in the ending inventory for that same period.

- On the balance sheet, if ending inventory is overstated, then both assets and shareholders' equity will be overstated. If ending inventory is understated, then both assets and shareholders' equity will be understated.

- Presenting inventory appropriately on the financial statements is important because inventory is usually the largest current asset (merchandise inventory) on the balance sheet and the largest expense (cost of goods sold) on the statement of earnings. The inventory on the balance sheet should be presented at the **lower of cost and net realizable value (LCNRV)**. For a merchandising company, **NRV** is the selling price less any costs required to make the goods ready for sale.

> study objective 4
>
> Demonstrate the presentation and analysis of inventory.

- The **LCNRV** rule is applied to the inventory at the end of the accounting period after specific identification, FIFO, or average has been used to determine the cost. To apply this rule, the following steps must be followed:

1. Determine the cost of the inventory.
2. Determine the NRV of the inventory.
3. Compare the values determined in steps 1 and 2. Use the lower value to report inventory on the financial statements.

The LCNRV rule should be applied to individual inventory items, rather than total inventory, although in certain cases, it can be applied to groups of similar items.

- The accounting entries associated with **NRV** are as follows:

Cost of Goods Sold
      Allowance to Reduce Inventory to NRV
(To record decline in inventory value from original cost to NRV)

The Allowance to Reduce Inventory to NRV account is a contra asset account to the Inventory account on the balance sheet. This is called the **allowance method** of recording inventory at the lower amount and is similar to the accumulated depreciation contra asset account. When there is clear evidence of an increase in NRV because of changed economic circumstances, the amount of the write-down is reversed as follows:

Allowance to Reduce Inventory to NRV

    Cost of Goods Sold

(To reverse previous write-down of inventory)

It must be noted that recovering the loss up to the original cost is permitted, but **may never exceed the original cost.**

- The **inventory turnover ratio** can help in managing inventory levels. It is calculated by dividing cost of goods sold by average inventory. (Average inventory is calculated by adding together the beginning and the ending inventories of a period and dividing the sum by two.) If a company's cost of goods sold is $50,000 and its average inventory is $16,000, then its inventory turnover is 3.13 times (rounded). This means that the company sells its entire inventory about three times every accounting period.

- **Days in inventory** is calculated by dividing the inventory turnover into 365. Using the same example as above, $365 \div 3.13 = 116.6$ days. This means that it takes the company about 117 days to sell its inventory.

- **Both the inventory turnover and days in inventory ratios must be compared with something to be meaningful.** They may be compared with the same company's numbers from prior periods or with the numbers of other companies in the same industry.

- Both of the inventory cost formulas, FIFO and average, described earlier in the chapter for a perpetual inventory system, may be used in a periodic inventory system.

- Using the following data, we calculate the ending inventory and cost of goods sold under each of the cost formulas using a periodic inventory system. Under a periodic system, the different dates of each of the sales is ignored. Instead, at the end of the period, an assumption is made that the entire pool of cost is available for allocation between cost of goods sold and ending inventory.

study objective 5

Apply the inventory cost formulas—FIFO and average—under a periodic inventory system.

Date	Units	Unit Cost	Total Cost
Feb. 1	300	$4	$ 1,200
Mar. 9	400	5	2,000
May 8	600	6	3,600
June 3	500	7	3,500
	1,800		$10,300

A physical count shows that there are 550 units in ending inventory. The February 1 units are the beginning inventory, and $10,300 is the cost of goods available for sale. To allocate the costs, the first step involves the calculation of the ending inventory, and the second step involves the calculation of cost of goods sold.

FIFO:

There are 1,250 units that were sold; therefore, there are 550 units remaining in ending inventory. (1,800 units – 1,250 units)

The ending inventory consists of the most recent purchases (remember, under FIFO, the first goods in are the first goods out, and so what is left in ending inventory is the last goods to be received). To get to 550, begin counting with the June 3 purchase.

June 3	500	×	$7	=	$3,500
May 8	50	×	6	=	300
	550				$3,800

The cost of goods sold is calculated by subtracting the ending inventory from the cost of goods available for sale. If you subtract what is still on hand from the total goods available for sale, the difference must be the amount sold. The cost of goods sold calculation is as follows:

Cost of goods available for sale	$10,300
Less: Ending inventory	3,800
Cost of goods sold	$ 6,500

Average:

To calculate an average unit cost, divide cost of goods available for sale of $10,300 by the total units available for sale, 1,800. The average unit cost is $5.722. Please note, too, that the company never paid $5.722 for any units purchased: This is simply a weighted average unit cost.

This unit cost is applied to ending inventory as follows:

Ending inventory:	550	×	$5.722	=	$3,147

The cost of goods sold calculation is as follows:

Cost of goods available for sale	$10,300
Less: Ending inventory	3,147
Cost of goods sold	$ 7,153

Chapter Self-Test

As you work through the questions and problems, remember to use the **Decision Toolkit** discussed and used in the text:

1. *Decision Checkpoints*: At this point, you ask a question.
2. *Info Needed for Decision*: You make a choice regarding the information needed to answer the question.
3. *Tool to Use for Decision*: At this point, you review just what the information chosen in step 2 does for the decision-making process.
4. *How to Evaluate Results*: You conduct an evaluation of information for answering the question.

Note: The notation (SO1) means that the question was drawn from study objective number one. All questions marked with an asterisk (*) relate to material in Appendix 6A.

Multiple Choice

Please circle the correct answer.

(SO1)   1. The taking of a physical inventory count in a perpetual inventory system is done for the following reasons:
  - a.   to check the accuracy of the perpetual records and to determine the inventory lost due to theft or shrinkage.
  - b.   to determine the cost of goods sold.
  - c.   to determine the inventory on hand.
  - d.   to determine the ownership of the goods.

(SO1)   2. Goods held on consignment are
  - a.   never owned by the consignee.
  - b.   included in the consignee's ending inventory.
  - c.   kept for sale on the premises of the consignor.
  - d.   included as part of no one's ending inventory.

(SO1)   3. If goods are shipped F.O.B. destination, then which of the following parties includes in its inventory the goods while they are in transit?
  - a.   Shipping company
  - b.   Buyer
  - c.   Seller
  - d.   Both the buyer and the seller include the goods in their inventory

(SO1)   4. Ceil gives goods on consignment to Jerry who agrees to try to sell them for a 25 percent commission. At the end of the accounting period, which of the following parties includes in its inventory the consigned goods?
  - a.   Ceil
  - b.   Jerry
  - c.   Both Ceil and Jerry
  - d.   Neither Ceil nor Jerry

(SO1)   5. Which of the following methods of cost determination actually parallels the physical flow of goods?
  - a.   NRV
  - b.   FIFO
  - c.   Average cost
  - d.   Specific identification

(SO2)   6. Which are known as cost formulas?
  - a.   Specific identification
  - b.   Average cost
  - c.   FIFO
  - d.   Both (b) and (c)

(SO2)   7. Assume that a company uses a perpetual inventory system and the specific identification method to determine costs. Assume that this company purchases the following: a diamond necklace for $19,000; a diamond tiara for $14,000;

diamond earrings for $8,000; and a diamond ring for $10,000. During June, the company sells the diamond tiara for $20,000 and the diamond necklace for $25,000. What is the company's cost of goods sold for June?

   a. $19,000
   b. $14,000
   c. $33,000
   d. $18,000

8. Assume the same data used in #7. What is the company's ending inventory at the end of June? (SO2)

   a. $33,000
   b. $18,000
   c. $29,000
   d. $45,000

9. Under a perpetual inventory system, a company can use either the FIFO or average cost formula, if its goods are interchangeable. What is one of the objectives that the company should consider in making a choice between FIFO and average? (SO3)

   a.   Choose a method that corresponds as closely as possible to the physical flow of goods.
   b.   Report an inventory cost on the balance sheet that is close to the inventory's earliest or oldest costs.
   c.   Use different cost methods for all inventories having a similar nature and usage in the company.
   d.   The method selected does not need to correspond to the physical flow of goods.

10. Which cost determination method provides the best statement of earnings valuation? (SO3)

   a.   FIFO
   b.   Specific identification
   c.   Average cost
   d.   All are equal

11. Using the lower of cost and net realizable value (LCNRV) rule is an example of the accounting concept of (SO4)

   a.   revenue recognition.
   b.   materiality.
   c.   matching.
   d.   full disclosure.

12. Net sales are $80,000; cost of goods sold is $30,000; and average inventory is $20,000. The inventory turnover is (SO4)

   a.   4.00 times.
   b.   2.67 times.
   c.   1.50 times.
   d.   0.25 times.

(SO3)   13. If the beginning inventory is overstated, then the current year's
   a.   cost of goods sold is overstated.
   b.   cost of goods sold is understated.
   c.   ending inventory is overstated.
   d.   ending inventory is understated.

(SO3)   14. A company reports net earnings of $50,000 in 2009 and $75,000 in 2010. Later, it was discovered that two errors were made: the ending inventory in 2009 was understated by $10,000, and the ending inventory in 2010 was overstated by $5,000. The corrected net earnings are
   a.   2009: $60,000; 2010: $60,000.
   b.   2009: $60,000; 2010: $80,000.
   c.   2009: $40,000; 2010: $80,000.
   d.   2009: $40,000; 2010: $60,000.

(SO4)   15. On January 1, a company had an inventory of $14,000. On December 31 of the same year, the company had an inventory of $18,000. Sales for the year were $400,000, and the gross profit margin was 30 percent. What is the company's inventory turnover for the year?
   a.   7.5 times
   b.   20.0 times
   c.   17.5 times
   d.   15.6 times

16. Using the information in #15 above, calculate the number of days of inventory (rounded to the nearest day) that the company has.
   a.   18 days
   b.   21 days
   c.   23 days
   d.   49 days

(SO2)   17. The results under _____ in a perpetual inventory system are the same as in a periodic inventory system.
   a.   average cost
   b.   FIFO
   c.   specific identification
   d.   none of these

Please use the following data for questions 18 and 19, where a periodic inventory system is used:

Date	Units	Unit Cost	Total Cost
Feb. 5	200	$2	$ 400
Mar. 6	500	4	2,000
Apr. 9	400	6	2,400
June 7	300	7	2,100
	1,400		$6,900

On June 30, there are 350 units in ending inventory.

(SO5)   *18. What is the cost of the ending inventory using the FIFO cost formula in a periodic inventory system?
   a. $1,000
   b. $1,726
   c. $2,400
   d. $5,177

*19. What is the cost of goods sold using the average cost formula in a periodic   (SO5)
inventory system?
   a. $1,000
   b. $1,726
   c. $2,400
   d. $5,177

Problems

1.   Jensen Corporation has just completed a physical inventory count at year end,   (SO1)
     December 31, 2009. Only the items on the shelves, in storage, and in the receiving
     area were counted and costed, using the FIFO cost formula. The ending invento-
     ry amounted to $88,000. During the audit, the following additional information
     was discovered:

   a.   Some office supplies in the amount of $400 were included in the inventory count.
        These supplies will be used in the office and will not be available for sale.

   b.   On December 27, 2009, Jensen shipped goods to a customer. The goods costing
        $900 were sold for $1,200. The goods were shipped F.O.B. destination and were
        received by the customer on January 3, 2010. Because the goods were not on the
        shelves, Jensen excluded them from the physical inventory count.

   c.   On the date of the inventory, Jensen received notice from a supplier that goods
        ordered earlier, at a cost of $3,500, had been delivered to the transportation
        company on December 28, 2009; the terms were F.O.B. shipping point. Because
        the shipment had not arrived on December 31, 2009, it was excluded from the
        physical inventory.

   d.   On December 31, 2009, there were goods in transit to customers, with terms
        F.O.B. shipping point, amounting to $750 (expected delivery on January 8, 2010).
        Because the goods had been shipped, they were excluded from the physical
        inventory count.

   e.   On December 31, 2009, Jensen shipped $1,200 worth of goods to a customer,
        F.O.B. destination on January 5, 2010. Because the goods were not on hand, they
        were not included in the physical inventory count.

   f.   Jensen, as the consignee, had goods on consignment that cost $3,700. Because
        these goods were on hand as of December 31, 2009, they were included in the
        physical inventory count.

   Analyze the above information and calculate a corrected amount for the ending
   inventory. Explain the basis for your treatment of each item.

2.   A company has the following transactions for the month of May: (SO2)

Date	Explanation	Units	Unit Cost	Total Cost
May 1	Beginning inventory	3,000	$4	$12,000
12	Purchase	7,000	5	35,000
20	Sale	8,000		
25	Purchase	3,200	6	19,200
30	Sale	4,300		
				$66,200

Determine the cost of goods sold and ending inventory under a perpetual inventory system using (a) FIFO and (b) average.

3.   A company, in its first year of operations, has the following inventory transactions for the year:

Date	Units Purchased	Unit Cost	Units Sold
Jan. 5	500	$5.00	
Feb. 10	800	6.75	
Mar. 6			1,000
June 15	700	7.00	
July 16			400
Aug. 12	500	8.00	
Sep. 11	300	10.00	
Oct. 25			500
Nov. 25	200	12.00	
Dec. 20			500

(SO2)   a.   Assume a perpetual inventory system using average cost. What is the cost of goods sold for the March 6 sale?

(SO2)   b.   Assume a perpetual inventory system using FIFO. What is the cost of goods sold for the March 6 sale?

(SO5)   *c.   Assume a periodic inventory system using FIFO. What is the cost of goods sold for the year?

(SO5)   *d.   Assume a periodic inventory system using average cost. What is the cost of goods sold for the year?

4.   A company has the following statement of earnings:

	2009	2010
Sales	$50,000	$70,000
Cost of goods sold	30,000	45,000
Gross profit	20,000	25,000
Operating expenses	14,000	15,000
Earnings before income tax	6,000	10,000
Income tax expense (25%)	1,500	2,500
Net earnings	$4,500	$7,500

After the preparation of the above statements, it was discovered that the ending inventory on December 31, 2009, was understated by $3,000. The value of the ending inventory on December 31, 2010, was correct. The company uses a perpetual inventory system, and the inventory, before the understatement was discovered, was $8,000 for 2009 and $10,000 for 2010.

(SO4)   a.   Recalculate the statement of earnings to reflect the correct inventory amount.

b. Calculate the effect of the inventory correction on the gross profit margin.   (SO4 in Chapter 5)

c. Calculate the effect of the inventory correction on the profit margin.   (SO4 in Chapter 5)

5. Please refer to the Domtar and Cascades financial statements found in
    the appendices at the end of this study guide for information for answer-
    ing the following questions. Do not forget to use the **Decision Toolkit**
    approach for help in the problem solving.

a. Cascades uses the average cost formula and Domtar uses the last-in, first-out   (SO3)
    (LIFO) cost formula. Why do you think that Domtar uses a different cost
    formula than Cascades?

b. For both Domtar and Cascades, calculate the inventory turnover and days in   (SO4)
    inventory for 2007.

c. Assume that the industry ratios were as follows for 2007:   (SO4)

    Inventory turnover   6.6
    Days in inventory   55

    Compare the performance of Domtar and Cascades according to how they have
    managed their inventories in 2007.

Solutions to Self-Test

Multiple Choice

1. a   Answers b and c deal with the periodic inventory system. Answer d is
        incorrect—counting inventory will not determine the ownership of the
        items.

2. a   Under a consignment arrangement, the holder of the goods (called the
        consignee) does not own the goods.

3. c   When goods are shipped F.O.B. destination, the seller retains title to the
        goods until they reach the buyer's place of business. Since the seller has title,
        he pays the shipping costs.

4. a   Consigned goods are always the property of the person who has put them
        out on consignment. They are Ceil's; Jerry never has title to the goods.

5. d   FIFO and average cost both assume a flow of costs that may not be the
        same as the actual physical flow of goods, unlike the specific identification
        method. NRV is not a cost determination method.

6. d   FIFO and average are known as "cost formulas" because they assume a flow
        of costs that may not be the same as the actual physical flow of the goods,
        unlike the specific identification method. Consequently, both b and c are
        correct answers.

7. c $14,000 + $19,000 = $33,000

8. b $8,000 + $10,000 = $18,000

9. a   The following objectives should be considered:

1. Choose a method that corresponds as closely as possible to the physical flow of goods.

2. Report an inventory cost on the balance sheet that is close to the inventory's recent cost.

3. Use the same method for all inventories having a similar nature and usage in the company.

10. b   Specific identification exactly matches costs and revenues on the statement of earnings.

11. c   Because of the matching principle, a loss in the value of the inventory should be deducted from (matched with) revenues in the period when the loss occurs, not in the period when the inventory is sold.

12. c $30,000 ÷ $20,000 = 1.5

13. a   An error in beginning inventory does not have an effect on ending inventory of the same year.

14. a   2009: $50,000 + $10,000 = $60,000

2010: $75,000 − $10,000 − $5,000 = $60,000

15. c   The percentage for cost of goods sold = 100% − 30% = 70%

Cost of goods sold = 70% × $400,000 = $280,000

$$\text{Inventory turnover} = \frac{\text{Cost of goods sold}}{\text{Average inventory}}$$

$$= \frac{\$280,000}{(\$14,000 + \$18,000) \div 2} = 17.5 \text{ times}$$

16. b   365 ÷ 17.5 = 21 days

17. b   Although the calculation format may differ, the results under FIFO in a perpetual inventory system are the same as in a periodic inventory system.

*18. c

June 7	300	×	$7	= $2,100
Apr. 9	50	×	6	= 300
	350			$2,400 ending inventory

*19. d $6,900 ÷ 1,400 = $4.93 (rounded)/unit × 1,050 units = $5,177

Problems

1.

$88,000 Unadjusted ending inventory amount

a. −$400. The office supplies are not for sale and are to be excluded from ending inventory.

b. +$900. Goods should be included as Jensen owns them until they are received by the customer on January 3.

c.   +$3,500. Goods belong to Jensen. Title passed when supplier delivered the goods to the transportation company.

d. $0. Because the goods were shipped F.O.B. shipping point, Jensen no longer has title to these goods. The items were properly excluded from ending inventory.

e.   +$1,200. Goods were shipped F.O.B. destination. Jensen retains title until the customer receives them.

f.   −$3,700. These goods are owned by the consignor, not the consignee, and should not be included in Jensen's inventory.

$89,500 corrected ending inventory amount ($88,000 − $400 + $900 + $3,500 + $1,200 − $3,700)

2.

a.   FIFO—Perpetual

	Purchases			Cost of Goods Sold			Balance		
Date	Units	Cost	Total	Units	Cost	Total	Units	Cost	Total
May 1							3,000	$4	$12,000
12	7,000	$5	$35,000				3,000 7,000	4 5 }	47,000
20				3,000 5,000	$4 5 }	$37,000	2,000	5	10,000
25	3,200	6	19,200				2,000 3,200	5 6 }	29,200
30				2,000 2,300	5 6 }	23,800	900	6	5,400
	10,200		$54,200	12,300		$60,800			

Hint: Check that the cost of goods sold and ending inventory equals the cost of goods available for sale: $60,800 + $5,400 = $66,200 ($12,000 + $54,200)

b.   Average—Perpetual

	Purchases			Cost of Goods Sold			Balance		
Date	Units	Cost	Total	Units	Cost	Total	Units	Cost	Total
May 1							3,000	$4.00	$12,000
12	7,000	$5	$35,000				10,000	4.70	47,000
20				8,000	$4.70	$37,600	2,000	4.70	9,400
25	3,200	6	19,200				5,200	5.50	28,600
30				4,300	5.50	23,650	900	5.50	4,950
	10,200		$54,200	12,300		$61,250			

Hint: Check that the cost of goods sold and ending inventory equals the cost of goods available for sale: $61,250 + $4,950 = $66,200 ($12,000 + $54,200)

3.

a.   The cost of goods sold for the March 6 sale is $6,077. The full perpetual inventory schedule is shown below for the average cost formula.

	Purchases			Cost of Goods Sold			Balance		
Date	Units	Cost	Total	Units	Cost	Total	Units	Cost	Total
Jan. 5	500	$5.00	$2,500				500	$5.00	$2,500
Feb. 10	800	6.75	5,400				1,300	6.08	7,900
Mar. 6				1,000	$6.08	$6,077	300	6.08	1,823
June 15	700	7.00	4,900				1,000	6.72	6,723
July 16				400	6.72	2,689	600	6.72	4,034
Aug. 12	500	8.00	4,000				1,100	7.30	8,034
Sep. 11	300	10.00	3,000				1,400	7.88	11,034
Oct. 25				500	7.88	3,941	900	7.88	7,093
Nov. 25	200	12.00	2,400				1,100	8.63	9,493
Dec. 20				500	8.63	4,315	600	8.63	5,178

The cost of goods sold, under the perpetual inventory system using average cost, is shown in the above table each time a sale is made. Total cost of goods sold is $17,022 ($6,077 + $2,689 + $3,941 + $4,315).

b.   Under a perpetual inventory system, the cost of goods sold is calculated each time a sale is made. The cost of goods sold, under FIFO, for the 1,000 units sold on March 6 is:

Jan. 5:	500	units	×	$5.00	=	$2,500
Feb. 10:	500	units	×	$6.75	=	3,375
	1,000					$5,875

*c.   Under a periodic inventory system, the individual sales dates are ignored. Instead, at the end of the period, we assume that the entire pool of cost of goods available for sale is allocated between cost of goods sold and ending inventory. The calculation of the cost of goods available for sale is shown in the following table:

Date	Units Purchased	Unit Cost	Total Cost
Jan. 5	500	$5.00	$ 2,500
Feb. 10	800	6.75	5,400
June 15	700	7.00	4,900
Aug. 12	500	8.00	4,000
Sep. 11	300	10.00	3,000
Nov. 25	200	12.00	2,400
Total goods available for sale	3,000		$22,200

The total sales are 1,000 + 400 + 500 + 500 = 2,400 units.
The ending inventory is: 3,000 − 2,400 units = 600 units.
The ending inventory, under FIFO, consists of the most recent purchases as follows:

Nov. 25	200	×	$12	=	$2,400
Sep. 11	300	×	10	=	3,000
Aug. 12	100	×	8	=	800
	600				$6,200

The cost of goods sold is calculated by subtracting the ending inventory from the cost of goods available for sale as follows:

Cost of goods available for sale	$22,200
Less: ending inventory	6,200
Cost of goods sold	$16,000

*d. The ending inventory, under average cost, consists of the number of units in ending inventory times the weighted average unit cost of the units purchased, as follows:

Weighted average unit cost is:

$$\frac{\$22,200}{3,000 \text{ units}} = \$7.40 \text{ per unit}$$

Ending inventory is: 600 units × $7.40 = $4,440

The cost of goods sold is calculated by subtracting the ending inventory from the cost of goods available for sale as follows:

Cost of goods available for sale	$22,200
Less: ending inventory	4,440
Cost of goods sold	$17,760

4.

a. If ending inventory is understated by $3,000 in 2009, then cost of goods sold is overstated in 2009 because of the inverse relationship between cost of goods sold and ending inventory. Furthermore, the beginning inventory for 2010 will also be understated in 2010 because the ending inventory in 2009 is carried forward to 2010. As a result, the cost of goods sold for 2010 is understated by $3,000. Assuming the ending inventory is calculated correctly at the end of the second year, 2010, this error stops but has had a 2-year effect. The following statement of earnings reflects the inventory correction:

	2009		2010	
	Incorrect	Correct	Incorrect	Correct
Sales	$50,000	$50,000	$70,000	$70,000
Cost of goods sold	30,000	27,000	45,000	48,000
Gross profit	20,000	23,000	25,000	22,000
Operating expenses	14,000	14,000	15,000	15,000
Earnings before income tax	6,000	9,000	10,000	7,000
Income tax expense (25%)	1,500	2,250	2,500	1,750
Net earnings	$4,500	$6,750	$7,500	$5,250

($2,250)	$2,250
Net earnings understated	Net earnings overstated

The combined net earnings for 2 years is correct because the errors cancel each other out.

In this illustration, the understatement of ending inventory results, in the same year, in an overstatement of the cost of goods sold and an understatement of gross profit, earnings before income tax, and net earnings. It also results in an understatement of the cost of goods sold in 2009 and an overstatement of gross profit, earnings before income tax, and net earnings for that year.

b.

Gross profit margin = Gross profit ÷ Net sales

	2009	2010
Before inventory correction:		
$20,000 ÷ $50,000	40.0%	
$25,000 ÷ $70,000		35.7%
After inventory correction:		
$23,000 ÷ $50,000	46.0%	
$22,000 ÷ $70,000		31.4%

c.

Profit margin = Net earnings ÷ Net sales

	2009	2010
Before inventory correction:		
$4,500 ÷ $50,000	9.0%	
$7,500 ÷ $70,000		10.7%
After inventory correction:		
$6,750 ÷ $50,000	13.5%	
$5,250 ÷ $70,000		7.5%

5.

a. Domtar may use LIFO because the nature of its inventories, and the economic benefits they produce, differ from those of Cascades. It should be noted that LIFO is not permitted for use in Canada or internationally, although it is permitted for use in the United States. Domtar reports using U.S. generally accepted accounting principles, which is why it is able to choose to use LIFO.

b. Domtar: average inventory = (U.S. $936 million + U.S. $520 million) ÷ 2 = U.S. $728 million
   Inventory turnover = cost of goods sold ÷ average inventory
   U.S. $4,757 million ÷ U.S. $728 million = 6.5 times
   Days in inventory = 365 ÷ inventory turnover
   365 ÷ 6.5 = 56 days

   Cascades: average inventory = ($555 million + $548 million) ÷ 2 = $552 million
   Inventory turnover = cost of goods sold ÷ average inventory
   $3,201 million ÷ $552 million = 5.8 times
   Days in inventory = 365 ÷ inventory turnover
   365 ÷ 5.8 = 63 days

c. Domtar's inventory ratios are close to the industry average of 6.6 times for the inventory turnover and 55 days in inventory. Cascades ratios are worse than the industry averages. This means that Cascades had a more difficult time in managing its inventory levels as compared with Domtar. Of course, differences could also be explained by the use of different inventory cost formulas, which will be discussed in more detail in an intermediate accounting course.

chapter 7

Internal Control and Cash

Chapter Overview

Chapter 7 discusses the importance of managing cash and how to control it. The chapter discusses the essential features of an internal control system and describes how these controls apply to cash receipts and disbursements. You will learn how to prepare a bank reconciliation and how to report cash on the balance sheet. Finally, you will learn the basic principles of cash management and tools for help in managing and monitoring cash.

Review of Specific Study Objectives

- Good internal control systems have five primary components, listed below:

  1. Control Environment: It is the responsibility of the management to make it clear that the organization values integrity, and that unethical activity will not be tolerated (often referred to as "setting the tone at the top").
  2. Risk Assessment: Companies must identify and analyze the various factors that create risk for the business and determine how to manage these risks.
  3. Control Activities: To reduce the occurrence of fraud, the management must design policies and procedures to address the specific risks faced by the company.

4. Information and Communication: The system must capture and communicate all pertinent information both down and up the organization and communicate it to appropriate external parties.
5. Monitoring: Internal control systems must be monitored periodically for their adequacy. Significant deficiencies need to be reported to the management and/or the board of directors.

---

study objective 1

Explain the activities that help achieve internal control.

● We will focus on the **control** component because these activities form the backbone of a company's plan to address the risks it faces. Control activities include the following:

1. Authorization of Transactions and Activities: Control is most effective when only one person is responsible for a given task. Therefore, it is important to establish who in the organization has responsibility and authority to perform transactions.
2. Segregation of Duties: The responsibility for related activities should be assigned to different individuals. This should decrease the potential for errors and irregularities. Related purchasing activities include ordering merchandise, receiving goods, and paying (or authorizing payment) for merchandise. Related sales activities include making a sale, shipping (or delivering) the goods, and billing the customer.
3. Documentation: Procedures should be established for documents. Wherever possible, documents should be prenumbered, and all documents should be accounted for. Source documents should be forwarded promptly to the accounting department to ensure accurate and timely recording of a transaction.
4. Physical Controls: Their use is essential to protect assets and records. Physical controls include mechanical and electronic controls to safeguard assets and enhance the accuracy and reliability of the accounting records.
5. Independent Checks of Performance: The four control activities that we just discussed—authorization of transactions and activities, segregation of duties, documentation, and physical controls—must be reviewed independently and frequently. These reviews should take place internally and externally, as described below.
    a. Internal Reviews: Independent internal reviews are especially useful in comparing accounting records with existing assets to ensure that nothing has been stolen. For independent internal reviews to be beneficial, three measures are recommended:
        1. The review should be done periodically or on a surprise basis.
        2. The review should be done by an employee who is independent of the personnel responsible for the information.
        3. Discrepancies and exceptions should be reported to a management level that can take appropriate corrective action.
    b. External Reviews: An important type of external review is conducted by the external auditors. External auditors, in contrast to internal auditors, are independent of the company. They are professional accountants hired by a company to report on whether or not the company's financial statements fairly present its financial position and results of operations.
6. Human Resource Controls: Other control measures include the following:
    a. Conduct thorough Background Checks: An inexpensive measure any company can take to reduce employee theft and fraud is for the human resources department to conduct thorough background checks.

    b.   Bonding of Employees who Handle Cash: Bonding involves acquiring insurance protection against theft of assets by dishonest employees.

    c.   Rotating Employees' Duties, and Requiring Employees to Take Vacations: These measures help to deter employees from attempting theft because the employees know that they cannot permanently conceal their theft.

- Internal controls generally provide reasonable assurance that assets are safeguarded and that the accounting records are accurate and reliable. In constructing the system, a company tries to have the best system at the lower cost. It attempts to have the benefits of the system outweigh the costs. There are, however, **limitations of any internal control system**. One involves the human element—a dishonest or incompetent employee can render the system ineffective, and two or more employees may collude to circumvent the system. (Performing a thorough background check when considering hiring a person is crucial.) The size of the company is also a factor. A large company has the resources, both human and financial, to put into place a sophisticated system of internal control. A small company may be very limited in both areas and must do the best it can with what it has.

- **Cash** consists of coins, currency (paper money), cheques, money orders, and money on hand or on deposit in a bank or similar depository. If a bank will accept an item at face value for deposit, then it is cash. Debit card transactions and bank credit card receipts, such as VISA, MasterCard, and American Express, are considered cash, but nonbank credit card receipts are not. Because cash is readily convertible into other assets, easily concealed and transported, and highly desired, internal control over cash is absolutely necessary. Cash does not include postdated cheques, staledated (more than 6 months old) cheques, or returned cheques (due to insufficient funds). Postage stamps or IOUs from employees also are not cash.

> study objective 2
>
> Apply control activities to cash receipts and payments.

- Generally, internal control over cash receipts is more effective when cash receipts are deposited intact into the bank account on a daily basis or are made by **electronic funds transfer.** Electronic funds transfer (EFT) is a way of transferring money electronically from one bank account directly to another without any paper money changing hands. Debit and credit card transactions, mentioned above, are examples of EFTs.

- A company must have effective control over cash receipts. The control activities were explained earlier and apply to cash receipts as follows:

1. Authorization of Transactions and Activities: Only designated personnel should be authorized to handle cash receipts.
2. Segregation of Duties: Different individuals receive cash, record cash receipts, and deposit or hold cash.
3. Documentation: A company must use remittance devices, cash register tapes, and deposit slips.
4. Physical Controls: A company should store cash in safes and bank vaults with limited access, and use cash registers.
5. Independent Checks of Performance: A company should have supervisors who count receipts daily, and have an accountant compare total receipts to bank deposits daily.
6. Human Resource Controls: A company should conduct background checks, bond personnel who handle cash, and require employees to take vacations.

- Generally, internal control over cash payments is more effective when payments are made by cheque or by EFT. The control activities that apply to cash payments are as follows:

  1. Authorization of Transactions and Activities: Only authorized personnel should sign cheques or issue electronic payments.
  2. Segregation of Duties: Different individuals approve and make payments, and ensure that cheque signers do not record cash payments.
  3. Documentation: Cheques should be prenumbered and used in sequence, and they should be issued only if an invoice has been approved.
  4. Physical Controls: A company should store cash in safes and bank vaults with limited access, and print cheques electronically.
  5. Independent Checks of Performance: Cheques and invoices should be compared, and a monthly bank reconciliation should be prepared.
  6. Human Resource Controls: A company should conduct background checks, bond personnel who handle cash, and require employees to take vacations.

study objective 3

Prepare a bank reconciliation.

- **The use of a bank contributes significantly to good internal control over cash**. A company can safeguard its cash by using a bank as a depository and clearing house for its cash, cheques received and written, and electronic funds received and paid. Use of a bank minimizes the amount of currency that must be kept on hand and control is strengthened because a double record of all transactions is kept.

- A company receives monthly bank statements and must reconcile the ending balance on the statement with the ending balance in the general ledger account "Cash." The two numbers are often not the same because of time lags (the bank has recorded something that the company has not, or vice versa) and errors made by either the bank or the company.

- In reconciling a bank account, it is customary to reconcile the balance per books and balance per bank to their adjusted (correct) cash balances. The reconciliation should be prepared by someone who has no other responsibilities for cash.

- The following are adjustments made to the column called "Balance per bank statement":

  1. Deposits in transit (deposits that the company has recorded but the bank has not) are always added to the balance per bank column.
  2. Outstanding cheques (cheques recorded by the company that have not yet been paid by the bank) are always subtracted from the balance per bank column.
  3. Errors may either be added to or subtracted from the column depending on the nature of the error.

- The following are adjustments made to the column called "Balance per books":

  1. Any unrecorded credit memoranda and other deposits should be added to the balance per books. For example, if the bank statement shows EFTs from customers paying their accounts on-line, unless they had previously been recorded by the company, these amounts will be added to the balance per books.
  2. Any unrecorded debit memoranda and other payments should be deducted from the balance per books. For example, if the bank statement shows bank service charges, this amount is deducted from the balance per books. Normally electronic payments will have already been recorded by the company. However, if

this has not been the case, then these payments must also be deducted from the balance per books.

3. Errors may either be added to or subtracted from the column depending on the nature of the error.

- The **key** question to ask when preparing a bank reconciliation is: *"Who knows about the transaction and has already recorded it, and who does not yet know about it?"* For example, with respect to bank service charges, the bank knows about them and has already subtracted them from the company account, reflecting this on the bank statement, but the company does not know the exact amount of the charges until it receives the statement.

- After the bank reconciliation has been prepared, each reconciling item in the balance per books column must be recorded by the company in a journal entry. (Bank personnel record any adjustments in the balance per bank statement column.) After the entries are journalized and posted, the balance in the Cash account should equal the total shown on the bank reconciliation.

- **Cash** is reported on the balance sheet and the cash flow statement. When presented on the balance sheet, cash on hand and cash in banks is combined and reported simply as Cash. Cash is listed first in the current assets section because it is the most liquid of assets. The sources and uses of cash are shown on the cash flow statement and reconciled to the ending cash balance reported on the balance sheet.

study objective 4

Explain the reporting and management of cash.

- Some companies label the first current asset **"Cash and cash equivalents."** A cash equivalent is a short-term, highly liquid investment that is readily convertible to cash and so near its maturity that its market value is relatively insensitive to changes in interest rates. Examples include treasury bills and money market funds, and short-term notes that normally have maturities of 3 months or less when purchased.

- If cash is restricted for a special purpose, then it should be reported separately as **"restricted cash."** If it is to be used within the next year, then it is reported as a current asset; if it is to be used at a time beyond 1 year, then it is reported as a noncurrent asset.

- In making loans to depositors, banks commonly require borrowers to maintain minimum cash balances. These minimum balances, called **compensating balances**, provide the bank with support for the loans. They are a form of restriction on the use of cash. A compensating balance should be reported as a noncurrent asset.

- The management of cash is critical to a company's success. A company's objective in the management of cash is to have sufficient cash to meet payments as they become due but to minimize the amount of non–revenue-generating cash on hand.

- There are six principles of cash management:

1. Increase the speed of collection on receivables. A company wants to receive cash as speedily as possible so that it can have the use of this money.
2. Keep inventory levels low. A company wants to minimize the costs associated with the carrying of inventory as much as possible.
3. Delay payment of liabilities. A company wants to pay its bills on time but not too early. It certainly wants to take advantage of all cash discounts offered.

4. Plan the timing of major expenditures. A company tries to make major expenditures when it has excess cash, usually during the off-season.
5. Invest idle cash. Cash that does not earn a return does a company little good. Idle cash should be invested in highly liquid (easy to sell) and risk-free (there is no concern that the party will default on its promise to pay principal and interest) investments.
6. Prepare a cash budget. A cash budget is a critical tool in effective cash management. It helps a company plan its cash needs by showing its anticipated cash flows.

Chapter Self-Test

As you work through the questions and problems, remember to use the **Decision Toolkit** discussed and used in the text:

1. *Decision Checkpoints:* At this point, you ask a question.
2. *Info Needed for Decision:* You make a choice regarding the information needed to answer the question.
3. *Tool to Use for Decision:* At this point, you review just what the information chosen in step 2 does for the decision-making process.
4. *How to Evaluate Results:* You conduct an evaluation of information for answering the question.

Note: The notation (SO1) means that the question was drawn from study objective number one.

Multiple Choice

Please circle the correct answer.

(SO1)   1. Which of the following statements is correct?
   a. Control is most effective when two or three people are given responsibility for the same task.
   b. The person who has custody of assets should not perform the record-keeping for the assets.
   c. The person who has custody of assets should also perform the record-keeping for the assets.
   d. It is a waste of company resources to have an employee perform independent internal review.

(SO1)   2. Which of the following statements is incorrect?
   a. Related purchasing activities should be assigned to different individuals.
   b. Safeguarding of assets is enhanced by the use of physical controls.
   c. Independent checks of performance should be done by an employee independent of the personnel responsible for the information.
   d. The use of prenumbered documents is not an important control activity.

(SO1)   3. The custodian of a company asset should
   a. have access to the accounting records for that asset.
   b. be someone outside the company.

    c.   not have access to the accounting records for that asset.
    d.   be an accountant.

4. Each of the following is a feature of a control activity, *except*   (SO1)
    a.   documentation of procedures.
    b.   allowing employees to defer their vacation.
    c.   holding one person responsible for a specific task.
    d.   keeping cash locked up in a safe.

5. Having one person responsible for the related activities of making a sale,   (SO2)
shipping goods to a customer, and billing the customer
    a.   is a good example of ensuring that transactions are recorded properly.
    b.   decreases the potential for errors and fraud.
    c.   is an example of good internal control.
    d.   increases the potential for errors and fraud.

6. An employee authorized to sign cheques should *not*   (SO2)
    a.   record cash deposits.
    b.   receive company mail.
    c.   record cash payments transactions.
    d.   approve sales transactions.

7. Which of the following is not considered cash?   (SO2)
    a.   Coins
    b.   Money orders
    c.   Short-term investment in another company's shares
    d.   Chequing account

8. A company has the following items: cash on hand, $1,000; cash in a chequing   (SO2, 4)
account, $3,000; cash in a savings account, $5,000; postage stamps, $50; and
120-day treasury bills, $10,000. How much should the company report as cash
on the balance sheet?
    a. $9,000
    b. $9,050
    c. $19,000
    d. $19,050

9. Effective internal control over cash payments include   (SO2)
    a.   the use of prenumbered cheques.
    b.   the storage of blank cheques in a secure place.
    c.   the separation of authorization of cheques and the actual writing of the
cheques.
    d.   All of the above are part of effective internal control over cash payments.

10. Which one of the following is one of the primary components of a good internal   (SO1)
control system?
    a.   Risk assessment
    b.   Documentation

          c.   Human resource controls
          d.   Segregation of duties

(SO3)   11.   Fiddler Corporation gathered the following information in preparing its June bank reconciliation:

Cash balance per books, June 30	$3,500
Deposits in transit	150
Electronic deposit	850
Bank charge for cheque printing	20
Outstanding cheques	2,000
NSF cheque	170

The adjusted cash balance per books on July 30 is
    a. $4,160
    b. $4,010
    c. $2,310
    d. $2,460

(SO3)   12.   Which of the following is added to the balance per books side of a bank reconciliation?
    a.   An outstanding cheque for $300.
    b.   An electronic deposit of $500 made by a customer.
    c.   A deposit in transit of $150.
    d.   A bank service charge for $50 for cheque printing.

(SO3)   13.   Cooper Corporation showed a balance in its Cash account of $1,250 when it received its monthly bank statement. It found the following reconciling items: deposits in transit, $256; outstanding cheques, $375; NSF cheque in the amount of $102; bank service charges of $27; and an EFT into the bank account for $850. What is the adjusted cash balance Cooper will show on its bank reconciliation?
    a. $1,131
    b. $1,852
    c. $1,971
    d. $1,981

(SO3)   14.   Which of the following items should be added to the balance per bank on a bank reconciliation?
    a.   A returned $200 cheque from the bank for insufficient funds.
    b.   Deposit of $600 incorrectly recorded by the bank as $60.
    c.   Deposit for $991 incorrectly recorded in the company's books for $919.
    d.   Cheque for $87 recorded as $78 in company's books.

(SO4)   15.   Which of the following bank reconciliation items would *not* result in an adjusting entry?
    a.   An error made by the company in recording a cheque.
    b.   Outstanding cheques.
    c.   Interest revenue earned on a bank account.
    d.   Collection of a note by the bank.

16. Cash equivalents include   (SO4)
    a.   short-term, highly liquid investments.
    b.   a note receivable, due in 3 months.
    c.   a 1-year guaranteed investment certificate.
    d.   investment securities, such as investment in shares of other companies.

17. On which two financial statements is Cash reported?   (SO4)
    a.   Balance sheet and cash flow statement
    b.   Balance sheet and statement of earnings
    c.   Balance sheet and statement of retained earnings
    d.   Statement of earnings and cash flow statement

18. If cash is restricted as to its use and will be used within the next year, then it   (SO4)
    should be
    a.   included in Cash on the balance sheet.
    b.   reported as a current liability on the balance sheet.
    c.   reported as a noncurrent asset on the balance sheet.
    d.   reported as a current asset separate from Cash and Cash Equivalents on the
         balance sheet.

19. Keeping inventory levels low and planning the timing of major expenditures are   (SO4)
    two basic principles of
    a.   internal control.
    b.   cash management.
    c.   inventory management.
    d.   share capital management.

20. With respect to cash management, most companies try to   (SO4)
    a.   keep as much spare cash on hand as possible in case of emergency.
    b.   keep a lot of cash in a non–interest-bearing chequing account because that
         type of account has the lowest fees.
    c.   invest idle cash, even if only overnight.
    d.   invest idle cash in illiquid investments because that is where money earns
         the greatest return.

21. The minimum cash balance required by borrowers is called   (SO2)
    a.   a compensating balance.
    b.   cash equivalent.
    c.   a liability.
    d.   financing.

Problems

1. You have been asked to help the Basil Corporation with its internal control pro-   (SO3)
    blems. Basil has 12 employees. There has not been any staff rotation between
    positions for at least 6 years because management believes that "the training costs
    of doing this would be too high." The company has a small Stores Department
    with one person who also works in the accounting department. That individual
    orders and receives goods and also pays the invoices. There is another person in
    the Accounting Department who handles all revenues. That individual makes

deposits to the bank when "the deposit is large enough to make it worthwhile to go to the bank." That person also opens the mail and holds any cash or cheques in a desk drawer until the deposit is made.

Identify four weaknesses in internal control and make recommendations to correct the weaknesses.

(SO3)   2.   The following information is available for the J By J Corporation as of June 30, 2009, to assist you in preparing its bank reconciliation.

(i)   Balance per bank, June 30, $1,617.
(ii)   Balance per books, June 30, $2,151.
(iii) Outstanding cheques at June 30 totalled $559.
(iv)   Deposits in transit at June 30, totalled $802.
(v)   An NSF cheque for $67 that was returned by the bank. The cheque was originally received by the company from a customer who made a payment on account.
(vi)   The bank statement showed bank service charges totalling $35 plus a $40 charge for processing the NSF cheque.
(vii) An electronic deposit of $760 was made by a customer in payment of her account.
(viii) On June 15, the company issued a cheque for $1,587 to a supplier on account. The cheque, which cleared the bank in June, was incorrectly journalized by the company for $1,578 by the company.
(ix)   Included with the cancelled cheques was a cheque issued by the G By G Corporation for $100 that was incorrectly charged to J By J Corporation by the bank.
(x)   An electronic payment of $800 was made for insurance for the month of June. This payment was not recorded in the company's books.

a.   Prepare a bank reconciliation for J By J Corporation as of June 30, 2009, using the above data.
b.   Prepare any journal entries required by the reconciliation.

(SO3)   3.   The bank reconciliation prepared by Star Corporation at July 31 showed the following outstanding cheques:

#101	$245
#113	560
#114	465
#117	657

A list of cheques and other debits recorded by the bank and the company during August follows:

Bank Statement
Cheques Paid and Other Debits
August 31

Date	Cheque Number	Amount
August 1	101	$245
2	121	352
5	122	678

11	114	465
13	123	560
15	Returned cheque—NSF	440
15	NSF fee	40
17	124	137
19	126	267
21	127	432
30	130	765
31	EFT, payment of insurance	568
31	Service charge	20

Cash Payments Journal
August 31

Date	Cheque Number	Amount
August 1	121	$352
3	122	687
6	123	560
9	124	137
13	125	287
14	126	267
16	127	432
20	128	206
22	129	925
24	130	765
29	131	429

Additional information:

The bank did not make any errors and the company did not record the EFT payment for insurance and the NSF cheque in its books.

a.   List the outstanding cheques at August 31.
b.   List any other item that must be included in the bank reconciliation for August.

4.   Please refer to the Domtar and Cascades financial statements found in the appendices at the end of this study guide for information for answering the following questions. Do not forget to use the **Decision Toolkit** approach for help in the problem solving.   (SO4)

a.   What is the name of the first current asset on each company's balance sheet? Please explain the two components.
b.   For each company, how much did Cash and Cash Equivalents increase or decrease from 2006 to 2007?
c.   How did Domtar and Cascades use their cash in 2007?

Solutions to Self-Test

Multiple Choice

1. b   Only one person should have responsibility for a task, and custody and record-keeping should always be separated. Internal reviews, or checks of performance, are a critical function, certainly not a waste of resources.

2. d   The use of prenumbered documents is very important.

3. c   The custodian of the asset cannot also be responsible for performing the record-keeping functions for the asset. These duties (custody and record-keeping) are related and must be performed by different individuals in accordance with the "Segregation of Duties" control activity.

4. b   Employees should take their vacation, not defer it. Answers a, c, and d are all examples of control activities.

5. d   When the same individual is responsible for related activities, the potential for errors and irregularities is increased.

6. c   These two duties (cheque signing and recording cash payments) are related and must be performed by different individuals in accordance with the "Segregation of Duties" control activity.

7. c   The short-term investment in another company's shares is not a cash equivalent.

8. a $1,000 + $3,000 + $5,000 = $9,000. Postage stamps are office supplies and are expensed when purchased. Treasury bills, due in 4 months, are short-term investments.

9. d   Use of prenumbered cheques forms part of "documentation"; storage of blank cheques forms part of "physical controls"; and separation of signing and writing cheques forms part of "segregation of duties."

10. a   The other answers (b, c, and d) form part of control activities.

11. a $3,500 + $850 – $20 – $170 = $4,160.

12. b   The outstanding cheque and the deposit in transit are dealt with on the balance per bank side, and the service charge is subtracted from the balance per books side.

13. c $1,250 – $102 – $27 + $850 = $1,971.

14. b   All of the other items would be recorded on the balance per books side.

15. b   Outstanding cheques are deducted from the bank balance side of the bank reconciliation and thus do not require an adjusting entry.

16. a   Cash equivalents are short-term, highly liquid (easily sold) investments. Short-term notes receivable, a 1-year GIC, and investments in shares of other companies do not fall in this category.

17. a   Cash does not appear on the statement of earnings and the statement of retained earnings.

18. d Restricted cash that is expected to be used within the next year is reported as a current asset. To be included in Cash, cash must be unrestricted.

19. b There are six basic principles of cash management. Keeping inventories low and planning for the timing of major expenditures are two of them.

20. c Keeping spare cash on hand or in a non–interest-bearing account is not taking advantage of cash's interest-earning ability. It is unwise to invest in illiquid investments because they cannot be converted into cash when the need arises.

21. a In making loans to depositors, banks commonly require borrowers to maintain minimum cash balances. These minimum balances are called compensating balances.

Problems

1. a. There is no rotation of employees, which means that the company is more susceptible to employee fraud. The company should institute a rotation system where a few employees at a time would change jobs. That action would deter employee fraud as it would be more difficult to permanently conceal fraudulent activity. (This falls under "Human Resource Controls.")

   b. The weakness of having one person do ordering and receiving of goods and paying the invoice involves segregation of duties. These three activities are referred to as "related activities." When one person is responsible for such related activities, the potential for errors and irregularities is increased. To remedy this weakness, separate individuals should do these different jobs. If the company cannot afford the required additional employees, then it should reorganize the jobs to at least remove the invoice paying function from the ordering and receiving function. The invoice paying could be done by the individual who handles the sales and cash handling functions, and perhaps the mail handling function could then be assigned to the stores person.

   c. Internal control over cash receipts is violated by not depositing cash daily. The weakness is further exacerbated by keeping cash in an unlocked desk drawer. Cash should be deposited daily unless the amount of cash on some days is insignificant. In any event, any cash should be held in a locked safe or locked filing cabinet. The company should also examine the possibility of having its customers pay their accounts through EFT as that would limit the amount of paper money on hand.

   d. The opening of mail with deposits should be done with two people present. That would prevent the possibility of an employee keeping the deposit. The supervisor or another person should be present when mail is opened.

2.

a.

J BY J CORPORATION
Bank Reconciliation
June 30, 2009

Balance per bank statement		$1,617
Add: deposits in transit	$802	
Cheque error	100	902
		2,519
Less: outstanding cheques		559
Adjusted cash balance per bank		$1,960
Cash balance per books		$2,151
Add: electronic deposit		760
		2,911
Less: NSF cheque	$ 67	
Bank service charges ($35 + $40)	75	
Electronic payment—insurance	800	
Cheque recording error ($1,587 – $1,578)	9	
		951
Adjusted cash balance per book		$1,960

b.   Journal entries are recorded only for the "cash balance per books" side of the bank reconciliation. Bank personnel record journal entries for the "balance per bank" side.

June 30	Cash	760	
	Accounts Receivable		760
	(To record electronic deposit)		
30	Accounts Receivable ($67 + $40)	107	
	Cash		107
	(To record NSF cheque and related service charge)		
30	Bank Charges Expense	35	
	Cash		35
	(To record cheque printing costs)		
30	Accounts Payable	9	
	Cash		9
	(To record cheque error)		
30	Insurance Expense	800	
	Cash		800
	(To record electronic payment for insurance)		

3.

a. The outstanding cheques at August 31 are:

Cheque Number	Amount
113	$560
117	657
125	287
128	206
129	925
131	429
	$3,064

b. Adjustments must be made to the books side of the bank reconciliation as follows:

1. The company recorded Cheque #122 as $687. The cheque should have been recorded for $678. The company therefore over-deducted from its cash general ledger account by $9. That amount must be shown as an addition to the books side of the bank reconciliation.

2. The following items were not recorded in the company's books and must therefore be shown as subtractions to the books side of the bank reconciliation.

- NSF cheque	$440
- NSF fee	40
- EFT payment	568
- Service charge	20

4.

a. For both companies, the first current asset is cash and cash equivalents. Cash represents all coins, currency, and amounts in bank accounts. Cash equivalents are short-term highly liquid investments.

b. Domtar: The amount has increased by U.S. $70 million. (U.S. $71 million – U.S. $1 million)

Cascades: The amount has decreased by $9 million. ($34 million – $25 million)

c. The cash flow statement indicates that Domtar obtained cash from investing financing activities through a business acquisition. This infusion of cash along with cash generated from operating activities allowed the company to pay off some of its debts.

Cascades, on the other hand, used up cash ($40 million) to discontinue some of its operations. That factor, along with some use of funds from investing in plant and equipment, was primarily responsible for the decrease in its cash and cash equivalents for the year.

A summary for 2007 follows:

	Domtar (USD millions)	Cascades (CAD millions)
Cash flows provided by operating activities	$ 606	$ 89
Cash flows used by investing activities	485	(136)
Cash flows provided by financing activities	(1,025)	79
Net increase in cash and cash equivalents before adjustments	66	32
Cash from discontinued operations		(40)
Other adjustments	4	(1)
Net increase (decrease) in cash and cash equivalents	$ 70	$ (9)

chapter 8

Reporting and Analyzing Receivables

Chapter Overview

In this chapter, you will learn how to recognize and value accounts receivable, including how to record both estimated and actual bad debts. You will also learn how receivables are reported on the financial statements and managed.

- The term "receivables" refers to amounts due from individuals and companies. They are claims that are expected to be collected in cash and are frequently classified as accounts receivable, notes receivable, and other receivables.

- **Accounts receivable** are amounts owed by customers on account, and they result from the sale of goods and services.

- **Notes receivable** are claims where formal instruments of credit are issued as evidence of the debt. Notes and accounts receivable that result from sales transactions are called trade receivables.

- **Other receivables** include credit card receivables, interest receivable, loans to company officers, advances to employees, recoverable sales taxes, and income taxes. They are classified and reported as separate items in the current or noncurrent assets section of the balance sheet, according to their due dates.

Recognizing Accounts Receivable

- For a service organization, accounts receivable are recorded when service is provided on account.

- For a merchandiser, accounts receivable are recorded at the point of sale of merchandise on account.

- Receivables are reduced by sales returns.

- A **subsidiary accounts receivable ledger** is used to help companies with a large number of customers to organize and track individual customer balances. The subsidiary accounts receivable ledger keeps track of individual account balances by customer, and the total of these balances agrees with the overall accounts receivable balance contained in the general ledger. Thus, the general ledger contains only one Accounts Receivable account, which acts as a control account to the subsidiary ledger.

Valuing Accounts Receivable

- Receivables are reported on the balance sheet as a current asset; however, determining the amount to report is sometimes difficult because some receivables will become uncollectible. For example, a credit customer may not be able to pay. In such a case, the credit loss is debited to Bad Debts Expense, a statement of earnings account. The key issue in valuing accounts receivable is when to recognize these credit losses. If the company waits until it knows for sure that the specific account will not be collected, it could end up recording the bad debts expense in a different period than when the revenue was recorded.

- To avoid the potential of mismatching expenses to revenue, the allowance method is used to record estimated uncollectibles. A feature of this method is that uncollectible accounts receivable are estimated and matched against sales in the same accounting period in which the sales occurred. It also ensures that receivables are stated at their net realizable value, which is the amount that is actually expected to be received.

- The allowance method has three essential features:

  1. Recording Accounts Receivable at their Net Realizable Value: Uncollectible accounts receivable are estimated and matched against sales in the accounting period in which sales occur. The adjusting journal entry to record estimated uncollectibles is as follows:

Bad Debts Expense	XXX	
Allowance for Doubtful Accounts		XXX

     (To record estimate of uncollectible accounts)

     Bad Debts Expense is reported on the statement of earnings as an operating expense. Allowance for Doubtful Accounts is reported on the balance sheet as a contra asset account to Accounts Receivable. When it is subtracted from accounts receivable, the difference represents the net realizable value of the accounts receivable at the statement date.

     The amount recorded in this journal entry is an estimate. At this point, the company does not know which customer will not pay its bill. While there are several acceptable ways to estimate uncollectible accounts, most companies use a percentage of the outstanding receivables to determine the allowance for doubtful accounts.

Under the percentage of receivables basis, management establishes a percentage relationship between net amount of receivables and expected losses from uncollectible accounts. This percentage can be applied to total receivables, or to various classifications of receivables. For the latter approach, a schedule is prepared in which customer balances are classified by length of time they have been unpaid. Because of its emphasis on time, this schedule is called an aging schedule, and its completion is called aging of accounts receivable. The longer the period unpaid, the higher is the percentage.

Consider the following example. Edison Inc. aged its receivables and calculated that estimated bad debts totalled $2,500. At the time, the Allowance for Doubtful Accounts had a credit balance of $300. The required adjusting entry is:

Bad Debts Expense	2,200	
Allowance for Doubtful Accounts		2,200
(To record estimate of uncollectible accounts)		

The Allowance account must have $2,500 in it after the adjusting entry is written. Since there is already a balance of $300, $2,200 must be added to the account to bring it up to that balance.

If the Allowance account had had a $400 debit balance in it before adjustment, then the adjusting entry would have been:

Bad Debts Expense	2,900	
Allowance for Doubtful Accounts		2,900
(To record estimate of uncollectible accounts)		

Remember that the Allowance account must have $2,500 in it after the adjusting entry is written. If there is a debit balance of $400, then the account must be credited for $2,900 in order to have an overall credit balance of $2,500.

2. Recording the Write-off of an Uncollectible Account: Actual uncollectibles are written off at the time the specific account is determined to be uncollectible. The journal entry to record the write-off of an uncollectible account is as follows:

Allowance for Doubtful Accounts	XXX	
Accounts Receivable		XXX
(To write off an uncollectible account)		

Bad Debts Expense is not used in this entry because it was used in the adjusting journal entry (in order to match revenues of the period to their related expense). The number in this entry is an actual, not an estimated, number; at this point, the company knows which customer is not paying its bill and the exact dollar amount of the bill.

Proper authorization of a write-off is critical. The entry to record a cash collection on an account requires a debit to Cash and a credit to Accounts Receivable. If an employee wished to steal money from customers paying into their accounts, to hide it from the company the employee could use the write-off entry. The write-off entry would allow the employee to steal the cash and to close out the customer's account balance.

Net realizable value is the same after a write-off as it was before a write-off. This is because both accounts receivable and the allowance account are reduced by the same amount.

3. Recovery of an Uncollectible Account: When an account previously written off is subsequently collected, the original write-off is reversed and the collection recorded. Neither the write-off nor the subsequent recovery has an impact on the statement of earnings, and, thus, matching is not distorted.

Two journal entries are required to record the recovery of an amount previously written off: The first reinstates the customer's account, and the second records the cash collection.

Accounts Receivable	XXX	
Allowance for Doubtful Accounts		XXX
(To reverse the write-off of an account)		
Cash	XXX	
Accounts Receivable		XXX
(To record collection on account)		

The first entry is simply a reversal of the original write-off entry. While the net effect of the two entries is a debit to Cash and a credit to the allowance account, it is important to reinstate the receivable and then show its collection for an information trail on the customer.

<table>
<tr><td>

study objective 3

Explain how notes receivable are recognized and valued in the accounts.

</td><td>

- Credit may also be granted in exchange for a formal credit instrument known as a promissory note. A promissory note is a written promise to pay a specified amount of money on demand or at a definite time. The maker of a note is the party making the promise to pay; the payee is the party to whom payment is to be made.

</td></tr>
</table>

- Notes receivable give the holder a stronger legal claim to assets than do accounts receivable; both types of *receivables* can readily be sold to another party. The majority of notes arise from lending transactions.

- The formula for calculating interest is as follows:

Interest = Principal × Rate × Time

The principal is the face value of the note, the rate is the annual interest rate, and the time is a fraction (in terms of 1 year). The interest on a $12,000, 3-month note with an interest rate of 4 percent is $120, calculated as follows:

$120 = $12,000 × 4% × 3/12 months

- A note receivable is recorded at its principal value, and no interest revenue is recorded when the note is accepted because the revenue recognition principle does not recognize revenue until earned. If a note is accepted in settlement of an open account, then the entry is a debit to Notes Receivable and a credit to Accounts Receivable. If a note is exchanged for cash, then the entry is a debit to Notes Receivable and a credit to Cash. Short-term notes are normally held to their maturity date, at which time, the principal value plus any outstanding interest is due. Interest may be collected periodically (e.g., each month) or at maturity. Occasionally, a maker defaults on a note.

- A note is honoured if it is paid in full at the maturity date. Consider again the note mentioned above: $12,000, 3-month note with an interest rate of 4 percent with total interest of $120 due at maturity. On the maturity date, the holder records the following journal entry:

Cash	12,120	
Notes Receivable		12,000
Interest Revenue		120
(To record collection of note)		

If the note had been issued on December 1 and the holder had a December 31 year end, then the holder would have accrued interest on December 31 with the following entry:

Interest Receivable	40	
Interest Revenue		40
(To record accrued interest: $12,000 × 4% × 1/12)		

On the maturity date, March 1, the following entry would be recorded:

Cash	12,120	
Notes Receivable		12,000
Interest Receivable		40
Interest Revenue		80

- A note is dishonoured if it is not paid in full at maturity. If the $12,000, 4 percent, 3-month note had not been paid on March 1, then the following journal entry would have been required:

Accounts Receivable	12,120	
Notes Receivable		12,000
Interest Revenue		120

While the note no longer has legal validity on the due date, the holder of the note records the entire amount as a receivable, signalling his intention to try to collect from the maker of the note. If the holder later determines that the account is not collectible, then he will write off the account by debiting the allowance account and crediting Accounts Receivable.

Like accounts receivable, notes receivable are reported at their net realizable value. Valuing short-term notes receivable is the same as valuing accounts receivable. The calculations and estimations involved in determining net realizable value and in recording the proper amount of bad debts expense and related allowance are similar.

- Short-term receivables are reported in the current assets section of the balance sheet following cash and short-term investments. Although only the net realizable value must be disclosed, it is helpful to report both the gross amount of receivables and the allowance for doubtful accounts either on the balance sheet or in the notes to the financial statements.

study objective 4

Explain the statement presentation of receivables.

- Bad Debts Expense appears on the statement of earnings as an operating expense. Interest Revenue is shown under other revenues in the non-operating section of the statement of earnings item.

- A company must disclose any particular problem with receivables, such as significant risk of uncollectible accounts.

- Managing receivables involves five steps:

  1. Determine who to extend credit to.
  2. Establish a payment period.
  3. Monitor collections.
  4. Evaluate the liquidity of receivables.
  5. Accelerate cash receipts from receivables when necessary.

- Determining who receives credit is a critical issue for a company. If a credit policy is too generous, then the company may extend credit to risky customers. If the policy is too tight, then it may lose sales. If a company requires references from new customers, then it must check out the references before it extends credit and, after credit is extended, continue to monitor the financial health of customers.

- When a company establishes a payment period, it must make sure to communicate the policy to customers. The payment period should be consistent with the period offered by competitors.

- A company needs to monitor collections. An aging schedule helps to do this in the following ways: it helps to establish the allowance for bad debts, it aids in the estimation and timing of future cash inflows, it provides information about the collection experience of the company, and it identifies problem accounts. If a company has significant concentrations of credit risk, it is required to disclose this risk in the notes to the financial statements. A concentration of credit risk is a threat of nonpayment from a single customer or class of customers that could adversely affect the company's financial health.

- To help evaluate its receivables balance, a company calculates the receivables turnover ratio by dividing net credit sales by average gross accounts receivable. (Average receivables are calculated by adding together the beginning and ending balances of receivables and dividing the sum by two.) If net credit sales total $25,000 and average receivables total $5,000, then the receivables turnover is five times, meaning that the company collects its receivables five times during the accounting period.

- This ratio measures the number of times receivables are collected during the period. A decreasing ratio should be of concern to a company, particularly if its competitors' ratios are holding steady or increasing.

- To calculate the average collection period, the company divides the receivables turnover into 365 days. Using the numbers above, the average collection period is 73 days ($365 \div 5$). A general rule is that the collection period should not greatly exceed the credit-term period.

- In the normal course of events, receivables are collected in cash and then removed from the books. However, as credit sales grow in size and significance, collection of receivables may slow down. There are two typical ways that a company can use to accelerate the receipt of cash from receivables: use the receivables to secure a loan or sell the receivables.

- A company can speed up flow from receivables by going to a bank and borrowing money using receivables as collateral. Quite often, these arrangements occur through an operating line of credit.

- A company frequently sells its receivables to another company to shorten the cash-to-cash operating cycle. There are three reasons for the sale of receivables: they may be a very large asset that a company wishes to convert to cash; they may be the only reasonable source of cash; and billing and collection are time-consuming and costly for companies.

- A common way to accelerate receivables collection is to transfer receivables to investors in return for cash through a process called securitization. This topic is normally covered in detail in an intermediate accounting course. Another way to accelerate receivables collection is to sell receivables to a factor, which is a finance company or bank that buys receivables from businesses for a fee and then collects the payments directly from the customers.

- A retailer may allow its customers to use credit cards to charge purchases, and its acceptance of a national credit card is another form of selling the receivable by the retailer. Use of such credit cards translates to more sales with zero bad debts for the retailer.

  Sales resulting from the use of nonbank credit cards are treated as credit sales by the retailer and recorded as credit cards receivable. On the other hand, bank credit cards are considered cash sales by the retailer and recorded as cash rather than as a receivable. Issuing banks charge the retailer a fee. If a jewellery store sells $5,000 of jewellery to customers who are using bank credit cards, and its bank charges a fee of 4 percent, then the jewellery store records the following entry:

Cash	4,800	
Credit Card Expense ($5,000 × 4%)	200	
Sales		5,000
(To record credit card sales)		

- A retailer may also allow its customers to use debit cards to charge purchases. The difference between debit and credit is that debit cards allow customers to spend only what is in their bank account. Credit cards, on the other hand, give a customer access to money made available by a bank or other financial institution, just like a loan. The entries to record a debit card sale are identical to those shown above for bank credit card sales.

Chapter Self-Test

As you work through the questions and problems, remember to use the **Decision Toolkit** discussed and used in the text:

1. *Decision Checkpoints:* At this point, you ask a question.
2. *Info Needed for Decision:* You make a choice regarding the information needed to answer the question.
3. *Tool to Use for Decision:* At this point, you review just what the information chosen in step 2 does for the decision-making process.
4. *How to Evaluate Results:* You conduct an evaluation of information for answering the question.

Note: The notation (SO1) means that the question was drawn from study objective number one.

Multiple Choice

Please circle the correct answer.

(SO1)   1. Accounts and notes receivable that result from sales transactions are called
   a.   other receivables.
   b.   non-trade receivables.
   c.   trade receivables.
   d.   noncurrent receivables.

(SO1)   2. Interest receivable and loans to company officers are included in
   a.   other receivables.
   b.   trade receivables.
   c.   notes receivable.
   d.   accounts receivable.

(SO1)   3. For a service organization, a receivable is recorded
   a.   when the customer pays the bill.
   b.   when service is provided on account.
   c.   30 days after service is provided.
   d.   when the bill is sent to the customer 1 week after service is provided.

(SO1)   4. A subsidiary accounts receivable ledger
   a.   is used by corporations that have subsidiary companies.
   b.   provides supporting detail to the general ledger.
   c.   replaces the main general ledger accounts receivable account.
   d.   is used by all companies.

(SO2)   5. The entry to record estimated uncollectibles is
   a.   Bad Debts Expense
           Accounts Receivable
   b.   Allowance for Doubtful Accounts
           Accounts Receivable
   c.   Accounts Receivable
           Allowance for Doubtful Accounts
   d.   Bad Debts Expense
           Allowance for Doubtful Accounts

(SO2)   6. The entry to record the write-off of an uncollectible account is
   a.   Bad Debts Expense
           Accounts Receivable
   b.   Allowance for Doubtful Accounts
           Accounts Receivable

c.   Accounts Receivable

Allowance for Doubtful Accounts

d.   Bad Debts Expense

Allowance for Doubtful Accounts

7. Before a write-off of an uncollectible account, Accounts Receivable had a $10,000   (SO2)
debit balance, and the Allowance for Doubtful Accounts had a $500 credit bal-
ance. After a write-off of $100, the net realizable value is
a. $10,000.
b. $9,500.
c. $9,400.
d. $9,300.

8. The Allowance for Doubtful Accounts has a $400 credit balance. An aging   (SO2)
schedule shows that total estimated bad debts is $3,600. The adjusting entry will
require a debit and a credit for
a. $4,000.
b. $3,600.
c. $3,200.
d.   some other amount.

9. The Allowance for Doubtful Accounts has a $400 debit balance. An aging sched-   (SO2)
ule shows that total estimated bad debts is $3,600. The adjusting entry will
require a debit and a credit for
a. $4,000.
b. $3,600.
c. $3,200.
d.   some other amount.

10. When an account is written off using the allowance method for uncollectible ac-   (SO2)
counts, the
a.   net realizable value of total accounts receivable will increase.
b.   net accounts receivable will decrease.
c.   allowance account will increase.
d.   net realizable value of total accounts receivable will remain the same.

11. A company issues a 4-month, 9 percent note for $30,000. The total interest on the   (SO3)
note is
a. $90.
b. $900.
c. $2,700.
d. $3,000.

12. The journal entry written on the maturity date by the holder of a 3-month, 4   (SO3)
percent, $15,000 note, with interest due at maturity, will include a
a.   debit to Cash for $15,150.
b.   credit to Notes Receivable for $15,150.

c.   debit to Interest Revenue for $150.
d.   credit to Cash for $15,150.

(SO3)   13. A company holds a 4-month, 5 percent, $21,000 note that was dishonoured on the maturity date. Interest is due at maturity. If eventual collection is expected, the journal entry on the maturity date will include a
a.   debit to Accounts Receivable for $21,350.
b.   credit to Notes Receivable for $21,350.
c.   debit to Cash for $21,350.
d.   debit to Notes Receivable for $21,000.

(SO3)   14. A promissory note has two key parties as follows:
a.   debtor and a bank
b.   debtor and the sender
c.   receiver and the sender
d.   payee and the maker

(SO3)   15. The total interest on a $5,000, 5 percent, 3-month note receivable is
a. $62.50.
b. $83.33.
c. $250.00.
d. $125.00.

(SO4)   16. Accounts receivable are valued and reported on the balance sheet
a.   at the gross amount.
b.   when a customer makes a payment.
c.   at net realizable value.
d.   in the Other Assets category.

(SO4)   17. Bad Debts Expense is reported on the statement of earnings as
a.   an operating expense.
b.   part of net sales.
c.   part of cost of goods sold.
d.   a contra-revenue account.

(SO5)   18. Which of the following is a step involved in the management of accounts receivable?
a.   Manage credit risk.
b.   Establish a payment period.
c.   Calculate bad debts expense.
d.   Recognize an accounts receivable when the work has been done on account.

(SO5)   19. A threat of nonpayment from a single customer or class of customers that could adversely affect the financial health of a company is called
a.   accounts receivable concentration risk.
b.   notes receivable concentration risk.
c.   credit risk.
d.   a concentration of credit risk.

20. Net credit sales are $800,000, average gross receivables total $150,000, average   (SO5)
    inventory totals $200,000, and the allowance for doubtful accounts totals $8,000.
    The receivables turnover is
    a.   100 times.
    b.   5.3 times.
    c.   4.0 times.
    d.   1.3 times.

21. Please use the information from question number 20. The average collection   (SO5)
    period is
    a.   100 days.
    b.   75 days.
    c.   69 days.
    d.   5.3 days.

22. Kerrison Corporation sold $6,000 of merchandise to customers who charged   (SO5)
    their purchases with a bank credit card. Kerrison's bank charges it a 4 percent fee.
    The journal entry to record the credit card sales will include a
    a.   debit to Cash for $5,760.
    b.   credit to Sales for $5,760.
    c.   debit to Cash for $6,000.
    d.   credit to Credit Card Expense for $240.

23. The receivables turnover ratio is used to analyze   (SO5)
    a.   credit worthiness.
    b.   profitability.
    c.   solvency.
    d.   liquidity.

Problems

1.   Please record journal entries for the following items for Morrison
     Corporation.

a.   At the end of the accounting period on June 30, Morrison prepares an aging   (SO2)
     schedule of accounts receivable that shows total estimated bad debts of $5,200.
     On this date, the Allowance for Doubtful Accounts has a debit balance of $300,
     and Accounts Receivable has a balance of $85,000.

b.   On July 5, Morrison receives word that Sperry Ltd. has declared bankruptcy, and   (SO2)
     Morrison writes off its account receivable of $800.

c.   On September 12, Sperry notifies Morrison that it can pay its $800 debt and   (SO2)
     includes a cheque for the entire amount.

d.   What is the net realizable value of accounts receivable after the entry in (a) is   (SO2)
     written? What is the net realizable value after the write-off in (b)?

a–c

Date	Account Titles	Debit	Credit

2.   The December 31, 2009 balance sheet of Master Retailer Limited had Accounts Receivable of $650,000 and a credit balance in Allowance for Doubtful Accounts of $12,500. The accounting manager has determined that 5 percent of the receivables will be uncollectible.

During 2010, the following transactions occurred:

1.	Sales on account	1,150,000
2.	Sales returns and allowances	20,000
3.	Collections from customers	900,000
4.	Accounts written off	10,000
5.	Previously written off accounts subsequently collected	2,500

(SO2)   a.   Record the 2010 summary transactions.

b.   Record any required adjusting journal entry(ies) at December 31, 2010.

Date	Account Titles	Debit	Credit

3. A company's partial balance sheet, at December 31, appears as follows before adjusting entries for 2010 have been made:

		2010		2009
Current Assets				
Cash		$ 50,000		$ 60,000
Short-term investments		40,000		30,000
Notes receivable		80,000		75,000
Accounts receivable	$90,000		$80,000	
Less: allowance for doubtful accounts	15,000	75,000	10,000	70,000
Other current assets		90,000		95,000
Total current assets		$335,000		$330,000

a. The $80,000 note shown above for 2010 represents a 3-month, 4.5 percent interest bearing note issued on November 1, 2010. Interest is due at maturity. Prepare any required adjusting entry.   (SO3)

(SO3)   b. Journalize the entry that would be required when the note is collected at maturity in 2011, assuming that the adjusting entry in (a) was made.

(SO2)   c. An aging of accounts receivable prepared on December 31, 2010, indicates that bad debts are estimated to be $17,000. Prepare any required adjusting entry.

(SO5)   d. Calculate the receivables turnover and the average collection period for 2010, assuming net credit sales for 2010 are $501,500.

4. The following accounts appear in the general ledger of Majestic Corporation at December 31, 2009 with the following balances:

Accounts Receivable	$125,000
Accumulated Depreciation	60,000
Allowance for Doubtful Accounts	18,000
Depreciation Expense	10,000
Cash	90,000
Dividends	8,000
Equipment	200,000
Merchandise Inventory	100,000
Notes Payable	50,000
Office Supplies	1,000
Prepaid Expenses	12,000
Sales	250,000
Sales Returns and Allowances	10,000
Short-Term Notes Receivable	75,000
Short-Term Investments	80,000

(SO4)   Prepare the partial balance sheet presentation for current assets of Majestic Corporation.

5. Please refer to the Domtar and Cascades financial statements found in the appendices at the end of this study guide for information for answering the following questions. **Do not** forget to use the **Decision Toolkit** approach for help in the problem solving.

(SO1)   a. What is the percentage increase or decrease in accounts receivable from 2006 to 2007?

(SO5)   b. For both Domtar and Cascades, calculate the receivables turnover and average collection period for 2007. Assume sales are net credit sales and use net receivables rather than gross receivables in your calculations.

(SO5)   c. Compare your results obtained in (b).

Solutions to Self-Test

Multiple Choice

1. c   Other and non-trade receivables are basically the same thing and arise from such items as interest and loans to company officers. Accounts receivable are always current assets.

2. a   Trade receivables arise from sales transactions, notes receivable are written promises and usually include interest, and accounts receivable are amounts owed by customers on account.

3. b   A receivable is recorded before the customer pays the bill. The receivable should be recorded when the service is performed, not at some other specific date.

4. b   The subsidiary ledger provides supporting detail to the general ledger, freeing it from excessive detail.

5. d   The allowance for doubtful accounts is used when estimating uncollectibles.

6. b   Under the allowance method, every accounts receivable write-off entry is debited to the allowance account and not to Bad Debts Expense.

7. b   The net realizable value is $9,500 ($10,000 − $500) before the write-off and $9,500 ($9,900 − $400) after.

8. c $3,600 is the amount that must be in the Allowance account after adjustment. Since it already has a credit balance of $400, only $3,200 is needed to raise the balance to $3,600.

9. a $3,600 is the amount that must be in the Allowance account after adjustment. Since it has a debit balance of $400, $4,000 is needed to raise the balance to $3,600.

10. d   Both the accounts receivable and the contra asset account, allowance for doubtful accounts, decrease by the same amount, thus resulting in no change to net realizable value of accounts receivable.

11. b $30,000 \times 9\% \times 4/12$ months = $900

12. a   The journal entry is:

Cash	15,150	
Notes Receivable		15,000
Interest Revenue		150
($15,000 \times 4\% \times 3/12 = $150)		

13. a   The journal entry is:

Accounts Receivable	21,350	
Notes Receivable		21,000
Interest Revenue		350
($21,000 \times 5\% \times 4/12 = $350)		

14. d   In a promissory note, the party making the promise to pay is called the maker; the party who will be paid is called the payee.

15. a $5,000 \times 5\% \times 3/12 = 62.50$

16. c   Although only the net realizable value of receivables must be disclosed, it is helpful to report both the gross amount of receivables and the allowance for doubtful accounts either in the statement or in the notes to the financial statements.

17. a   Bad debts expense is part of operations.

18. b   There are five steps in managing accounts receivable:

1. Determine who to extend credit to.

2. Establish a payment period.

3. Monitor collections.

4. Evaluate the liquidity of receivables.

5. Accelerate cash receipts from receivables when necessary.

19. d   If a company sells services or products to only a few customers, it has a concentration of credit risk.

20. b   Net credit sales ÷ Average gross receivables = $800,000 ÷ $150,000 = 5.3 times

21. c   365 ÷ Receivables turnover = 365 ÷ 5.3 = 69 days

22. a   The journal entry is:

Cash	5,760	
Credit Card Expense	240	
Sales		6,000

23. d   The receivables turnover is an important component of a company's overall liquidity.

Problems

1.

a.   June 30   Bad Debts Expense   5,500

                        Allowance for Doubtful Accounts   5,500

              (To record the estimate of uncollectible accounts: $300 + $5,200)

b.   July 5   Allowance for Doubtful Accounts   800

                        Accounts Receivable—Sperry   800

              (To write off the Sperry account)

c.   Sep. 12   Accounts Receivable—Sperry   800

                        Allowance for Doubtful Accounts   800

               (To reinstate Sperry account)

              Cash   800

                        Accounts Receivable—Sperry   800

               (To record collection on Sperry account)

d.

	Before Write-off	After Write-off
Accounts receivable	$85,000	$84,200
Less: allowance for doubtful accounts	5,500	4,700
Net realizable value	$79,500	$79,500

The net realizable value does not change because both accounts are reduced by the same amount.

2.

a.

(1)   Accounts Receivable   1,150,000

        Sales   1,150,000

        (To record credit sales)

(2)   Sales Returns and Allowances   20,000

        Accounts Receivable   20,000

        (To record credits to customers)

(3)	Cash	900,000	
	Accounts Receivable		900,000
	(To record collection of receivables)		

(4)	Allowance for Doubtful Accounts	10,000	
	Accounts Receivable		10,000
	(To write off specific accounts)		
(5)	Accounts Receivable	2,500	
	Allowance for Doubtful Accounts		2,500
	(To reverse write-off of account)		
	Cash	2,500	
	Accounts Receivable		2,500
	(To record collection of account)		

    b.   Percentage of receivables basis:

Accounts Receivable		Allowance for Doubtful Accounts	
650,000	20,000	10,000	12,500
1,150,000	900,000		2,500
2,500	10,000		Bal. 5,000
	2,500		
Bal. 870,000			

Required balance ($870,000 × 5%)	$43,500
Balance before adjustment	5,000
Adjustment required	$38,500

Dec. 31	Bad Debts Expense	38,500	
	Allowance for Doubtful Accounts		38,500
	(To record bad debt expense)		

3.

a.	Dec. 31, 2010	Interest Receivable	600	
		Interest Revenue		600
		$80,000 \times 4.5\% \times 2/12 = \$600$		
b.	Feb. 1, 2011	Cash	80,900	
		Interest Receivable		600
		Interest Revenue		300
		Notes Receivable		80,000
		Interest Revenue $= \$80,000 \times 4.5\% \times 1/12 = \$300$		
c.	Dec. 31, 2010	Bad Debts Expense	2,000	
		Allowance for Doubtful Accounts		2,000
		$\$17,000 - \$15,000 = \$2,000$		

d.   Receivables turnover $\dfrac{\$501,500}{(\$90,000 + \$80,000) \div 2}$ = 5.9 times

Average collection period $\dfrac{365}{5.9}$ = 62 days

4.

MAJESTIC CORPORATION
Balance Sheet (Partial)
December 31, 2009

Current assets		
Cash		$ 90,000
Short-term investments		80,000
Accounts receivable	$125,000	
Less: allowance for doubtful accounts	18,000	107,000
Short-term notes receivable		75,000
Merchandise inventory		100,000
Office supplies		1,000
Prepaid expense		12,000
Total current assets		$465,000

5. (Domtar $ in USD millions; Cascades $ in CAD millions)

a.   Domtar: The amount has increased by 59.4%.
$542 − $340 = $202 ÷ $340 = 59.4%
Cascades: The amount has decreased by 4.0%.
$624 − $650 = ($26) ÷ $650 = (4.0)%

b.   Domtar:
Average receivables = ($542 + $340) ÷ 2 = $441
Receivables turnover = net credit sales ÷ average receivables
$5,947 ÷ $441 = 13.5 times
Average collection period = 365 ÷ receivables turnover
365 ÷ 13.5 = 27 days

Cascades:
Average receivables = ($624 + $650) ÷ 2 = $637
Receivables turnover = net credit sales ÷ average receivables
$3,929 ÷ $637 = 6.2 times
Average collection period = 365 ÷ receivables turnover
365 ÷ 6.2 = 59 days

c.   The average collection period for Cascades is much longer than it is for Domtar (59 days compared with 27 days). To further evaluate the effectiveness of the accounts receivable collection policy, the credit period granted to customers would have to be examined for each company.

chapter 9

Reporting and Analyzing Long-Lived Assets

Chapter Overview

This chapter discusses the accounting for long-lived assets. You will learn about the amounts at which they are recorded in the accounting records and how to allocate their cost to expense using different depreciation methods. You will learn how to dispose of long-lived assets and methods used by companies for evaluating their use. Finally, you will learn how to report long-lived assets on the balance sheet.

Review of Specific Study Objectives

- The **cost principle** requires that property, plant, and equipment be recognized (recorded) at cost. Cost includes:

study objective 1

Determine the cost of property, plant, and equipment.

  1. The purchase price, less any discounts or rebates.
  2. The expenditures necessary to bring the asset to its required location and to make it ready for its intended use.

  All these costs are **capitalized** (recorded as property, plant, and equipment), rather than expensed, if it is probable that the company will receive an economic benefit in the future from the asset.

- **Operating expenditures** are costs that benefit the current period and are expensed.

- **Capital expenditures** are costs that benefit future periods and are included in a property, plant, and equipment account.

- Property, plant, and equipment are often divided into four classes:
  1. **Land**, such as a building site;
  2. **Land improvements**, such as driveways, parking lots, fences, and underground sprinkler systems;
  3. **Buildings**, such as stores, offices, factories, and warehouses; and
  4. **Equipment**, such as store checkout counters, cash registers, computers, office furniture, factory machinery, and delivery equipment.

The cost of land includes the cash purchase price and closing costs, such as survey and legal fees. All costs incurred in making land ready for its intended use increase the Land account: clearing, draining, filling, grading, and razing old buildings are included. If the land has a building on it that must be removed to make the site suitable for construction of a new building, all demolition and removal costs, less any proceeds from salvaged materials, are chargeable to the Land account. Once the land is ready for its intended use, recurring costs such as annual property taxes are expensed. Its cost is not amortized over the life of the asset because land has an unlimited useful life.

The cost of land improvements includes all expenditures necessary to make the improvements ready for their intended use. For example, constructing a parking lot includes paving, fencing, and lighting. Land improvements require maintenance and replacement to maintain their value to the company. Because of this, the cost of land improvements is depreciated over their limited useful lives.

The cost of buildings includes all expenditures relating to the purchase or construction of a building. If a building is purchased, then the costs include the purchase price and closing costs. In addition, any cost required to make the building ready for its intended use are also charged to the Building account. Such costs include remodelling rooms and offices and replacing or repairing the roof, floors, electrical wiring, and plumbing. If a building is constructed, then costs include the contract price, architects' fees, building permits, excavation costs, and interest costs incurred to finance the project. Specific rules exist to determine the amount of interest costs to capitalize; these are not discussed here as they are normally taught in an intermediate accounting course.

The cost of equipment includes the cash purchase price, freight charges, and insurance during shipping paid by the purchaser, as well as assembling, installing, and testing the unit. Fees, which occur after the equipment is operational, such as vehicle licences and accident insurance, are debited to an expense account or treated as an asset (prepaid expense).

The cost of property, plant, and equipment must also include an estimate of the cost of any obligation to dismantle, remove, or restore the long-lived asset when it is retired. Costs such as these must be estimated (using present-value concepts) and added to the asset account. The other side of the entry records a liability for the asset retirement obligation. These costs, and the liability, are recorded in the period when the legal obligation is created, which can be at the time the asset is acquired, or later when the asset is used. A more detailed discussion of asset retirement costs and their associated liabilities will be covered in a future accounting course. We will assume asset retirement costs are equal to zero in all of the examples this chapter.

- Companies often **lease** assets. In a lease, a lessor agrees to allow another party, the lessee, to use the asset for an agreed period of time at an agreed price. Some advantages of leasing include reduced risk of obsolescence, 100 percent financing, income tax advantages, and off-balance sheet financing, which involves the non-reporting of assets and liabilities. In an operating lease, the lessee uses the asset but does not record an asset or a liability. Instead, periodic lease payments are recorded as rent expense (or prepaid rent). Under a finance lease, the lessee uses the asset and does record an asset and a liability.

- Under international financial reporting standards, companies will have two models they can choose from to account for their property, plant, and equipment: the cost model or the revaluation model. We will cover the cost model in the following sections of the chapter.

- The **cost model** records property, plant, and equipment at cost at acquisition. Subsequent to acquisition, depreciation is recorded each period and the assets are carried at cost less accumulated depreciation.

- **Depreciation** is the process of allocating the cost of property, plant, and equipment asset to expense over its useful (service) life in a rational and systematic way. Such cost allocation is designed to properly match expenses with the pattern in which the asset's future economic benefits are expected to be used.

  The journal entry to record depreciation is:

  Depreciation Expense
      Accumulated Depreciation

  Depreciation Expense appears on the statement of earnings, and the Accumulated Depreciation account is a contra asset account, subtracted from the asset's original cost to give its carrying amount, on the balance sheet.

  Recognizing depreciation for an asset does not result in the accumulation of cash for the replacement of the asset.

  Depreciation is a process of cost allocation, not a process of asset valuation. Thus, the carrying amount (cost less accumulated depreciation) may differ significantly from the fair value of the asset.

  Land improvements, building, and equipment are depreciable assets, but land is not. Land has an indefinite useful life and often appreciates in value.

  Depreciable assets lose their utility because of wear and tear and obsolescence, the process by which an asset becomes out of date before it physically wears out.

  Three factors affect the calculation of depreciation: cost, useful life (an estimate of the productive, or service, life of the asset, expressed in terms of time, units of activity, or units of output), and residual value (an estimate of the asset's value at the end of its useful life).

- Depreciation is generally calculated using one of these three methods:

  1. Straight-line
  2. Diminishing-balance
  3. Units-of-production

> **study objective 2**
>
> Explain and calculate depreciation.

Management of a company chooses the method that it feels best matches the estimated pattern in which the benefits of the asset are expected to be consumed, and then applies that method consistently.

Under the **straight-line method**, an equal amount of depreciation is expensed each year of the asset's useful life. Depreciable cost, which is the asset's cost less its residual value, is divided by the useful life to give the annual depreciation expense. A straight-line rate can also be calculated (100% ÷ useful life) and multiplied by the depreciable cost to give the annual depreciation expense.

Consider the following example. A company purchased a truck on January 2 for $58,000. The truck has a useful life of 5 years and a residual value of $8,000. The depreciable cost is $50,000 ($58,000 − $8,000), and annual depreciation expense is $10,000 (50,000 ÷ 5 years). The straight-line rate is 20 percent (100% ÷ 5 years); multiplying $50,000 by 20 percent also yields $10,000 per year. After 5 years, the total accumulated depreciation is $50,000, and the carrying amount of the asset is $8,000 ($58,000 − $50,000). Note that the carrying amount equals the residual value after all depreciation is taken. If this asset had been purchased on July 1, then depreciation for the year ended December 31 would have been $5,000 ($10,000 × 6/12).

The **diminishing-balance method** produces a decreasing annual depreciation expense over the useful life of the asset. It is called the "diminishing-balance" method because the periodic depreciation is calculated using the asset's carrying amount, which diminishes each year because accumulated depreciation increases. Annual depreciation expense is calculated by multiplying the carrying amount at the beginning of the year by the depreciation rate. The depreciation rate remains constant from year to year, but the carrying amount that the rate is applied to declines each year. In early years diminishing-balance depreciation expense will be higher than the straight-line depreciation expense, and in later years it will be less than straight-line. However, the total amount of depreciation (the depreciable cost) taken over an asset's life is the same, regardless of the method of depreciation used. A common way to apply the diminishing-balance method is to use a rate that is double the straight-line rate, thus producing double diminishing-balance. Just as is true for straight-line, depreciation under this method is a function of time.

Under the **units-of-production method**, useful life is expressed in terms of the total units of production or the use expected from the asset. Units of output, machine hours, kilometres driven, and hours flown can all be used. This method is excellent for factory machinery, vehicles, and airplanes.

● The following provides an example of the calculation of depreciation using the diminishing-balance method and the units-of-production method.

Under the diminishing-balance method, depreciation expense is calculated by multiplying the carrying amount of the asset by the straight-line rate. Residual value is initially ignored in the calculations. Later, depreciation stops when the carrying amount reaches the residual value. Double diminishing-balance is one of the forms of the diminishing-balance method: the rate is the straight-line rate multiplied by two. If an asset has a useful life of 4 years, then the straight-line rate is 25 percent (100% ÷ 4 years). Double that rate is 50 percent.

Assume that the asset with a 4-year useful life originally cost $50,000 and has a residual value of $5,000. Depreciation expense for the 4 years will be:

| | | | | | End of Year | |
Year	Carrying Amount Beginning of Year	Depreciation Rate	=	Depreciation Expense	Accumulated Depreciation	Carrying Amount
1	$50,000	50%		$25,000	$25,000	$25,000
2	25,000	50%		12,500	37,500	12,500
3	12,500	50%		6,250	43,750	6,250
4	6,250	50%		1,250	45,000	5,000
	Total depreciation expense:			$45,000		

Note that in year 4 only $1,250 of depreciation was taken, even though the carrying amount of $6,250 multiplied by 50 percent yields $3,125. Remember that the carrying amount must equal residual value at the end of the 4 years, and $3,125 would have violated that. In the final year, only depreciation that will make the total depreciation $45,000 ($50,000 − $5,000) is taken.

Depreciation under this method is a function of time. Therefore, an asset purchased during the year must have its depreciation prorated. If the asset above had been purchased on April 1, then depreciation for year 1 would have been $18,750 ($50,000 × 50% × 9/12). The carrying amount for year 2 would have been $31,250 ($50,000 − $18,750).

Under the units-of-production method, depreciable cost per unit is calculated and applied to actual units produced during the accounting period.

A company purchased an asset with a cost of $30,000; a residual value of $5,000; an estimated useful life of 5 years; and estimated units of output of 50,000. In year 1, the asset produced 12,000 units. Depreciation is calculated as follows:

$30,000 − $5,000 = $25,000 depreciable cost
$25,000 ÷ 50,000 units = $0.50 per unit
$0.50 per unit × 12,000 actual units = $6,000

Note that the useful life in years is not used in the calculation. Note, too, that this method starts with the depreciable cost, just as straight-line depreciation does. Since the units-of-production method is a function of usage and not of time, it is not necessary to prorate depreciation if the asset is purchased at a time other than the beginning of the accounting period.

Remember that all three methods produce the same total amount of depreciation over the life of an asset. It is the timing of the expense that differs among the methods.

- When an item of property, plant, and equipment includes individual components for which different depreciation methods or rates are appropriate, the cost should be allocated to the asset's significant components and each component should be depreciated separately.

Further discussion of calculating depreciation for the different parts of an asset will be left to a later accounting course. For simplicity, we will assume in this text that all of the components of the depreciable asset have the same useful life and we will therefore depreciate each asset as a whole.

study objective 3

Describe other accounting issues related to depreciation.

- The Canada Revenue Agency (CRA) allows corporate taxpayers to deduct a specified amount of depreciation expense when calculating taxable income. The depreciation allowed for income tax purposes is calculated on a class (group) basis, using the single diminishing-balance, and is termed capital cost allowance (CCA). For accounting purposes, a company should choose the depreciation method that best reflects the pattern in which the asset's future economic benefits are consumed.

- In some instances, the fair value may fall significantly below the carrying amount of property, plant, and equipment. Recall that the carrying amount is the asset's cost less any accumulated depreciation since its acquisition. If such a case arises, an **impairment loss** must be recorded. An impairment loss is the amount by which the carrying amount of an asset exceeds its recoverable amount.

  The journal entry to record an impairment loss is:

  Loss on Impairment

      Accumulated Depreciation

  The impairment loss is recorded on the statement of earnings as part of continuing operations and not under "other expenses."

- As mentioned earlier, companies can choose the cost model or the **revaluation model** to account for their property, plant, and equipment. Under the revaluation model, the carrying amount of property, plant, and equipment is its fair value less any subsequent accumulated depreciation (which includes any subsequent impairment losses). This model can be applied only to assets whose fair value can be reliably measured and revaluations must be carried out often enough that the carrying amount is not materially different from the asset's fair value at the balance sheet date.

- It may become necessary to **revise periodic depreciation** during an asset's useful life for the following reasons:

  1. **Capital expenditures during the asset's useful life.** After purchasing an asset the company will incur costs as it continues to use the asset. Companies apply the same rules during an asset's useful life as when the asset was purchased, to determine which costs are capital expenditures and which costs are operating expenditures.

     If a cost, such as ordinary repairs and maintenance, benefits the company only in the current period, the cost is an operating expenditure and is recorded as an expense in the statement of earnings. If the cost, such as a replacement of a major part or an addition to a building, will benefit future periods then it is a capital expenditure and is added to the cost of the asset in the balance sheet. As capital expenditures during the asset's useful life increase the cost of a long-lived asset, the depreciation calculations will have to be revised.

  2. **Impairment losses.** As described in the previous section, an impairment loss will result in the reduction of the asset's carrying amount. Since the carrying value is reduced, the depreciation calculations will also need to be revised.

  3. **Changes in estimated useful life or residual value.** Management should regularly review its estimates of useful life and residual value. For example, wear and tear or obsolescence might indicate that annual depreciation is either not enough or too much. Capital expenditures may increase the useful life of the asset and/or is residual value. Impairment losses might signal a reduction in useful life and/or

residual value. Regardless of the reason for the change, a change in estimated useful life or residual value will cause a revision to the depreciation calculations.

4. **Changes to the pattern in which the economic benefits of the asset are consumed.** As discussed earlier, management must review the choice of depreciation methods at least annually. If the pattern in which the future benefits will be consumed is expected to change, then the depreciation method must change as well. A change in methods will obviously result in a revision to depreciation calculations.

● Revising depreciation is known as a change in estimate. Changes in estimates are made in current and future years but not to prior periods. This means that prior years' financial statements do not have to be restated. Continual restatement would undermine confidence in the financial statements.

Significant changes in estimates must be disclosed in the financial statements.

The calculation for revised depreciation is covered in other accounting courses.

● Regardless of the method of disposal, depreciation must be brought up to date, if necessary. Then, when the disposal journal entry is written, the asset account is credited for its cost, and the related Accumulated Depreciation account is debited.

study objective 4
Account for the disposal of property, plant, and equipment.

If the disposal is a sale, then the carrying amount of the asset is compared with the proceeds of the sale. If the proceeds exceed the carrying amount, then there is a gain on the sale. If the proceeds are less than the carrying amount, then there is a loss on the sale.

Consider the following example. A company sells a piece of machinery for $5,000. The machinery's original cost was $10,000. The up-to-date accumulated depreciation is $6,000. The journal entry to record the sale is as follows:

Cash	5,000	
Accumulated Depreciation	6,000	
Machinery		10,000
Gain on Disposal		1,000
(To record sale of machinery at a gain)		

The carrying amount of the asset is $4,000 ($10,000 − $6,000). Since the company received $5,000 for the asset, it sold the asset for a $1,000 gain. Gain on Disposal appears in the "Other Revenues" section of the statement of earnings.

If the company had sold the asset for $2,000, then it would have incurred a loss of $2,000 ($4,000 carrying amount − $2,000 cash proceeds). The journal entry is as follows:

Cash	2,000	
Accumulated Depreciation	6,000	
Loss on Disposal	2,000	
Machinery		10,000
(To record sale of machinery at a loss)		

Loss on Disposal appears in the "Other Expenses" section of the statement of earnings.

If the disposal is a retirement, then it is recorded as a sale in which no cash is received. The asset is credited for its cost, Accumulated Depreciation is debited for the proper amount, and a loss is debited for the carrying value of the asset on the date of retirement. A retirement will never result in a gain. If the asset in the two journal entries above is simply retired, then the journal entry is as follows:

Accumulated Depreciation	6,000	
Loss on Disposal	4,000	
Machinery		10,000

(To record retirement of machinery)

- In an exchange of assets, a new asset is typically purchased by trading in an old asset, on which a trade-in allowance is given toward the purchase price of the new asset. An additional cash payment is usually also required for the difference between the trade-in allowance and the purchase price of the new asset. Accounting for exchange transactions is complex and is left for future accounting courses.

study objective 5

Identify the basic accounting issues for intangible assets and goodwill.

- **Intangible assets** are rights, privileges, and/or competitive advantages that result from ownership of long-lived assets that do not possess physical substance. An intangible asset must be identifiable, which means it must meet one of the two following criteria:

  1. It can be separated from the company and sold whether or not the company intends to do so.
  2. It is based on contractual or legal rights, regardless of whether or not it can be separated from the company.

  Since goodwill cannot be separated from a company and sold, there are differences in the accounting for goodwill from other intangible assets.

- Intangible assets are recorded at cost. If an intangible asset has a finite or limited life, its amortizable amount (cost less residual value) should be allocated over the shorter of the (i) estimated useful life and (ii) legal life. Similar to depreciation, the company must use the amortization method that best matches the pattern in which the asset's future economic benefits are expected to be consumed. If that pattern cannot be reliably determined, the straight-line method should be used. The journal entry to record amortization includes a debit to amortization expense and a credit to accumulated amortization. If an intangible asset has an indefinite life, it is not amortized. However, its cost is reviewed and tested for an impairment loss annually, or more often, as circumstances dictate. If any impairment is evident, that is if the asset's fair value permanently falls below its carrying amount, the asset must be written down to its recoverable amount and an impairment loss recorded. If no impairment has occurred, the asset remains at its carrying amount until the following year, when it is evaluated again.

  As mentioned above, intangible assets are segregated into two categories—those with limited lives and those with indefinite lives—in order to determine whether or not the intangible assets should be amortized. The following represent intangible assets with limited lives.

- A **patent** is an exclusive right issued by the Canadian Intellectual Property Office of Industry Canada that allows the patent holder to manufacture, sell, or otherwise control an invention for a period of 20 years from the date of the application. The initial cost of a patent is the price paid to acquire the patent. The cost of the patent should be amortized over its 20-year legal life or its useful life, whichever is shorter.

- A **copyright** is granted by the Canadian Intellectual Property Office, giving the owner the exclusive right to reproduce and sell an artistic or published work. The legal life of a copyright is the life of the creator plus 50 years, and the cost is the cost of acquiring and defending it. Generally, the useful life of a copyright is significantly shorter than its legal life, and the copyright is therefore amortized over its useful life.

- **Research and development** (R&D) costs are not intangible assets, per se. But, they may lead to patents, copyrights, new processes, and new products. Research and development costs present two accounting problems: (i) it is sometimes difficult to determine the costs related to a specific project, and (ii) it is also hard to know the extent and timing of future benefits. As a result, accounting distinguishes between research costs and development costs.

  Research is original planned investigation that is done to gain new knowledge and understanding. All research costs should be expensed when incurred.

  Development is the use of research findings and knowledge for a plan or design before the start of commercial production. **Development costs with reasonably certain future benefits can be capitalized**. Management must have the technical feasibility, intention, and ability to complete the intangible asset and use or sell it; a future market must be defined; adequate resources must exist to complete the project; and management must be able to measure the costs related to the development of the intangible asset. All of these conditions must be met to capitalize development costs; otherwise they must be expensed.

- An intangible asset is considered to have an indefinite life when there is no foreseeable limit to the period over which the asset is expected to generate net cash inflows for the company. The following represent intangible assets with indefinite lives.

- A **trademark** or trade name is a word, phrase, jingle, or symbol that distinguishes or identifies a particular enterprise or product. Trademarks and trade names have tremendous value to companies and are vigorously defended. The creator or original user may obtain the exclusive legal right to a trademark or trade name by registering it with the Canadian Intellectual Property Office. Such registration provides continuous protection and may be renewed every 15 years as long as the trademark or trade name is in use. If it is developed internally rather than purchased, it cannot be recognized as an intangible asset on the balance sheet. Expenditures on internally developed trademarks or brands cannot be distinguished from the cost of developing the business as a whole. Thus the cost of an internally developed trademark or brand cannot be measured.

- A **franchise** is a contractual agreement under which the franchisor grants the franchisee the right to sell certain products, to render specific services, or to use certain trademarks or trade names, normally within a designated geographic area. Another type of franchise is granted by a governmental body and permits a company to use public property in performing its services. When costs can be identified with the acquisition of the franchise or licence, an intangible asset should be recognized. These rights have indefinite lives and are not amortized.

  Annual payments, often proportionate with sales, are sometimes required under a franchise agreement. These are called royalties and are recorded as **operating expenses** in the period in which they are incurred.

- **Goodwill** represents the value of all favourable attributes that relate to a company. These include excellent management, a desirable location, skilled employees, good customer relations, high-quality products, fair pricing policies, and harmonious relations with labour unions. Unlike other assets such as investments or property, plant, and equipment, which can be sold individually in the marketplace, goodwill can be identified only with the business as a whole.

  Goodwill is recorded only when there is a purchase of an entire business, at which time an independent valuation can be determined. The cost of the goodwill is measured by comparing the cost of the business acquired to the fair value of its net identifiable assets (assets less liabilities). If the cost is greater than the net identifiable assets, then the purchaser has paid for something that is not identifiable. The purchaser has paid for something that cannot be separated and sold—goodwill. Because a transaction occurs, the cost of the goodwill purchased can be measured and therefore recorded as an asset.

  Because goodwill has an indefinite life, it is not amortized. Since goodwill is measured using the fair value of a company, a subjective evaluation that can easily change, it must be tested annually for impairment and a loss recognized, if appropriate.

<table>
<tr><td>

study objective 6

Illustrate how long-lived assets are reported in the financial statements.

</td><td>

- Long-lived assets are normally reported under the headings "Property, Plant, and Equipment" and "Intangible Assets." Sometimes intangible assets are listed separately, following Property, Plant, and Equipment, with no separate caption. Goodwill must be separately disclosed; other intangibles can be grouped together for reporting purposes.

</td></tr>
</table>

- Either on the balance sheet or in the notes, the cost of each of the major classes of assets should be disclosed, as well as the accumulated depreciation for assets that are depreciated and accumulated amortization for intangible assets that are amortized. In addition, the depreciation and amortization methods used and the useful lives or rates must be described.

- Under international financial reporting standards, companies will also have to disclose if they are using the cost or the revaluation model for each class of assets, and include a reconciliation of the carrying amount at the beginning and end of the period for each class of long-lived assets in the notes to the financial statements. This means they must show all of the following for each class of long-lived assets: (i) additions; (ii) disposals; (iii) depreciation or amortization; (iv) impairment losses; and (v) reversals of impairment losses. If a company uses the revaluation model, it must also disclose any increases or decreases from revaluations as well as other information about the revaluation.

- The depreciation expense and impairment losses are reported in the operating section of the statement of earnings. The cash flows resulting from the purchase or sale of long-lived assets are reported in the investing section of the cash flow statement.

<table>
<tr><td>

study objective 7

Describe the methods for evaluating the use of assets.

</td><td>

- Two measures are used to analyze assets: return on assets and asset turnover.

  1. The **return on assets ratio** measures the overall profitability of a company. It is calculated by dividing net earnings by average total assets. The return on assets ratio indicates the amount of net earnings generated by each dollar invested in assets. Thus, the higher the return on assets, the more profitable the company.

</td></tr>
</table>

2. The **asset turnover ratio** indicates how efficiently a company is able to generate sales with a given amount of assets. It is calculated by dividing net sales by average total assets. It shows how many dollars of sales are generated by each dollar invested in assets. The higher the ratio, the more efficiently the company is operating. If the ratio is 1.25 times, then this means that for each dollar invested in assets, the company generates sales of $1.25. Asset turnover ratios vary considerably among industries.

• To complete the analysis of the sales-generating ability of a company's assets, the profit margin, discussed in Chapter 5, can be used in conjunction with the asset turnover ratio to explain the return on assets ratio. The relationship is as follows:

$$\text{Profit Margin} \quad \times \quad \text{Asset Turnover} \quad = \quad \text{Return on Assets}$$

$$\frac{\text{Net Earnings}}{\text{Net Sales}} \quad \times \quad \frac{\text{Net Sales}}{\text{Average Total Assets}} \quad = \quad \frac{\text{Net Earnings}}{\text{Average Total Assets}}$$

This relationship has important implications for management. If a company wants to increase its return on assets, it can do so either by increasing the margin it generates from each dollar of goods that it sells (profit margin), or by trying to increase the volume of goods that it sells (asset turnover).

Chapter Self-Test

As you work through the questions and problems, remember to use the **Decision Toolkit** discussed and used in the text:

1. *Decision Checkpoints:* At this point, you ask a question.
2. *Info Needed for Decision:* You make a choice regarding the information needed to answer the question.
3. *Tool to Use for Decision:* At this point, you review just what the information chosen in step 2 does for the decision-making process.
4. *How to Evaluate Results:* You conduct an evaluation of information for answering the question.

Note: The notation (SO1) means that the question was drawn from study objective number one.

Multiple Choice

Please circle the correct answer.

1. A company purchases a used delivery van for $20,000. The logo of the company   (SO1)
    is painted on the side of the van for $600. The van licence is $60. The van undergoes safety testing for $110. What does the company record as the cost of the new van?
    a. $20,600
    b. $20,660
    c. $20,710
    d. $20,770

(SO1)   2. Massey Corporation purchased a piece of land for $50,000. It paid legal fees
            of $9,000. An old building on the land was torn down at a cost of $2,000 and
            proceeds from the scrap were $500. The total to be debited to the Land account is
            a. $61,000.
            b. $60,500.
            c. $59,000.
            d. $50,000.

(SO1)   3. Newcome Corporation installed a new parking lot for its employees at a cost of
            $10,000. The $10,000 should be debited to
            a.   Repairs and Maintenance Expense.
            b.   Land.
            c.   Land Improvements.
            d.   Parking Lot.

(SO1)   4. Oliver Corporation purchased a piece of equipment for $20,000. It paid shipping
            charges of $500 and insurance during transit of $200. Installation and testing of the
            new equipment cost $1,000. The total to be debited to the Equipment account is
            a. $20,000.
            b. $20,500.
            c. $20,700.
            d. $21,700.

(SO2)   5. Which of the following is *not* a depreciable asset?
            a.   Land
            b.   Building
            c.   Driveway
            d.   Equipment

(SO2)   6. Which of the following is a way to express the estimated useful life of a depreciable
            asset?
            a.   5 years
            b.   10,000 machine hours
            c.   30,000 units
            d.   All of the above are expressions of useful life

(SO2)   7. At the beginning of the year, Powers Corporation purchased a piece of machinery
            for $50,000. It has a residual value of $5,000; an estimated useful life of 9 years; and
            estimated units of output of 90,000 units. Actual units produced during the first
            year were 11,000. Depreciation expense for the first year under the straight-line
            method is
            a. $5,556.
            b. $5,500.
            c. $5,300.
            d. $5,000.

(SO2)   8. Which of the following statements is correct?
            a.   Straight-line depreciation is an accelerated method of depreciation.
            b.   The total amount of depreciation for an asset is the same, regardless of the
                 method used.

c.   The total amount of depreciation for an asset differs depending on the method used.

d.   In the later years of an asset's useful life, straight-line depreciation gives a lower expense than does diminishing-balance.

9. Which of the following statements is correct?   (SO3)

a.   Once depreciation expense is set, it may never be changed for an asset.

b.   When a change in estimate for depreciation is required, the change is made to prior periods.

c.   When a change in estimate for depreciation is required, the change is made in current and future years but not to prior periods.

d.   When a change in estimate for depreciation is required, the change is made to prior periods and in current and future years.

10. When the carrying amount of a long-lived asset exceeds its recoverable amount,   (SO3)
     it is called

a.   an impairment loss.

b.   a write-down.

c.   earnings management.

d.   a capital expenditure.

11. Which of the following methods will result in the highest depreciation in the first   (SO3)
    year?

a.   Diminishing-balance

b.   Time valuation

c.   Straight line

d.   Double diminishing-balance

12. A company sold for $3,000 a machine that had a cost of $10,000 and   (SO4)
     accumulated depreciation of $7,500. The company had a

a.   loss of $500.

b.   gain of $500.

c.   gain of $3,000.

d.   loss of $7,000.

13. A company sold for $2,000 a machine that had a cost of $10,000 and   (SO4)
     accumulated depreciation of $7,500. The company had a

a.   loss of $500.

b.   gain of $500.

c.   gain of $2,000.

d.   loss of $8,000.

14. Quick Corporation retired a piece of equipment, which had a cost $8,000 and   (SO4)
     accumulated depreciation of $7,000. The journal entry to record the retirement
     will include a

a.   debit to Gain on Disposal for $1,000.

b.   credit to Gain on Disposal for $1,000.

c.   credit to Loss on Disposal for $1,000.

d.   debit to Loss on Disposal for $1,000.

(SO5)   15. Which of the following gives the recipient the right to manufacture, sell, or otherwise control an invention for a period of 20 years?
a.   Patent
b.   Copyright
c.   Trademark
d.   Licence

(SO5)   16. A company successfully defended its copyright on a piece of literature at a cost of $75,000. The journal entry to record that cost includes a debit to
a.   Legal Fees Expense for $75,000.
b.   Intangible Assets for $75,000.
c.   Copyright for $75,000.
d.   Research and Development Expense for $75,000.

(SO5)   17. At the beginning of the year, Righter Corporation purchased for $10,000 a patent with a legal life of 8 years. Righter estimates that the useful life of the patent will be 4 years. Amortization expense on the patent for the year is:
a. $2,500.
b. $1,250.
c. $588.
d. $250.

(SO6)   18. With respect to long-lived assets, which of the following must be disclosed in the financial statements or notes to the financial statements?
a.   The balances of major classes of assets.
b.   Accumulated depreciation by major classes of assets.
c.   Depreciation methods used.
d.   All of the above must be disclosed.

(SO6)   19. An impairment loss is reported
a.   as a note to the financial statements.
b.   in the operating activities section in the cash flow statement.
c.   as a special item in the statement of retained earnings.
d.   in the operating expenses section in the statement of earnings.

(SO7)   20. A company's average total assets is $200,000; depreciation expense is $10,000; and accumulated depreciation is $60,000. Net sales total $250,000. The asset turnover is
a.   0.8 times.
b.   1.25 times.
c.   3.33 times.
d.   4.17 times.

(SO7)   21. The return on assets ratio
a.   indicates how efficiently a company uses its assets.
b.   measures the overall profitability of a company.
c.   indicates whether assets should be replaced.
d.   measures the liquidity of a company.

22. A company can increase its return on assets by   (SO7)
     a.   decreasing its average assets and holding its net sales and net earnings
           constant.
     b.   increasing its average assets and holding its net sales and net earnings
           constant.
     c.   increasing its net sales and holding its net earnings and average total assets
           constant.
     d.   decreasing its net earnings and holding its net sales and average total assets
           constant.

23. On January 3, 2009, Powers Corporation purchased a piece of machinery for   (SO2)
     $50,000. It has a residual value of $5,000, an estimated useful life of 9 years, and
     estimated units of output of 90,000 units. Actual units produced during the first
     year were 11,000. Depreciation expense for 2009 under the units-of-production
     method is
     a. $5,556.
     b. $5,500.
     c. $5,300.
     d. $5,000.

24. On January 4, 2009, Sacks Corporation purchased a piece of equipment   (SO2)
     for $20,000. It has a residual value of $4,000 and an estimated useful life of
     8 years. Depreciation expense for 2009 under the double diminishing-balance
     method is
     a. $5,000.
     b. $4,000.
     c. $2,000.
     d.   None of the above is the correct amount.

25. The carrying amount of a building is calculated as follows: (SO2)
     a.   Original cost of asset less its residual value.
     b.   Fair value of asset less its accumulated depreciation.
     c.   Original cost of asset less its accumulated depreciation.
     d.   Fair value of asset less its residual value.

Problems

1.   Townsend Corporation owns a piece of machinery that it had purchased 3 years   (SO2, 4)
     ago for $40,000. The machinery has an estimated residual value of $5,000 and an
     estimated useful life of 10 years. At the end of 2008, the Accumulated Deprecia-
     tion account had a balance of $10,500. On April 1, 2010, the corporation sold the
     machinery for $27,000.

Record the following journal entries:

     a.   The depreciation entry on December 31, 2009.
     b.   The entry or entries to record the sale on April 1, 2010.
     c.   If Townsend had simply retired the machinery on April 1, 2010, then what
           would the journal entry or entries have been?

Date	Account Titles	Debit	Credit

(SO1, 2, 4)   2.   The Sligo Corporation adjusts and closes its account at the end of each calendar year and uses the straight-line method of depreciation on all its machinery equipment. On January 2, 2007, machinery was purchased for cash at a cost of $45,000. Useful life was estimated to be 10 years and residual value $8,000.

On June 29, 2010, Sligo decided to lease new, more efficient machinery; consequently, the machinery described above was sold on this date for $33,350 cash.

Prepare the following journal entries:

    a.   to record the purchase of the machinery.
    b.   to record depreciation for 2007, 2008, and 2009.
    c.   to record the disposal of the machinery on June 29, 2010.

Date	Account Titles	Debit	Credit

3.   Assume that a company purchases machinery at a cost of $100,000 on April 1,   (SO2)
     2009. The machinery has a 5-year useful life and a residual value of $8,000. The
     company uses the diminishing-balance of depreciation at twice the straight-line
     rate. The company's year ends on December 31.

     a.   Prepare a 5-year depreciation schedule.
     b.   Prepare a journal entry to record depreciation for 2010.
     c.   Prepare a journal entry to record depreciation for 2014.

4.   The following account balances are provided for the Vic Corporation as of   (SO6)
     December 31, 2009:

Cash	$200,000
Accounts receivable	260,000
Accumulated depreciation—equipment	300,000
Accumulated depreciation—building	370,000
Accumulated amortization—patents	10,000
Allowance for doubtful accounts	70,000
Building	900,000
Equipment	800,000
Goodwill	150,000
Inventories	180,000
Land	700,000
Patents	40,000
Prepaid expenses	30,000
Short-term investments	90,000

Prepare the assets section of the balance sheet for Vic Corporation as of December 31,
2009.

5.   Please refer to the Domtar and Cascades financial statements found in the ap-
     pendices at the end of this study guide for information for answering the follow-
     ing questions. Do not forget to use the **Decision Toolkit** approach for help in the
     problem solving.

     a.   What line items concerning property, plant, and equipment and intangible   (SO1, 2, 6)
          assets and depreciation and amortization can be found on Domtar and
          Cascades' statement of earnings, balance sheet, and cash flow statement for
          2007?
     b.   Calculate the profitability of both companies for 2007, breaking down each   (SO7)
          company's return on assets ratio into its profit margin and asset turnover
          components.
     c.   Compare the performance of Domtar and Cascades for 2007 using the   (SO7)
          information obtained in (b). The return on assets for the industry in 2007
          was 2.3 percent.

Solutions to Self-Test

Multiple Choice

1. c $20,000 + $600 + $110 = $20,710. The cost of the licence would be recorded as an expense.

2. b $50,000 + $9,000 + $2,000 − $500 = $60,500

3. c Using an expense account is incorrect because the parking lot will benefit future periods. Land does not have a limited useful life, as does a parking lot. Typically a company will not call an account "Parking Lot" but will use "Land Improvements."

4. d $20,000 + $500 + $200 + $1,000 = $21,700

5. a The other three are depreciable.

6. d Answer a applies to straight-line method of depreciation and answers b and c apply to units-of-production method.

7. d ($50,000 − $5,000) ÷ 9 years = $5,000

8. b Straight-line gives an even amount of depreciation for each year of an asset's useful life. In the later years of an asset's useful life, straight-line gives a higher expense than does diminishing-balance.

9. c Depreciation methods may be changed. A change in estimate never affects prior periods, only current and future periods.

10. a Earnings management involves timing the recognition of gains and losses to achieve certain results. A capital expenditure is money spent on an asset after its purchase. A write-down is what is done when there is an impairment.

11. d Methods such as the double diminishing-balance method that produce higher depreciation expense in the early years than in the later years are known as accelerated depreciation methods.

12. b The carrying amount is $2,500 ($10,000 − $7,500). Since the proceeds exceed the carrying amount by $500, there is a gain.

13. a The carrying amount is $2,500 ($10,000 − $7,500). Since the carrying amount exceeds the proceeds by $500, there is a loss.

14. d Since the carrying amount is $1,000 ($8,000 − $7,000), there is a Loss on Disposal, and losses are always debited.

15. a A copyright protects literary and artistic works. A trademark is a word, phrase, jingle, or symbol that distinguishes or identifies an enterprise or product. A licence is an operating right.

16. c The money spent for a successful legal defence of an intangible asset is debited to the asset account. Use of an expense account is inappropriate.

17. a $10,000 ÷ 4 years. The shorter period is used.

18. d Either on the balance sheet or in the notes, the cost of each of the major classes of assets should be disclosed, as well as the accumulated depreciation for assets that are depreciated and accumulated amortization for intangible assets that are amortized. In addition, the depreciation and amortization methods used and the useful lives or rates must be described, as well as whether the company is following the cost or the revaluation model.

19. d   Depreciation expense and impairment losses are presented in the operating section of the statement of earnings.

20. b   Asset turnover = net sales ÷ average total assets; $250,000 ÷ $200,000 = 1.25 times

21. b   The return on assets ratio measures overall profitability.

22. a   Return on assets = profit margin × asset turnover
Decreasing the average assets increases the asset turnover and therefore the return on assets ratio.

23. b $50,000 − $5,000 = $45,000 ÷ 90,000 units = $0.50/unit × 11,000 actual units = $5,500

24. a   The double diminishing-balance rate is 25 percent [(100% ÷ 8 years) × 2], and $20,000 × 25 percent = $5,000.

25. c   The carrying amount of a depreciable asset is cost less accumulated depreciation.

Problems

1.   a.

Dec. 31, 2009	Depreciation Expense	3,500	
	Accumulated Depreciation—Machinery		3,500
	(To record annual depreciation)		

$40,000 − $5,000 = $35,000 ÷ 10 years = $3,500

Note: The company must use straight-line depreciation because the Accumulated Depreciation account at the end of 3 years after the asset is purchased is $10,500. On a straight-line basis, that equals 3 years × 3,500.

Apr. 1, 2010	Depreciation Expense	875	
	Accumulated Depreciation—Machinery		875
	(To bring depreciation up to date)		

$3,500 annual depreciation × 3/12 = $875

b.

Apr. 1, 2010	Cash	27,000	
	Accumulated Depreciation—Machinery	14,875	
	Machinery		40,000
	Gain on Disposal		1,875
	(To record disposal at a gain)		

Accumulated depreciation =
$10,500 + $3,500 + $875 = $14,875

Carrying Amount =
$40,000 − $14,875 = $25,125

Gain = $27,000 − $25,125 = $1,875

c.

Apr. 1, 2010	Depreciation Expense	875	
	Accumulated Depreciation—Machinery		875

(To bring amortization up to date)

$3,500 annual depreciation × 3/12 = $875

	Loss on Disposal	25,125	
	Accumulated Depreciation—Machinery	14,875	
	Machinery		40,000

(To record retirement of asset)

Accumulated Depreciation =
$10,500 + $3,500 + $875 = $14,875

Carrying Amount =
$40,000 − $14,875 = $25,125

The loss on disposal equals the carrying amount of the machinery.

2.   a.

Jan. 2, 2007	Machinery	45,000	
	Cash		45,000

(To record purchase of machinery)

b.

Dec. 31, 2007	Depreciation Expense	3,700	
	Accumulated Depreciation—Machinery		3,700

(To record depreciation for 2007)

$45,000 − $8,000 = $37,000 ÷ 10 years = $3,700

Dec. 31, 2008	Depreciation Expense	3,700	
	Accumulated Depreciation—Machinery		3,700

(To record depreciation for 2008)

Dec. 31, 2009	Depreciation Expense	3,700	
	Accumulated Depreciation—Machinery		3,700

(To record depreciation for 2009)

c.

June 29, 2010	Depreciation Expense	1,850	
	Accumulated Depreciation—Machinery		1,850

(To bring depreciation up to date prior to disposal of machinery: $3,700 ÷ 2 = $1,850)

Cash	33,350	
Accumulated Depreciation—Machinery	12,950	
Machinery		45,000
Gain on Disposal		1,300
(To record disposal at a gain)		

Accumulated depreciation =
$3,700 + $3,700 + $3,700 + $1,850 = $12,950

Carrying amount =
$45,000 − $12,950 = $32,050

Gain = $33,350 − $32,050 = $1,300

3.   a.

Year	Carrying Amount Beginning of Year	Depreciation Rate	=	Depreciation Expense	End of Year Accumulated Depreciation	End of Year Carrying Amount
						$100,000
2009	$100,000	40%^{1}		$30,000^{2}	$30,000	70,000
2010	70,000	40%		28,000	58,000	42,000
2011	42,000	40%		16,800	74,800	25,200
2012	25,200	40%		10,080	84,880	15,120
2013	15,120	40%		6,048	90,928	9,072
2014	9,072	40%		1,072^{3}	92,000	8,000
	Total depreciation expense:			$92,000		

Note 1: $1 \div 5 = 20\% \times 2 = 40\%$.

2: The machinery was purchased on April 1, 2009, therefore 9 months of depreciation apply in 2009: ($100,000 × 40% × 9/12 = $30,000).

3: Calculation of $3,628.80 ($9,072 × 40%) is adjusted to $1,072 so carrying amount will equal residual value.

b.

Dec. 31, 2010	Depreciation Expense	28,000	
	Accumulated Depreciation—Machinery		28,000
	(To record depreciation for 2010)		

c.

Dec. 31, 2014	Depreciation Expense	1,072	
	Accumulated Depreciation—Machinery		1,072
	(To record depreciation for 2014)		

4.

VIC CORPORATION
Balance Sheet (Partial)
December 31, 2009

Current assets

Cash		$200,000
Accounts receivable	$260,000	
Less: allowance for doubtful accounts	70,000	190,000
Short-term investments		90,000
Inventories		180,000
Prepaid expenses		30,000
Total current assets		690,000

Property, plant, and equipment

Land		700,000
Building	$900,000	
Less: accumulated depreciation	370,000	530,000
Equipment	$800,000	
Less: accumulated depreciation	300,000	500,000
Total property, plant, and equipment		1,730,000

Intangible assets

Patents	$40,000	
Less: accumulated amortization	10,000	30,000

Goodwill		150,000
Total assets		$2,600,000

5. (Domtar $ in USD millions; Cascades $ in CAD millions)

a. Domtar:

Depreciation and amortization of $471, impairment of property, plant, and equipment of $92, and impairment of goodwill of $4 on the statement of earnings; property, plant, and equipment of $9,685, accumulated depreciation of $4,323, goodwill of $372, and intangible assets, net of amortization, of $111 on the balance sheet; and additions to property, plant, and equipment of $116 offset by proceeds from disposals of property, plant, and equipment of $29 on the cash flow statement.

Cascades:

Depreciation and amortization of $208 on the statement of earnings; property, plant, and equipment of $1,886, intangible assets of $130, and goodwill of $312 on the balance sheet; and the purchase of property, plant, and equipment of $167 offset by proceeds from disposal of property, plant, and equipment of $7 on the cash flow statement.

b.

Profit Margin	$\times$	Asset Turnover	$=$	Return on Assets

$\dfrac{\text{Net Earnings}}{\text{Net Sales}}$	$\times$	$\dfrac{\text{Net Sales}}{\text{Average Total Assets}}$	$=$	Return on Assets

Domtar:	$\dfrac{\$70}{\$5,947}$	$\times$	$\dfrac{\$5,947}{(\$7,748 + \$3,998) \div 2}$		
	1.2%	$\times$	1.0 times	$=$	1.2%
Cascades:	$\dfrac{\$95}{\$3,929}$	$\times$	$\dfrac{\$3,929}{(\$3,769 + \$3,911) \div 2}$		
	2.4%	$\times$	1.0 times	$=$	2.4% *

* *Note*: Some rounding discrepancies may exist.

c.   Both companies' asset turnover ratios were the same but Cascades' profit margin of 2.4 percent was significantly better than Domtar's 1.2 percent. As a result, Cascades, return on assets was better than that of Domtar's and the industry average of 2.3 percent in 2007 while Domtar's return was below average.

chapter 10

Reporting and Analyzing Liabilities

Chapter Overview

Chapter 10 discusses the two basic types of liabilities—current and long-term. In the former category, you will learn about an operating line of credit, notes payable, sales taxes payable, property taxes payable, payroll, and current maturities of long-term debt. In the latter category, you will learn about notes payable and bonds payable. For both categories, you will learn about financial statement presentation and analysis. Finally, you will learn how to apply the effective interest method of amortizing bond discounts and premiums.

Review of Specific Study Objectives

- A **current liability** is a debt that will be paid within 1 year from existing current assets or through the creation of other current liabilities. A debt that does not meet both criteria is classified as a long-term liability.

study objective 1

Account for current liabilities.

- Current liabilities include an operating line of credit; notes payable; accounts payable; unearned revenue; accrued liabilities, such as taxes, salaries and wages, and interest; and the current portion of long-term debt.

- An **operating line of credit** is set up at a company's bank to help the company manage its temporary cash shortfalls. This means that the company has been pre-authorized by the bank to borrow money, up to a pre-set limit, when it is needed. Security, called collateral, is usually required by the bank as protection in the event of a default on the loan. Collateral normally includes some or all of the company's current assets. Line of credit borrowings are normally on a short-term basis, repayable immediately upon request—that is, on demand, by the bank.

- A number of companies show a negative or overdrawn cash balance at year end as a result of using their line of credit. No special entry is required to record the overdrawn amount. The normal credits to Cash will simply accumulate and are reported as **bank indebtedness** in the current liability section of the balance sheet and with a suitable note disclosure.

- **Notes payable** are obligations in the form of written notes. They give written documentation of a liability and usually require the borrower to pay interest. If a note is due for payment within 1 year of the balance sheet, then it is classified as a current liability.

- Consider the following example. Robinson Ltd. borrows $20,000 and issues a 3-month, 6-percent note on May 1. Interest plus principal are repayable at maturity. The entry on May 1 is:

Cash	20,000	
Notes Payable		20,000
(To record issue of note)		

If Robinson prepares financial statements on June 30, necessitating adjusting entries, then the adjusting entry for accrued interest is:

Interest Expense	200	
Interest Payable		200
(To record accrued interest: $20,000 \times 6\% \times 2/12$)		

On the maturity date, August 1, the following entry is recorded:

Notes Payable	20,000	
Interest Payable	200	
Interest Expense	100	
Cash		20,300
(To record payment of note plus interest)		

Total interest on the note is $300, and the maturity value is $20,300. The interest payable of $200 must be taken off the books, since it is no longer payable, and the interest expense is the third month's interest ($20,000 \times 6\% \times 1/12$). Recall from Chapter 4 that interest is calculated for short-term notes by multiplying the principal amount by the annual interest rate by the fraction of the year. That is, the 6 percent is an annual interest rate and must be adjusted for the monthly time period. Interest rates are always expressed as an annual (1 year) rate, regardless of the term of the note.

There are usually **sales taxes:** Goods and Services Tax (GST), Provincial Sales Tax (PST), or Harmonized Sales Tax (HST) on items sold. In Quebec, the PST is known as the Quebec Sales Tax (QST). In many provinces, sales taxes are collectively known as Retail Sales Tax (RST).

The retailer serves as a collection agent for the taxing authority, usually the provincial and federal governments, and must periodically remit to these governments the sales taxes collected. When an item is sold, the amount of the sale and the amount of each of the sales taxes collected are usually rung up separately on the cash register. If $500 of merchandise is sold, the GST percentage is 5 percent, and the PST percentage is 8 percent, then the following entry records the sale:

Cash	565	
Sales		500
GST Payable		25
PST Payable		40
(To record sales and sales taxes)		

- When these two sales taxes are remitted to the governments, the entry is:

GST Payable	25	
PST Payable	40	
Cash		65
(To remit sales taxes to tax agencies)		

- Businesses that own property pay **property taxes** annually. It is difficult to determine the property tax expense because the amount due for the current year is unknown until the bill is received, usually sometime in the spring of each year.

To illustrate, assume that a company's year end is December 31 and that it makes adjusting entries only annually. This company receives its property tax bill of $8,400 on March 1, and it is due to be paid on May 31. On March 1, when the property tax bill is received, the company records the property tax expense and liability for the 2 months that have already passed.

Mar. 1	Property Tax Expense ($8,400 × 2/12)	1,400	
	Property Tax Payable		1,400
	(To record property tax expense for January and February)		

In May, when the company records the payment of the liability recorded on March 1, it also records the expense incurred to date for the months of March, April, and May. As at May 31, 5 months have passed and should be recorded as property tax expense. The remaining 7 months of the year are recorded as a prepayment, as shown in the following entry:

May 31	Property Tax Payable	1,400	
	Property Tax Expense ($8,400 × 3/12)	2,100	
	Prepaid Property Tax ($8,400 × 7/12)	4,900	
	Cash		8,400
	(To record payment of property tax expense for March through May, and amount prepaid for June through December)		

After the payment of the property tax, the company has a zero balance in its liability account but still has a prepayment. Since the company only makes adjusting entries annually, it would not adjust the prepaid property tax account until year end, December 31. At that time, it would make the following entry:

Dec. 31	Property Tax Expense	4,900	
	Prepaid Property Tax		4,900
	(To record property tax expense for June through December)		

- Every employer incurs liabilities relating to employees' salaries and wages. Amounts withheld from employees' paycheques, called withholding taxes, must be remitted to the appropriate authorities. Withheld amounts include federal and provincial income taxes, Canada Pension Plan (CPP) contributions, Employment Insurance (EI) premiums, and other amounts specified by employees, such as charitable contributions, union dues, and health insurance.

- Every employer incurs a second type of payroll-related liability. With every payroll, the employer incurs liabilities to pay various payroll costs that are levied, such as the employer's share of CPP and EI. In addition, the provincial governments mandate employer funding of a workplace health, safety, and compensation plan. Each of these contributions, plus such items such as paid vacations and employer-sponsored pensions, are collectively referred to as employee benefits.

- Payroll and payroll tax liability accounts are classified as current liabilities because they must either be paid to employees or remitted to government authorities or other third parties both periodically and in the near-term.

- Companies often have long-term debt of which a portion is due in the current period. If a company has a 10-year mortgage, then the portion due in the current period must be classified as current. These items are often identified on the balance sheet as "long-term debt due within the year." No adjusting entry is required. The proper classification is recognized when the balance sheet is prepared.

- **Long-term liabilities** are obligations that are expected to be paid after 1 year. They are often in the form of long-term notes or bonds.

study objective 2

Account for long-term notes payable.

- **Long-term notes payable** are similar to short-term notes payable, except that the terms of the note exceed 1 year.

- The following are types of notes:

    a. Secured notes have specific assets of the issuer pledged as collateral for the notes. Secured notes are also known as mortgages.
    b. Unsecured notes are issued against the general credit of the borrower. These are also known as debentures and are issued by corporations with good credit ratings.
    c. Convertible debt may be converted into common shares.

- A long-term note may be unsecured or secured. Secured notes are commonly known as mortgages. A **mortgage note payable** is widely used by individuals to purchase homes or by companies to acquire property, plant, and equipment.

- Most long-term notes are repayable in a series of periodic payments. These payments are known as **instalments** and are paid monthly, quarterly, semi-annually, or at another defined period. Each payment consists of (i) interest on the unpaid balance of the loan, and (ii) a reduction of the loan principal. Payments generally take one of two forms: (i) fixed principal payment plus interest, or (ii) blended principal and interest payments.

- Instalment notes with **fixed principal payments** are repayable in equal periodic amounts, **plus interest.** Interest may be either fixed or floating. A fixed interest rate will be constant over the term of the note. A floating (or variable) interest rate will change with fluctuating market rates. Floating rates are generally tied to changes in the prime rate.

Assume that on January 1, 2009, a company issues a 5-year, 6-percent, $114,000 note payable and that the interest rate is fixed. The entry to record that note is:

Jan. 1	Cash	114,000	
	Notes Payable		114,000
	(To record issue of 5-year, 6-percent note)		

The terms of the note provide for fixed principal payments of $1,900 ($114,000 ÷ 60 monthly periods) on the first of each month, plus interest of 6 percent on the outstanding principal balance.

On the first payment date—February 1—interest expense is $570 ($114,000 × 6% × 1/12). Similar to short-term notes, the 6 percent is an annual interest rate and must be adjusted for the monthly time period. The cash payment of $2,470 for the month of February is the total of the instalment payment of $1,900, which is applied against the principal, plus the interest of $570.

The entry to record the first instalment payment on February 1 is as follows:

Feb. 1	Interest Expense ($114,000 × 6% × 1/12)	570	
	Note Payable	1,900	
	Cash ($1,900 + $570)		2,470
	(To record monthly payment on note)		

An instalment payment schedule helps to organize the information that is required to prepare journal entries. A partial instalment payment schedule for the first few months, rounded to the nearest dollar, is shown as follows:

Instalment Payment Schedule— Fixed Principal Payments				
Interest Period	(A) Cash Payment (B + C)	(B) Interest Expense (D × 6% × 1/12)	(C) Reduction of Principal ($114,000 ÷ 60)	(D) Principal Balance (D − C)
Jan. 1				$114,000
Feb. 1	$2,470	$570	$1,900	112,100
Mar. 1	2,461	561	1,900	110,200
Apr. 1	2,451	551	1,900	108,300

- Instalment notes with **blended principal and interest payments** are repayable in equal periodic amounts, **including interest.** Blended principal and interest payments result in changing amounts of interest and principal applied to the loan. With fixed principal payments, the interest decreases each period (as the principal decreases). In contrast, with blended principal and interest payments, the portion applied to the loan principal increases each period.

To illustrate this option, assume that instead of fixed principal payments, the company repays its note in equal monthly instalments of $2,213. (The cash payment of $2,213 can be calculated mathematically or be determined using present value techniques, which are discussed later in the chapter.) As with the fixed principal payments illustrated above, monthly interest expense is calculated by multiplying the outstanding principal balance by the interest rate. For the first payment date—February 1—interest expense is $570 ($114,000 × 6% × 1/12). The instalment payment of $2,213 is fixed for each month, and includes interest and principal amounts that will vary. In February, the principal balance will be reduced by $1,643, which is the difference between the instalment payment of $2,213 and the interest amount of $570.

The entry to record the issue of the note payable is the same as in the previous section.

The entry to record the instalment payment uses the same accounts but different amounts. The first instalment payment on February 1 is recorded as follows:

Feb. 1	Interest Expense ($114,000 × 6% × 1/12)	570	
	Note Payable ($2,213 − $570)	1,643	
	Cash ($1,643 + $570)		2,213
	(To record monthly payment on note)		

A partial instalment payment schedule for the first few months, rounded to the nearest dollar, is shown as follows:

Interest Period	(A) Cash Payment (B + C)	(B) Interest Expense (D × 6% × 1/12)	(C) Reduction of Principal (A − B)	(D) Principal Balance (D − C)
Jan. 1				$114,000
Feb. 1	$2,213	$570	$1,643	112,357
Mar. 1	2,213	562	1,651	110,706
Apr. 1	2,213	554	1,659	109,047

study objective 3

Account for bonds payable.

- **A bond** is a form of interest-bearing note payable. Bonds are issued in small denominations (usually $1,000 or multiples of $1,000) and attract many investors.

- The following are types of bonds:

  a. Secured bonds have specific assets of the issuer pledged as collateral for the bonds.
  b. Unsecured bonds are issued against the general credit of the borrower. These are also known as debentures and are issued by corporations with good credit ratings.
  c. Convertible bonds may be converted into common shares.
  d. Redeemable (callable) bonds are subject to retirement at a stated dollar amount prior to maturity at the option of the issuer.

- A bond certificate is issued to investors to provide evidence of an investor's credit claim against the company. The certificate provides such information as the name of the issuer, the face value, the contractual interest rate, and the maturity date of the bond. The face value is the amount of principal due at the maturity date. The maturity date is the date that the final payment is due to the investor from the company. The contractual interest rate is the rate used to determine the amount of cash interest the borrower pays and the investor receives.

- Bonds may be issued at face value, at a discount (below face value), or at a premium (above face value).

- Bond prices are quoted as a percentage of the face value of the bond, such as 97 or 101. If a $1,000 bond sells at 97, then the issuing corporation receives 97 percent of the face value, or $970. If the bond sells at 101, then the corporation receives $1,010. These percentages applied to the face value of a bond represent the present value of a bond. We will show you shortly how to calculate present value.

- When a bond sells at face value (the contractual rate of interest equals the market interest rate), the journal entry to record the issue is a debit to Cash and a credit to Bonds Payable. When bond interest is paid, the debit is to Bond Interest Expense, and the credit is to Cash. If interest is accrued, then the debit is to Bond Interest Expense, and the credit is to Bond Interest Payable. Bonds Payable is reported as a long-term liability, and Bond Interest Payable is a current liability.

- When a bond is issued, if the contractual rate of interest exceeds the market rate of interest, then the bond is issued at a premium. If the contractual rate of interest is lower than the market rate of interest, then the bond is issued at a discount.

- Consider the following example. The Jays Corporation issued $500,000, 5-year, 5-percent bonds at 96 on January 1, 2009, with interest payable each July and January.

The journal entry on January 1, 2009, is as follows:

Cash ($500,000 × 96%)	480,000	
Bonds Payable		480,000
(To record issue of bonds)		

Note that Bonds Payable is always credited for the issue price of the bonds, which is also the carrying amount of the bonds. The credit to the Bonds Payable account is net of the bond discount ($500,000 – $20,000).

- Let us now assume that the Jays Corporation issued $500,000, 5-year, 5-percent bonds at 102 on January 1, 2009, with interest payable each July and January 1. The journal entry on January 1, 2009, is as follows:

Cash ($500,000 × 102%)	510,000	
Bonds Payable		510,000
(To record issue of bonds)		

The credit to the Bonds Payable account is net of the bond premium ($500,000 + $10,000). The $510,000 is the carrying amount of the bonds.

In the above examples, the issue price or fair value of the bond was determined by applying a percentage factor to the face value of the bond. This percentage factor represents the present value of all the cash flows associated with the bond or the value at which the bond sells in the marketplace. The present value depends on three factors: (i) the dollar amounts to be received, (ii) the length of time until the amounts are received, and (iii) the market rate of interest. The process of finding the present value is referred to as discounting the future amounts.

Present value tables, provided in Appendix 10A, can assist you in calculating the present value of the bonds. The following instructions will help you use the tables:

1.   Use Table 1 (the present value of $1) to determine the right factor to use to calculate the present value of the principal, which is a single sum.
2.   Use Table 2 (the present value of an annuity of $1) to calculate the present value of the interest, which recurs periodically (as an annuity).
3.   To find the right factor in each table, locate the factor at the intersection of the number of periods and the interest rate. When interest is paid semi-annually, remember to double the number of periods and halve the annual interest rate. For example, in the following Jays Corporation example, the 5-year term of the bonds means that there are 10 semi-annual interest periods. In addition, the effective interest rate of 6 percent when bonds are sold at a discount becomes 3 percent ($6\% \times 6/12$).
4.   The face value of the bonds and the contractual interest rate are used to calculate the interest payment. Note that while the contractual interest rate is used to determine the interest payment, the market interest rate is what is used to determine the present value.

To illustrate the use of present value tables to calculate the issue of a bond, the following example is used. Assume that Jays Corporation issues a $500,000, 5-year, 5-percent bond on January 1, 2009, with interest payable each July 1 and January 1. Also assume that the bonds are issued to yield a market rate of interest of 6 percent.

Present value of $500,000 received in 10 periods	
$500,000 × 0.7441 ($n = 10$, $i = 3$) (from Present Value of $1 table)	$372,050
Present value of $12,500 received for each of 20 periods ($500,000 × 5% × 6/12)	
$12,500 × 8.5302 ($n = 10$, $i = 3$) (from Present Value of Annuity table)	106,628
Present value (issue price) of bonds	$478,678

Note that the percentage applied to the face value of the bond to determine its selling price is:

Issue price = $478,678 ÷ $500,000 = 95.74%

The following journal entry reflects the January 1, 2009 transaction:

Cash	478,678	
Bonds Payable		478,678
(To record issue of bonds)		

Once the bond has been issued, the Jays Corporation is obligated to pay interest to the bondholders on a semi-annual basis. As discussed earlier, the discount on the bonds payable will need to be amortized. The following steps are required to calculate the amortization of the discount.

1. Calculate the **bond interest expense**: Multiply the carrying amount of the bonds at the beginning of the interest period by the effective interest rate.
2. Calculate the **bond interest paid** (or accrued): Multiply the face value of the bonds by the contractual interest rate.
3. Calculate the **amortization amount**: Determine the difference between the amounts calculated in steps (1) and (2).

The bond discount amortization schedule is shown below for the amortization of the $21,322 discount on bonds payable. All figures have been rounded to the nearest dollar for simplicity.

	(A) Interest Payment ($500,000 × 5% × 6/12)	(B) Interest Expense (Preceding Bond Carrying Amount × 6% × 6/12)	(C) Discount Amorti- zation (B − A)	(D) Un- amortized Discount (D − C)	(E) Bond Carry- ing Amount ($500,000 − D)
Semi-Annual Interest Period					
Issue Date				$21,322	$478,678
1	$12,500	$14,360	$1,860	19,462	480,538
2	12,500	14,416	1,916	17,546	482,454
3	12,500	14,474	1,974	15,572	484,428
4	12,500	14,533	2,033	13,539	486,461
5	12,500	14,594	2,094	11,445	488,555
6	12,500	14,657	2,157	9,288	490,712
7	12,500	14,721	2,221	7,067	492,933
8	12,500	14,788	2,288	4,779	495,221
9	12,500	14,857	2,357	2,422	497,578
10	12,500	14,927	2,422[1]	0	500,000

JAYS CORPORATION
Bond Discount Amortization Schedule
Effective Interest Method

[1]$5 difference due to cumulative rounding.

The journal entry for the first interest date on July 1, 2009, is as follows:

Bond Interest Expense	14,360	
Bonds Payable		1,860
Cash		12,500

(To record payment of interest and amortization of discount)

The discount is an additional cost of borrowing and, according to the matching principle, should be recorded as bond interest expense over the life of the bonds. This is referred to as amortizing the discount. Amortizing a discount results in an increase in interest expense and an increase in the carrying amount of the bonds.

The journal entry for the second interest date on December 31, 2009, is as follows. While the interest expense and amortization amounts vary, the cash payment remains a constant $12,500 every interest period.

Bond Interest Expense	14,416	
Bonds Payable		1,916
Cash		12,500

(To record payment of interest and amortization of discount)

Note that the amount of periodic interest expense increases over the life of the bond when bonds are issued at a discount. The reason is that a constant percentage is applied to an increasing bond carrying amount to calculate interest expense. The bond carrying amount is increasing because of the amortization of the discount.

If a bond premium existed rather than a discount, as is the case here, the premium would be considered a reduction in the cost of borrowing. It reduces bond interest expense over the life of the bonds. Amortizing a premium results in a decrease in interest expense and a decrease in the carrying amount of the bonds.

The bond amortization schedule would be constructed in the same manner for a bond issued at a premium. The only difference would be that periodic interest expense decreases over the life of the bond when bonds are issued at a premium. The reason is that a constant percentage is applied to a decreasing bond carrying amount to calculate interest expense. The carrying amount is decreasing because of the amortization of the premium.

- At maturity, the carrying amount of the bonds equals the face value, and the journal entry to redeem the bonds involves a debit to Bonds Payable and a credit to Cash.

- If bonds are redeemed before maturity, it is necessary to (i) update any unrecorded interest, (ii) eliminate the carrying amount of the bonds at the redemption date, (iii) record the cash paid, and (iv) recognize the gain or loss on redemption. If $500,000 of bonds with a carrying amount of $496,000 are redeemed at 101 by the company, the following entry is required:

Bonds Payable	496,000	
Loss on Redemption ($505,000 − $496,000)	9,000	
Cash ($500,000 × 101%)		505,000

(To record redemption of bonds)

study objective 4

Identify the requirements for the financial statement presentation and analysis of liabilities.

The loss or gain on bond redemption is reported in the statement of earnings, as Other Expenses or Revenues.

- **Current liabilities** are reported as the first category in the liabilities section of the balance sheet. Each of the principal types of current liabilities is listed separately within the category, and important data relating to them are disclosed in the notes to the financial statements. Similar to current assets, current liabilities are generally listed in their order of maturity.

- **Long-term liabilities** are reported separately immediately following current liabilities. Summary data regarding debts may be presented on the balance sheet, while detailed data (such as interest rates, maturity dates, conversion privileges, and assets pledged as collateral) should be shown in a supporting schedule in the notes.

- Information regarding cash inflows and outflows during the year that resulted from the principal portion of debt transactions is provided in the financing activities in the **cash flow statement**. Interest expense is reported in the operating activities section, even though it resulted from debt transactions.

- **Liquidity ratios** measure the short-term ability of a company to pay its maturing obligations and to meet unexpected needs for cash. A commonly used measure of liquidity is the **current ratio** (current assets divided by current liabilities). The current ratio can be misleading because some items, such as receivables and inventory may not be very liquid and are included in the numerator. Consequently, the current ratio should be supplemented by other ratios, such as the receivables turnover and inventory turnover.

- Many companies keep few liquid assets on hand because they cost too much to hold and, thus, must rely on other sources of liquidity. One such source is an **operating bank line of credit**, as discussed earlier in this chapter.

- **Solvency ratios** measure the ability of a company to repay its long-term debt and survive over a long period of time. One solvency ratio is **debt to total assets**, calculated by dividing total liabilities by total assets. This ratio indicates the extent to which a company's debt could be repaid by liquidating its assets. To supplement the information provided by the debt-to-total-assets ratio, the **times interest earned ratio** is used. It is calculated as follows: earnings before interest expense and income tax expense (EBIT) by interest expense. This ratio calculates how many times the company has earned its interest payments in an accounting period, thus providing an indication of a company's ability to meet interest payments as they come due.

- A concern for analysts when they evaluate a company's liquidity and solvency is whether that company has properly recorded all of its obligations. **Contingent liabilities and off-balance sheet financing** are two examples of unrecorded debt.

- **Contingent liabilities** are events with uncertain outcomes. A good example of a contingency is a lawsuit, and other contingencies are product warranties and environmental problems. If it is probable that the contingency will occur and the company can reasonably estimate the expected loss, then the **company should accrue the loss** by debiting a loss account and crediting a liability account. If both conditions are not met, then the **company discloses the loss in the notes to the financial statements**.

- **Off-balance sheet financing** refers to a situation where liabilities are not recorded on the balance sheet. One very common type of off–balance sheet financing results from leasing transactions, which were discussed in Chapter 9.

Chapter Self-Test

As you work through the questions and problems, remember to use the **Decision Toolkit** discussed and used in the text:

1. *Decision Checkpoints:* At this point, you ask a question.
2. *Info Needed for Decision:* You make a choice regarding the information needed to answer the question.
3. *Tool to Use for Decision:* At this point, you review just what the information chosen in step 2 does for the decision-making process.
4. *How to Evaluate Results:* You conduct an evaluation of information for answering the question.

Note: The notation (SO1) means that the question was drawn from study objective number one.

Multiple Choice

Please circle the correct answer.

(SO1)   1.   The journal entry to record the accrual of the employer's share of Canada Pension Plan (CPP) would include a
    a.   credit to CPP Payable.
    b.   debit to Wages Expense.
    c.   credit to Payroll Tax Expense.
    d.   debit to CPP Payable.

(SO1)   2.   A retailer who collects GST from its customers would
    a.   debit GST Payable.
    b.   debit GST Expense.
    c.   credit GST Payable.
    d.   credit GST Revenue.

(SO1)   3.   Which of the following is a criterion for the classification of a liability as current?
    a.   It is a debt that can be paid from existing current assets.
    b.   It is a debt that can be paid through the creation of other current liabilities.
    c.   It must be paid within 1 year.
    d.   All of the above are criteria for the classification of a liability as current.

(SO2)   4.   Monthly payments on an instalment note consist of
    a.   interest expense only.
    b.   principal repayment only.
    c.   interest expense and principal repayment.
    d.   neither interest expense nor principal repayment.

(SO2)   5.   The interest charged on an $80,000 note payable, at the rate of 5 percent on a 6-month note would be
    a. $4,000.
    b. $2,000.

    c. $3,000.

    d. $1,000.

6. A corporation issued a $50,000, 6-percent, 4-month note payable on July 1.   (SO2)
Interest is payable at maturity. If the corporation's year end is September 30,
then the adjusting entry for interest on that date is:

a.	Interest Expense	750	
	Notes Payable		750
b.	Interest Expense	750	
	Interest Payable		750
c.	Interest Expense	1,000	
	Notes Payable		1,000
d.	Interest Expense	1,000	
	Interest Payable		1,000

7. When the corporation in question (6) above pays the amount due on the   (SO2)
maturity date, the journal entry will include a
    a.   debit to Notes Payable for $51,000.
    b.   credit to Cash for $50,000.
    c.   debit to Interest Expense for $1,000.
    d.   debit to Interest Payable for $750.

8. On November 1, 2009, a company issued a note payable of $50,000, of which   (SO2)
$10,000 is repaid each year. What is the proper classification of this note on the
December 31, 2009, balance sheet?
    a. $10,000 current liability; $40,000 long-term liability
    b. $50,000 current liability
    c. $50,000 long-term liability
    d. $10,000 long-term liability; $40,000 current liability

9. Notes that are issued against the general credit of the borrower are called   (SO2)
    a.   unsecured notes.
    b.   secured notes.
    c.   mortgage notes.
    d.   convertible notes.

10. A corporation issues $1,000,000 of 4-percent, 5-year bonds. The 4-percent rate of   (SO3)
interest is called the _____ rate.
    a.   yield
    b.   effective
    c.   market
    d.   contractual

11. The fair value of a bond is equal to the   (SO3)
    a.   present value of the principal only.
    b.   present value of the principal and the interest payments.
    c.   present value of interest payments only.
    d.   face value of the principal only.

(SO3)   12.   When the contractual rate of interest exceeds the market rate of interest, the bond sells at
    a.   face value.
    b.   a discount.
    c.   a premium.
    d.   some amount other than those listed above.

(SO3)   13.   A premium on bonds is shown on a balance sheet
    a.   classified as a revenue account.
    b.   deducted from bonds payable, which is shown net of the premium.
    c.   classified as a shareholders' equity account.
    d.   added to bonds payable, which is shown net of the premium.

(SO3)   14.   When calculating the carrying amount of bonds payable
    a.   premium is subtracted from and discount is added to bonds payable.
    b.   discount is subtracted from and premium is added to bonds payable.
    c.   both discount and premium are subtracted from bonds payable.
    d.   both discount and premium are added to bonds payable.

(SO3)   15.   Bonds payable with a face value of $200,000 and a carrying amount of $196,000 are redeemed prior to maturity at 102. There is a
    a.   loss on redemption of $4,000.
    b.   gain on redemption of $4,000.
    c.   loss on redemption of $8,000.
    d.   gain on redemption of $8,000.

(SO4)   16.   A gain or loss on the early redemption of bonds payable is classified as a(n):
    a.   operating expense on the statement of earnings.
    b.   addition or subtraction to bonds payable on the balance sheet.
    c.   other expense or other revenue on the statement of earnings.
    d.   long-term liability on the balance sheet.

(SO4)   17.   A company's total debt is $250,000, while its total assets are $500,000. Earnings before interest expense and income tax is $300,000, and interest expense is $30,000. The company's times interest earned ratio is
    a.   10 times.
    b.   2 times.
    c.   50 percent.
    d.   10 percent.

(SO4)   18.   Rouse Corporation is being sued by a customer. At the balance sheet date, Rouse's lawyers feel that it is probable that the company will lose the lawsuit and that a reasonable estimate of the loss is $50,000. On the balance sheet date, Rouse should:
    a.   not disclose the lawsuit because a jury has not yet ruled.
    b.   disclose the lawsuit in the notes to the financial statements.
    c.   accrue the loss by debiting an expense and crediting a liability.
    d.   ask for a second opinion from an outside law firm.

19. Some companies finance assets without the liability showing on the balance sheet. This procedure is called (SO4)
   a. fraud.
   b. finance lease.
   c. off-balance sheet financing.
   d. capitalizing.

20. The ability of a company to survive over a long period of time is measured by (SO4)
   a. liquidity ratios.
   b. solvency ratios.
   c. profitability ratios.
   d. cash management ratios.

21. Which is a very common way to present current liabilities on the balance sheet? (SO4)
   a. Notes payable are always being listed first.
   b. Current maturities of long-term debt are always being listed first.
   c. By order of magnitude.
   d. By order of maturity date.

22. On January 1, a company issued $600,000 of 6-percent, 10-year bonds at 102, which reflects a 5-percent market rate of interest. Interest is payable on July 1 and January 1. On July 1 of the first year of the bond, the journal entry to record interest will include a (SO3)
   a. credit to Cash for $15,000.
   b. debit to Bonds Payable for $2,700.
   c. credit to Bonds Payable for $2,700.
   d. debit to Bond Interest Expense for $18,000.

23. What principle does the effective interest method satisfy? (SO3)
   a. Matching principle
   b. Revenue recognition principle
   c. Comparability principle
   d. Full disclosure principle

Problems

1. A company incurred the following transactions in the month of June: (SO1)

   June 1: The company borrowed $100,000 on a 1-year, 6-percent note on June 1. Interest is payable at maturity.

   June 20: The monthly payroll showed total wages of $10,000 and the following deductions from employees: CPP $800, EI $340, Income Tax $1,195, and Health Insurance Premiums $200. The employer's payroll costs were: CPP $800, and EI $476.

   June 30: Pre-tax sales for June totalled $125,000. The GST rate is 5 percent and the PST is 8 percent.

   June 30: The payroll deductions and health insurance premiums for June were remitted to the Receiver General and the health insurance organization, respectively.

   Record all the transactions required for June.

(SO1, 3)   2.   The Jansen Corporation incurred the following transactions:

a.   On May 1, the corporation issued a 6-month, 6-percent note in the amount of $20,000. Interest is payable at maturity. Record the adjusting entry for interest on June 30.

b.   On March 1, the corporation received its $10,020 property tax invoice for the calendar year due to be paid on May 31. Record the
   i.   entry on March 1 to record the receipt of the property tax bill.
   ii.   payment of the bill on May 31.
   iii. adjusting entry required on December 31, assuming the company makes adjusting entries only annually.

c.   On July 1, the corporation sold $400,000 of 6-percent, 10-year bonds at 101. The bonds pay interest every January 1 and July 1. Please record the entry for the issue of the bonds.

Date	Account Titles	Debit	Credit

(SO3)   3.   The Dove Corporation issues $100,000 of 10-year, 7-percent bonds for proceeds of $107,473, which reflects a 6-percent market rate of interest. The bonds pay interest semi-annually.

a.   Prepare the journal entry to record the issue of the bond.

b.   Prepare the journal entry to record the payment of interest and the amortization of any premium or discount for the first interest period.

Date	Account Titles	Debit	Credit

4.   The following selected general ledger account balances are provided for the   (SO4)
     Rebus Corporation as of December 31, 2009. This is the corporation's first year
     of operations.

Accounts payable	$15,000
Accounts receivable	70,000
Accumulated depreciation—building	10,000
Advertising expense	1,000
Allowance for doubtful accounts	20,000
Bad debt expense	2,000
Bonds payable	98,000
Building	350,000
Cash	140,000
Common shares	234,000
Depreciation expense	5,000
Dividends	10,000
Income tax expense	13,000
Interest expense	8,000
Interest payable	13,000
Land	100,000
Mortgage payable	175,000

Notes payable, 6 months	40,000
Payroll tax expense	1,000
PST payable	13,000
Retained earnings, January 1	15,000
Service revenue	75,000
Wages expense	10,000
Wages payable	2,000

a. Prepare a statement of earnings, a statement of retained earnings, and the balance sheet for Rebus Corporation for 2009, assuming $30,000 of the mortgage is payable next year.

b. Using appropriate ratios, comment on Rebus Corporation's liquidity and solvency.

5. Please refer to the Domtar and Cascades financial statements found in the appendices at the end of this study guide for information for answering the following questions. Do not forget to use the **Decision Toolkit** approach for help in the problem solving.

(SO2) a. What is Domtar's long-term debt in 2007, and how much did it increase or decrease from 2006?

(SO1) b. What percentage of total liabilities are current liabilities in 2007 for (i) Cascades and (ii) Domtar?

(SO4) c. Assess Domtar's and Cascades' solvency using the debt to total assets and times interest earned ratios for 2007 and 2006.

Solutions to Self-Test

Multiple Choice

1. a   The employer owes its share of CPP to the government, therefore a liability account, CPP Payable, is credited.

2. c   The employer owes GST collected from its customers to the federal government, therefore a liability account, GST Payable, is credited.

3. d   A current liability is a debt that will be paid within 1 year and from existing current assets or through the creation of other current liabilities.

4. c   Instalment payments consist of a mix of interest on the unpaid balance of the loan, and a reduction of the loan principal.

5. b $\$80,000 \times 5\% \times 6/12 = \$2,000$

6. b   Interest expense/payable: $\$50,000 \times 6\% \times 3/12 = \$750$

7. d The journal entry is:

Notes Payable	50,000	
Interest Payable	750	
Interest Expense	250	
Cash		51,000

8. a The $10,000 is a current maturity of long-term debt.

9. a Secured notes are secured by some sort of collateral and are also known as mortgage notes. Convertible notes are convertible into shares of stock at some future date.

10. d Yield, effective, and market rates are different terms for the same thing.

11. b Bonds involve two streams of cash flows: principal and interest.

12. c If the rates are the same, then the bond sells at face value. If the contractual rate is lower than the market rate, then the bond sells at a discount.

13. d Premium on bonds payable is added to bonds payable, with the net amount reported on the balance sheet.

14. b Premium is added to bonds payable; discount is subtracted from bonds payable.

15. c The company had to pay $204,000 for bonds with a carrying amount of $196,000. The difference between these two numbers is a loss on redemption.

16. c Losses and gains on bond redemption are reported in the statement of earnings as other expenses or revenues.

17. a The ratio is calculated by dividing earnings before interest expense and income tax by interest expense. In this case, $300,000 \div $30,000 = 10$ times.

18. c It is simply disclosed in the notes if both conditions (reasonable estimate and probable) are not met. Only if the possibility of loss is remote does the company do nothing.

19. c This procedure is allowed under certain circumstances, and finance leases are recorded as liabilities. Off-balance sheet financing should be considered by financial statement analysts.

20. b Solvency ratios measure the ability of a company to repay its long-term debt and survive over a long period of time.

21. d Similar to current assets, current liabilities are generally listed in their order of maturity.

22. b The journal entry is:

Bond Interest Expense ($612,000 \times 5\% \times 6/12$)	15,300	
Bonds Payable ($18,000 - $15,300$)	2,700	
Cash ($600,000 \times 6\% \times 6/12$)		18,000

23. a The effective interest method matches the carrying amount of the bonds, because interest changes proportionately as the carrying amount changes.

Problems

1.

Date	Account Titles	Debit	Credit
June 1	Cash	100,000	
	Notes Payable		100,000
	(To record issue of note)		
20	Wages Expense	10,000	
	CPP Payable		800
	EI Payable		340
	Income Tax Payable		1,195
	Health Insurance Payable		200
	Cash		7,465
	(To record payroll and employee deductions)		
20	Employee Benefits Expense	1,276	
	CPP Payable		800
	EI Payable		476
	(To record employee benefits)		
30	Cash ($125,000 + $6,250 + $10,000)	141,250	
	Sales		125,000
	GST Payable ($125,000 × 5%)		6,250
	PST Payable ($125,000 × 8%)		10,000
	(To record sales and sales taxes)		
30	CPP Payable ($800 + $800)	1,600	
	EI Payable ($340 + $476)	816	
	Income Tax Payable	1,195	
	Cash		3,611
	(To record remittance to Receiver General)		
30	Health Insurance Payable	200	
	Cash		200
	(To record remittance to health insurance organization)		
30	Interest Expense ($100,000 × 6% × 1/12)	500	
	Interest Payable		500
	(To accrue interest for the month of June on note payable)		

2. a.   June 30 Interest Expense   200

                          Interest Payable   200

                          (To record interest on note: $20,000 \times
                          6\% \times 2/12$)

    b. i.   Mar. 1 Property Tax Expense ($10,020 \times 2/12$)   1,670

                          Property Tax Payable   1,670

                          (To record property tax expense for
                          January and February)

        ii. May 31 Property Tax Payable   1,670
                      Property Tax Expense ($10,020 \times 3/12$)   2,505
                      Prepaid Property Tax ($10,020 \times 7/12$)   5,845

                          Cash   10,020

                          (To record payment of property tax
                          expense for March through May, and
                          amount prepaid for June through
                          December)

        iii. Dec. 31 Property Tax Expense   5,845

                          Prepaid Property Tax   5,845

                          (To record property tax expense for
                          June through December)

    c.   July 1 Cash   404,000

                          Bonds Payable   404,000

                          (To record sale of bonds at premium)

3. a.   Cash   107,473

                      Bonds Payable   107,473

                  (To record sale of bonds at premium)

    b.   Bond Interest Expense   3,224
            Bonds Payable   276

                      Cash   3,500

            Bond interest expense = $107,473 \times 6\% \times 6/12$

            Bonds payable = $3,500 - $3,224$

            Cash = $100,000 \times 7\% \times 6/12$

4.   a.

REBUS CORPORATION
Statement of Earnings
Year Ended December 31, 2009

Service revenue		$75,000
Operating expenses		
Wages expense	$10,000	
Payroll tax expenses	1,000	
Depreciation expense	5,000	
Advertising expense	1,000	
Bad debt expense	2,000	
Interest expense	8,000	
Total operating expenses		27,000
Earnings before income taxes		48,000
Income tax expense		13,000
Net earnings		$35,000

REBUS CORPORATION
Statement of Retained Earnings
Year Ended December 31, 2009

Retained earnings, January 1	$15,000
Add: net earnings	35,000
	50,000
Less: dividends	10,000
Retained earnings, December 31	$40,000

REBUS CORPORATION
Balance Sheet
December 31, 2009

Assets

Current assets		
Cash		$140,000
Accounts receivable	$70,000	
Less: allowance for doubtful accounts	20,000	50,000
Total current assets		190,000
Property, plant, and equipment		
Land		100,000
Building	$350,000	
Less: accumulated depreciation—building	10,000	340,000
Total property, plant, and equipment		440,000
Total assets		$630,000

Liabilities and Shareholders' Equity

Current liabilities

Accounts payable	$15,000	
Wages payable	2,000	
Interest payable	13,000	
PST payable	13,000	
Notes payable, 6 months	40,000	
Current portion of mortgage payable	30,000	
Total current liabilities		$113,000

Long-term liabilities

Bonds payable	$98,000	
Mortgage payable	145,000	
Total long-term liabilities		243,000
Total liabilities		356,000

Shareholders' equity

Common shares	$234,000	
Retained earnings	40,000	
Total shareholders' equity		274,000
Total liabilities and shareholders' equity		$630,000

b. The current ratio is $190,000 ÷ $113,000 = 1.7:1$, which means that there are 1.7 times current assets as there are current liabilities. At first glance, it would appear as though the company's liquidity is strong; however, we would want to prepare additional ratios, such as the receivables turnover ratio, before concluding on the company's liquidity.

The debt to total assets is $356,000 ÷ $630,000 = 56.5\%$, which means that 56.5 percent of total assets are financed by debt. The times interest earned ratio is used to supplement the debt to total assets ratio and is calculated as follows: ($35,000 + $13,000 + $8,000) ÷ $8,000 = 7$ times. (The formula is net earnings + income tax + interest divided by interest). Thus, the current earnings are currently more than sufficient to cover interest expense. Therefore, the solvency position looks favourable.

5. (Domtar $ in USD millions; Cascades $ in CAD millions)

a. Domtar's long-term debt is $2,213 in 2007 and $32 in 2006, for an increase of $2,181.

b. Current liabilities divided by total liabilities is as follows:
   (i) Cascades: $623 ÷ $2,570 = 24.2\%$
   (ii) Domtar: $895 ÷ ($895 + $2,213 + $1,003 + $440) = 19.7\%$

c. **Domtar:**
   Debt to total assets:
   2006: ($268 + $32 + $758 + $25) ÷ $3,998 = 27.1\%$
   2007: ($895 + $2,213 + $1,003 + $440) ÷ $7,748 = 58.7\%$

Times interest earned:
2006: There was no interest expense in 2006
2007: ($70 + $29 + $171) ÷ $171 = 1.6 times

Cascades:
Debt to total assets:
2006: $2,754 ÷ $3,911 = 70.4%
2007: $2,570 ÷ $3,769 = 68.2%

Times interest earned:
2006: ($3 + $6 + $79) ÷ $79 = 1.1 times
2007: ($95 + $11 + $102) ÷ $102 = 2.0 times

Domtar's restructuring, explained in the notes to its financial statements found in the Study Tools section of the textbook website, significantly increased its debt to total assets ratio from 27.1 percent in 2006 to 58.7 percent in 2007. Cascades' debt to total assets ratio, on the other hand, improved (decreased) slightly from 70.4 percent in 2006 to 68.2 percent in 2007.

For 2007 Cascades, times interest earned ratio of 2.0 was significantly better than Domtar's 1.6. This means Cascades is better able to handle its interest payments than is Domtar.

Note that discontinued operations has had an effect on Cascades' times interest earned ratio. We will learn more about the impact of discontinued operations in Chapter 14.

chapter 11

Reporting and Analyzing Shareholders' Equity

Chapter Overview

In this chapter, you will learn about the essential features of a corporation and how to account for common shares, preferred shares, and dividends. You will also learn about how to present the shareholders' equity section of the balance sheet. Finally, you will learn how to measure corporate performance using various ratios.

Review of Specific Study Objectives

- A **corporation** is a legal entity with most of the rights and privileges of a person.

- **Corporations** may be classified in a variety of ways. Two common classifications are by purpose, such as for-profit or not-for-profit (charitable or medical organizations), and by ownership (publicly held, which may have thousands of shareholders, and privately held, which have few shareholders and generally do not offer shares for sale to the public).

The following are **characteristics of a corporation**:

1. **Separate legal existence**, which means that a corporation acts under its own name and has most of the same rights as does a person. It may buy, own, or sell property, borrow money, enter into binding contracts, and sue or be sued, and it pays its own taxes.

study objective 1

Identify and discuss the major characteristics of a corporation.

2. **Limited liability of shareholders**, which means that the liability of shareholders is limited to the amount of their investment.
3. **Transferable ownership rights**, which means that a shareholder may buy or sell shares without approval of the corporation or other shareholders.
4. **Ability to acquire capital**, resulting from the issue of its shares.
5. **Continuous life**, which means that the life of the corporation is not affected by the withdrawal, death, or incapacity of a shareholder, employee, or officer.
6. **Corporation management**, meaning that shareholders manage the company indirectly through the board of directors.
7. **Government regulation**, both by federal and provincial governments, which can be burdensome from both time and money standpoints.
8. **Income taxes** are paid by corporations because they are separate legal entities. Some argue that corporate earnings are taxed twice (double taxation)—at the corporate level and again at the individual level when dividends are received. This is not quite true, as individuals receive a dividend tax credit to reduce some of the tax burden.

- A **corporation may sell ownership rights** in the form of shares. The shares of a company are divided into different classes, such as Class A, Class B, and so on. The different classes are usually identified by the generic terms **common shares** and **preferred shares.** If it has only one class of shares, then that class is identified as common shares. Each common shareholder has the following rights:

  1. The **right to vote** in the election of directors and to vote on matters requiring shareholder approval.
  2. The **right to share in corporate earnings** through receipt of dividends.
  3. The **right to share in distribution of assets upon liquidation of the corporation** in proportion to the shareholders' holdings.

- **Authorized share capital** is the amount of share capital that a corporation is authorized to sell as indicated in its articles of incorporation. It may be specified as an unlimited amount or a certain number. If a number is specified, the amount of authorized shares normally anticipates a company's initial and later capital needs. Issued shares are authorized shares that have been sold. No formal journal entry is required for authorized shares, but the number of shares authorized and issued must be disclosed in the shareholders' equity section of the balance sheet.

- A **corporation may sell its share capital** either directly to investors or indirectly through an investment banking firm. The first time a corporation's shares are offered to the public, the offer is called an initial public offering (IPO). The company receives the cash (less any issue fees) from the sale of the IPO shares whether done by a direct or indirect issue.

  Once these shares have been initially issued, they continue trading on the secondary market. That is, investors buy and sell shares to each other, rather than from the company. When shares are sold among investors, there is no impact on the company's financial position.

  Shares are traded on stock exchanges, such as the Toronto Stock Exchange (TSX).

- **Fair value of shares** is established by the interaction between buyers and sellers. In general, the price follows the trend of a company's earnings and dividends. Factors beyond a company's control (such as wars, trade embargoes, elections, recessions, and changes in interest rates) can also influence market prices.

One commonly reported measure of the fair value of a company's total equity is its market capitalization. The **market capitalization** of a company is calculated by multiplying the number of shares issued by the share price at any given date.

- Share capital is **legal capital** that cannot be distributed to shareholders. It must remain invested in the company for the protection of corporate creditors. Some countries, notably the United States, assign a par or stated value to shares to predetermine the amount of legal capital. The use of par or stated values for shares is either not required or prohibited in Canada.

study objective 2

Record share transactions.

- **No par value shares** are shares that have not been assigned a pre-set legal capital. When no par value shares are issued, all of the proceeds received are considered to be legal capital.

- **Contributed capital** is the amount shareholders paid or contributed to the corporation in exchange for share ownership. This includes **share capital**, in addition to other sources of capital affected by share transactions.

The following describes the issue of **no par value common shares.** As mentioned earlier, the entire proceeds is considered to be legal capital of the no par value shares. If 100 common shares are sold for $5 per share, then the journal entry is:

Cash	500	
Common Shares		500
(To record sale of 100 common shares for $5 per share)		

If another 100 common shares are sold for $7 per share, then the journal entry is:

Cash	700	
Common Shares		700
(To record sale of 100 common shares for $7 per share)		

Note that in each case the Common Shares account is credited with the entire proceeds of the sale.

- When shares are issued for a noncash consideration, they should be recorded at their **cash equivalent price**. The cash equivalent price is the fair value of the consideration (common shares) given up. If the fair value of the consideration cannot be determined (e.g., there is no active market for the shares), then the fair value of the consideration received must be used.

- **Reacquisition of shares** involves companies that purchase their own shares on the open market. A corporation may acquire its own shares to:

1. increase trading of the company's shares in the securities market in the hope of enhancing the company's value.
2. reduce the number of shares issued and thereby increase earnings per share and return on equity.
3. eliminate hostile shareholders by buying them out.

4. have additional shares available to issue to officers and employees under bonus and stock compensation plans, or for use in acquiring other companies.

When a company reacquires its own shares, the repurchased shares must be retired and cancelled, which effectively restores the shares to the status of authorized but unissued shares.

The difference between the price paid to reacquire the shares and their original cost is, in essence, a "gain" or "loss" on reacquisition. However, companies cannot realize a gain or suffer a loss from share transactions with their own shareholders, so these amounts are not reported on the statement of earnings. They are seen instead as an excess or deficiency that belongs to the original shareholders and are reported as an increase or decrease in contributed capital.

Assume that a company has 100,000 shares issued and $400,000 in its common share account and $20,000 in contributed capital. The company decides to reacquire 60,000 of its common shares on the open market. The following journal entry would be made if the company purchases its shares at $3.50 each.

Common Shares ($400,000 ÷ 100,000 = $4 × 60,000)	240,000	
Contributed Capital—Reacquisition of Common Shares		30,000
Cash (60,000 × $3.50)		210,000

The average cost of each common share is $4 ($400,000 ÷ 100,000), so the Common Shares account must be decreased for the cost of each share. The Contributed Capital account is increased by the difference between the cash paid ($3.50 per share) and the average cost of each share ($4 per share).

If the company repurchased its shares at $4.50 each instead of $3.50, the journal entry would be:

Common Shares ($400,000 ÷ 100,000 = $4 × 60,000)	240,000	
Contributed Capital—Reacquisition of Shares	20,000	
Retained Earnings ($40,000 – $20,000)	10,000	
Cash (60,000 × $4.50)		270,000

If a company reacquires its shares at a price that is greater than its average cost of the common shares, as shown above, the difference between the purchase price and average cost is first debited to contributed capital, if any exists (the account has a balance of $20,000 in this particular case), and then to retained earnings.

- **Preferred shares** have contractual provisions that may give them *preference or priority over common shares in certain areas,* usually in relation to dividends and to assets in the event of liquidation. Preferred shareholders usually have no voting rights. If a corporation issues 500 preferred shares for $30 per share, the journal entry is:

Cash	15,000	
Preferred Shares		15,000
(To record sale of 500 shares at $30 per share)		

- **Preferred shares** are *listed before common shares on the balance sheet* because of their preferences in the areas of dividends and liquidation.

- **Preferred shares have priority over common shares in the matter of dividends.**
  This does not guarantee that preferred shareholders will always receive the dividend.
  The dividend amount is stated as an annual amount per share; for example, $5
  preferred shares means that each preferred shareholder is eligible to receive $5 a year
  in dividends. Normally, dividends are paid quarterly, so shareholders would receive
  $1.25 ($5 ÷ 4) each quarter.

  Preferred shares may contain **a cumulative** dividend feature. This right means that
  preferred shareholders must be paid both current-year dividends and any unpaid
  prior-year dividends before common shareholders receive dividends. Preferred
  dividends not declared in a given period are called *dividends in arrears* and *should be
  disclosed in the notes* to the financial statements.

  Dividends in arrears are *not a liability*. No obligation exists until the board of directors declares the dividend. If preferred shares are **non-cumulative**, then *any dividend
  not declared and paid is forever lost.* Since this is very unattractive to investors, most
  companies do not issue non-cumulative preferred shares.

- **Preferred shareholders** also have a *preference in the event of liquidation of the
  corporation.* Creditors must be paid first, then preferred shareholders, then common
  shareholders. The preference may be for the legal capital value of the shares or for a
  specified liquidating value.

- **Convertible preferred shares** allow the shareholder to exchange preferred shares
  into common shares at a specified ratio.

- **Redeemable (callable) preferred shares** offer an option for the corporation to
  repurchase its shares from the shareholder in the future. **Retractable preferred
  shares** offer the option to the shareholder to resell its shares to the corporation
  in the future.

- A **dividend** is a pro rata (equal) distribution of a portion of a corporation's retained
  earnings to its shareholders.

- To pay a **cash dividend**, a corporation must have retained earnings, adequate cash,
  and dividends declared by the board of directors. While many companies pay a
  quarterly dividend, there are companies, called growth companies, that pay no
  dividends but reinvest earnings in the company so that it can grow.

> **study objective 3**
>
> Prepare the entries
> for cash dividends,
> stock dividends,
> and stock splits, and
> understand their
> financial impact.

- There are **three dates of importance for all dividends:** date of declaration, date of
  record, and date of payment. Journal entries are required on the first and third dates.
  For a **cash dividend**, the journal entry on the date of declaration will be as follows if
  a corporation declares a $0.25 per share cash dividend on 100,000 shares:

Cash Dividends	25,000	
Dividends Payable		25,000
(To declare a cash dividend of $0.25 per share on 100,000 shares)		

Dividends Payable is a current liability. It will normally be paid within the next
month.

On the **date of record**, ownership of the shares is determined for dividend purposes.
No journal entry is required.

On the **date of payment**, the following entry is required:

Dividends Payable	25,000	
Cash		25,000

(To record payment of a cash dividend)

Declaration and payment of a cash dividend reduce both shareholders' equity and total assets.

- A **stock dividend** is a distribution of the corporation's own shares to shareholders. A stock dividend results in a decrease in retained earnings and an increase in share capital. Total shareholders' equity will remain the same because dollar amounts are simply transferred from retained earnings to share capital accounts. A stock dividend is interesting because an investor really receives nothing extra on the day he receives the shares. His ownership percentage has not changed. In the future, however, if the share price rises, he will have more shares on which there may be price appreciation.

- **Corporations issue stock dividends to:**

1. satisfy shareholders' dividend expectations while conserving cash.
2. increase the marketability of the shares by reducing the price per share. A reduced market price makes it easier for more investors to buy the shares.
3. emphasize that a portion of equity has been permanently reinvested in the business and is unavailable for cash dividends.

Consider the **following example of a stock dividend**. A corporation has 500,000 common shares issued on the day on which the board of directors declares a 10 percent stock dividend. The fair value of the shares is $30 per share. Fifty thousand new shares (500,000 × 10%) will be issued. The journal entry on the **date of declaration is:**

Stock Dividends	1,500,000	
Common Stock Dividends Distributable		1,500,000

The calculation is as follows: 50,000 shares × $30 = $1,500,000

Common Stock Dividends Distributable is a shareholders' equity account. If a balance sheet is prepared after the dividend declaration, then the account will appear directly under the Common Shares account in the share capital section.

On the **date of payment**, the journal entry is:

Common Stock Dividends Distributable	1,500,000	
Common Shares		1,500,000

(To record distribution of stock dividend)

- Like a stock dividend, a **stock split** involves the issue of additional shares to shareholders according to their percentage ownership. Unlike a stock dividend, a stock split is usually much larger than a stock dividend. The **purpose of a stock split** is to increase the marketability of the shares by lowering the price per share. A corporation has 200,000 common shares issued; the price of the shares is $100 per share. The corporation declares a 2-for-1 stock split. The number of shares will double to 400,000 and the price will be reduced by half, to $50 per share. Note that the Common Shares account has $1 million in it both before and after the split. A stock split has no effect on total share capital, retained earnings, and total shareholders' equity, and no journal entry is required to record it.

- The **balance in retained earnings** is generally available for dividend declarations. There may be **retained earnings restrictions** that make a portion of the balance currently unavailable for dividends. Restrictions result from legal, contractual, or voluntary causes and are usually disclosed in the notes to the financial statements.

- Shareholders' equity transactions are reported in the balance sheet, statement of shareholders' equity, and cash flow statement. Contributed capital, retained earnings, and other comprehensive income are reported in the shareholders' section of the balance sheet. **Contributed capital** includes share capital and additional contributed capital. **Share capital** consists of preferred and common shares, and preferred shares are shown before common shares because of the former's preferential rights. Stock dividends distributable that exist at year end are also reported under share capital. **Additional contributed capital** includes amounts contributed from reacquiring and retiring shares. If a company has a variety of additional sources of contributed capital, it is important to distinguish each one by source.

study objective 4

Indicate how shareholders' equity is presented in the financial statements.

- **Retained earnings** are the cumulative net earnings (or loss) since incorporation that has been retained in the company (i.e., not distributed to shareholders). Just as net earnings is credited to the Retained Earnings account, net loss is debited to the account, even if an overall debit balance in the account results. A debit balance in Retained Earnings is called a deficit and is reported as a deduction in the shareholders' equity section of the balance sheet.

- **Comprehensive income** includes all changes in shareholders' equity during a period except for changes that result from the sale or repurchase of shares or from the payment of dividends. It includes:

1. the revenues, expenses, gains, and losses included in net earnings, and
2. the gains and losses that bypass net earnings but affect shareholders' equity. This category is referred to as "other comprehensive income." Some examples will be discussed in the next chapter.

Reporting other comprehensive income in a statement of comprehensive income, separately from net earnings and retained earnings, is done for two important reasons: (1) it protects earnings from sudden changes that would simply be caused by fluctuations in fair value, and (2) it informs the financial statement user of the gain or loss that would have occurred if the securities had actually been sold at year end.

- **Accumulated other comprehensive income** is the *cumulative* change in shareholders' equity that results from the gains and losses that bypass net earnings but affect shareholders' equity. Similar to retained earnings, which is the cumulative total of earnings retained in the business, accumulated other comprehensive income is the cumulative total of all past credits and charges to other comprehensive income. In other words, it starts with the balance at the beginning of the period and is increased by other comprehensive income and decreased by other comprehensive losses during the period, to arrive at the ending balance. It is this ending balance that is reported in the shareholders' equity section of the balance sheet.

In Canada, until recently, the financial statements included a statement of retained earnings, with detail about changes in other equity accounts disclosed in the notes to the statements. An alternate, and preferred, approach is to disclose changes affecting each shareholders' equity account in a **statement of shareholders' equity.** This statement discloses changes in total shareholders' equity for the period, as well as changes in each shareholders' equity accounts, including contributed capital, retained earnings, and accumulated other comprehensive income. When a statement of shareholders' equity is prepared, it explains any changes in retained earnings, which makes a statement of retained earnings unnecessary. In this, and subsequent chapters, we will now include the statement of shareholders' equity in our list of required financial statements. Our financial statement package now includes the statement of earnings, statement of comprehensive income (illustrated in Chapter 12), statement of shareholders' equity, balance sheet, and cash flow statement. All of these statements, except the balance sheet, cover the fiscal year. The balance sheet reports the company's financial position at the end of the fiscal year.

study objective 5

Evaluate dividend and earnings performance.

- To **measure a corporation's dividend record**, an investor can calculate the payout ratio.

  The **payout ratio** measures the percentage of earnings distributed in the form of cash dividends to common shareholders. It is calculated by dividing total cash dividends to common shareholders by net earnings. A company with a high growth rate typically has a low payout ratio because it reinvests earnings in the business.

- Another dividend measure is the **dividend yield.** It is calculated by dividing the dividend per share by the share price. It measures the earnings generated by each share for the shareholder, based on the market price of the share.

- As mentioned in Chapter 2, **earnings per share** is calculated by dividing net earnings available to the common shareholders by the weighted average number of common shares issued during the year. The numerator, net earnings available to the common shareholders, is calculated by subtracting any preferred dividends from net earnings. The denominator, the weighted average number of shares, is calculated by weighing the shares issued or purchased during each current period by the fraction of the year (or period) that they have been issued. If there is no change in the number of common shares issued during the year, the weighted average number of shares will be the same as the ending balance. If new shares are issued throughout the year, then these shares are adjusted for the fraction of the year they are outstanding to determine the weighted average number of shares.

  The earnings performance of a company is measured in several different ways. It is measured by the earnings per share ratio, discussed in an earlier chapter, and by the **return on common shareholders' equity.** The ratio shows how many dollars were earned for each dollar invested by common shareholders. It is calculated by dividing net earnings available to common shareholders (net earnings minus preferred share dividends) by average common shareholders' equity. The common shareholders' equity is total shareholders' equity, less the legal capital of any preferred shares.

Chapter Self-Test

As you work through the questions and problems, remember to use the **Decision Toolkit** discussed and used in the text:

1. *Decision Checkpoints*: At this point, you ask a question.
2. *Info Needed for Decision:* You make a choice regarding the information needed to answer the question.
3. *Tool to Use for Decision*: At this point, you review just what the information chosen in step 2 does for the decision-making process.
4. *How to Evaluate Results*: You conduct an evaluation of information for answering the question.

Note: The notation (SO1) means that the question was drawn from study objective number one.

Multiple Choice

Please circle the correct answer.

1. Which of the following is considered to be a disadvantage of the corporate form of business organization?   (SO1)
   a.   Limited liability of shareholders
   b.   Separate legal existence
   c.   Continuous life
   d.   Provincial and federal government regulation

2. Share capital that has not been assigned a legal value per share in the corporate charter is called: (SO1)
   a.   legal capital shares.
   b.   par value shares.
   c.   no par value shares.
   d.   stated value shares.

3. The amount per share that must be retained in the business for the protection of corporate creditors is called: (SO1)
   a.   legal capital.
   b.   par value.
   c.   market value.
   d.   stated value.

4. If 3,000 common shares are sold for $6 per share, then the journal entry includes a: (SO2)
   a.   credit to Investments for $18,000.
   b.   credit to Cash for $18,000.
   c.   credit to Retained Earnings for $18,000.
   d.   credit to Common Shares for $18,000.

5. If the following accounts have these balances: (SO4)
        Contributed Capital: $23,000
        Retained Earnings: $30,000
        Accumulated Other Comprehensive Income: $10,000

then Total Shareholders' Equity is:

a. $63,000.

b. $53,000.

c. $40,000.

d. $33,000.

(SO2)   6. Assume that a corporation has a total 20,000 common shares for which it received $100,000 and that it reacquires 2,000 of its common shares at a price of $4 per share. The journal entry to record the reacquisition of the 2,000 shares will include:

a.   debit Contributed Capital—Reacquisition of Common Shares $2,000.

b.   credit Contributed Capital—Reacquisition of Common Shares $2,000.

c.   credit Common Shares $10,000.

d.   debit Common Shares $8,000.

(SO2)   7. Which of the following statements is incorrect?

a.   Dividends cannot be paid to common shareholders while any dividend on preferred shares is in arrears.

b.   Dividends in arrears on preferred shares are not considered a liability.

c.   Dividends may be paid on common shares while dividends are in arrears on preferred shares.

d.   When preferred shares are non-cumulative, any dividend not declared in a year is lost forever.

(SO3)   8. On December 1, a corporation has declared a $1 cash dividend per share on its 500,000 common shares. The journal entry on the date of payment of the dividend, December 20, includes a debit to:

a.   Dividends Payable for $500,000.

b.   Cash Dividends for $500,000.

c.   Cash for $500,000.

d.   Common Stock Dividends Distributable for $500,000.

(SO3)   9. A corporation is authorized to sell 1,000,000 common shares and has 500,000 shares issued. The board of directors declares a 10 percent stock dividend. How many new shares will ultimately be issued as a result of the stock dividend?

a.   100,000.

b.   50,000.

c.   None. The corporation will pay the dividend in cash.

d.   None of the above is correct.

(SO3)   10. The board of directors of a corporation declares a 5 percent stock dividend while there are 20,000 common shares issued. On the declaration date, the fair value of each share is $40. The journal entry to declare the stock dividend includes a:

a.   debit to Retained Earnings for $1,000.

b.   debit to Cash for $40,000.

c.   credit to Common Stock Dividends Distributable for $40,000.

d.   credit to Common Shares for $40,000.

11. A corporation has 100,000 common shares issued with a fair value of $80 per share. If the board of directors declares a 2-for-1 stock split, then: (SO3)
    a.   the number of shares doubles and the fair value decreases to $40.
    b.   the number of shares and fair value remain the same.
    c.   the number of shares halves and the fair value doubles.
    d.   the number of shares and fair value both halve.

12. A retained earnings restriction: (SO3)
    a.   makes a portion of the balance of retained earnings unavailable for dividends.
    b.   may arise from legal, contractual, or voluntary causes.
    c.   generally is disclosed in the notes to the financial statements.
    d.   All of the above are correct.

13. Indicate the respective effects of the declaration of a cash dividend on the following balance sheet sections: (SO3)

	Total Assets	Total Liabilities	Total Shareholders' Equity
a.	Increase	Decrease	No change
b.	No change	Increase	Decrease
c.	Decrease	Increase	Decrease
d.	Decrease	No change	Increase

14. Accumulated other comprehensive income is shown in the: (SO4)
    a.   statement of earnings.
    b.   statement of comprehensive income.
    c.   shareholders' equity section of the balance sheet.
    d.   cash flow statement.

15. A corporation shows the following account balances: (SO4)

Retained Earnings	($10,000)
Common Stock Dividends Distributable	$20,000
Common Shares	$255,000
Accumulated Other Comprehensive Income	$50,000
Dividends Payable	$25,000

    What is the total shareholders' equity?
    a. $335,000
    b. $360,000
    c. $340,000
    d. $315,000

16. In the shareholders' equity section of the balance sheet: (SO4)
    a.   Dividends in arrears will appear as a restriction of Retained Earnings.
    b.   Preferred and common shares appear under the subsection Share Capital.
    c.   Common Stock Dividends Distributable will appear in its own subsection of shareholders' equity.
    d.   Common Stock Dividends Distributable will be classified as a contra account to Retained Earnings.

(SO4)   17.   The following is the complete list of categories that can appear in the shareholders' equity section of the balance sheet:
a.   retained earnings and common stock dividends distributable.
b.   share capital and retained earnings.
c.   preferred shares and common shares.
d.   contributed capital, retained earnings, and accumulated other comprehensive income.

Use the following information for questions 18–20.

Consider the following data for a corporation:

Gross earnings	$900,000
Net earnings	$800,000
Weighted average number of common shares	400,000
Common dividends per share	$0.75
Preferred dividends	$50,000
Price per preferred share	$25
Price per common share	$20
Preferred shares issued	110,000
Average common shareholders' equity	$3,000,000

(SO5)   18.   What is the return on common shareholders' equity?
a.   25%
b.   26.67%
c.   30%
d.   29.1%

(SO5)   19.   What is the dividend payout ratio for common shareholders?
a.   37.5%
b.   33.3%
c.   40%
d.   35%

(SO5)   20.   What is the dividend yield for common shareholders?
a.   3%
b.   3.75%
c.   3.25%
d.   4%

(SO5)   21.   During its past fiscal year, a corporation had net earnings of $175,000 and paid
preferred share dividends of $50,000 and common share dividends of $25,000.
It had 80,000 common shares issued at the beginning of the year and issued an
additional 40,000 shares half way through the year. What was the company's
earnings per share?
a. $0.83
b. $1.00
c. $1.04
d. $1.25

Problems

1. Windsor Corporation shows the following data:

Common shares, 500,000 no par value shares authorized, 300,000 shares issued	$1,700,000
Retained earnings	3,200,000

Record the following transactions:

a. Sold 10,000 common shares for $9 per share. (SO2)
b. Declared and distributed a 15 percent stock dividend. The fair value of the shares on this date was $12 per share. (SO3)
c. Sold 8,000 common shares for $15 per share. (SO2)
d. Declared a 2-for-1 stock split. On this date, the fair value of the shares was $18 per share. (SO3)
e. Declared and paid a $0.10 per share cash dividend. (SO3)

Date	Account Titles	Debit	Credit
	Cash	90 000	
	Common Shares		90 000
	Stock Dividends	558 000	
	Stock Dividends Distributable		558 000
	Stock Divids distributable	558 000	
	Common shares		558 000
	Cash	120 000	
	CCS		120 000
	Cash dividends		
	dividends payable		
	Dividends payable		
	Cash		

2. At June 30, 2009, the Atlantis Corporation had the following selected account balances:

Common shares, no par value, 100,000 shares issued	$500,000
Contributed capital—Reacquisition of common shares	20,000

Prepare the journal entry to record each of the two following independent situations:

a. On July 1, 2009, Atlantis reacquires 70,000 of its shares at $4 each.
b. On July 1, 2009, Atlantis reacquires 70,000 of its shares at $5.50 each.

Date	Account Titles	Debit	Credit
	Common Share	350 000	
	Contributed Cap-Reacquired Shares		70 000
	Cash		28 000
	Common Share	35 000	
	Contributed Cap		385 000 3174
	Cash		0

3. Axwell Corporation had the following shareholders' equity balances at December 31, 2009:

Common shares, no par value, 900,000 shares authorized;
   700,000 shares issued $6,610,000
Retained earnings   850,000
Accumulated other comprehensive income   188,000

The following selected information is available for the year ended December 31, 2009:

Issued 20,000 common shares for $200,000.

Reported net earnings of $360,000.

Declared dividends of $0.10 per share to shareholders of record on December 31, 2009.

Reported an unrealized gain (other comprehensive income) of $45,000.

The price per common share on December 31, 2009 was $10.

(SO4)   a. Prepare the statement of shareholders' equity at December 31, 2009.
(SO3, 5)   b. Calculate the dividend payout and dividend yield ratios and return on common shareholders' equity for 2009.

(SO5)   4. A company has the following shareholders' equity accounts on January 1, 2009:

$2 non-cumulative preferred shares (20,000 shares issued)	$1,050,000
Common shares (100,000 shares issued)	4,000,000
Retained earnings	3,750,000
Total shareholders' equity	$8,800,000

The following transactions occurred during 2009:

Mar. 1   Reacquired 4,800 common shares for $38 per share.

Jul. 1   Issued 12,000 common shares in exchange for land with a fair value of $525,000.

Sep. 20   Declared a preferred dividend to shareholders of record on October 17 payable on October 31.

Nov. 1   Issued 12,000 common shares for $45 per share.

Dec. 31   Net earnings for the year ended December 31, 2009 were $549,600.

Calculate earnings per share for year 2009.

5.   Please refer to the Domtar and Cascades financial statements found in the appendices at the end of this study guide for information for answering the following questions. Do not forget to use the **Decision Toolkit** approach for help in the problem solving.

a.   On which financial statement(s) is there information about shares?   (SO4)
b.   What is the dividend payout ratio for both Domtar and Cascades for 2007 and 2006?   (SO5)
c.   What is the return on common shareholders' equity for both Domtar and Cascades for 2007?   (SO5)

Solutions to Self-Test

Multiple Choice

1. d   The other three are considered to be advantages.

2. c   There is no such thing as legal capital shares. Par value shares have a specified (legal) value. Stated value shares are no par value shares assigned a stated value by the board of directors.

3. a   Par value is an arbitrary amount listed in the corporate charter, and fair value is the selling price of a share on a given day. Stated value is a value assigned to no par value shares by the board of directors. The legal capital is whatever is specified in the corporate charter or by the board of directors— par value, no par value, or stated value.

4. d   The journal entry is:
Cash   18,000
    Common Shares   18,000

5. a $23,000 + $30,000 + $10,000 = $63,000

6. b   The average cost per share is: $100,000 ÷ 20,000 = $5

The journal entry is:
Common Shares (2,000 × $5)   10,000
    Contributed Capital—Reacquisition of Common Shares   2,000
    Cash (2,000 × $4)   8,000

7. c　Dividends may not be paid on common shares as long as preferred dividends are in arrears.

8. a　The journal entry is:

Dividends Payable	500,000	
Cash		500,000

9. b　500,000 shares × 10% = 50,000 new shares

10. c　The journal entry is:

Retained Earnings	40,000	
Common Stock Dividends Distributable		40,000

20,000 × 5% = 1,000 new shares; 1,000 × $40 fair value = $40,000

11. a　With a 2-for-1 stock split, each shareholder receives one additional share for each one they currently own. The number of shares double (200,000), and fair value is reduced by half ($40).

12. d　Retained earnings restrictions result from contractual restrictions known as debt covenants and from voluntary restrictions authorized by the board of directors. No journal entry is necessary to record a retained earnings restriction, but they are disclosed in the notes to the financial statements.

13. b　The accounting entry for the declaration of a cash dividend is:

Cash Dividends
　　Dividends Payable

Cash dividends is a retained earnings account that reduces shareholders' equity, and dividends payable is a liability account that is increased by this transaction.

14. c　**Accumulated other comprehensive income** is the cumulative change in shareholders' equity that results from the gains and losses that bypass net earnings but affect shareholders' equity. Other comprehensive income, reported on the statement of comprehensive income, is added to the beginning balance of accumulated other comprehensive income to determine the ending balance of accumulated other comprehensive income, which is reported in the shareholders' equity section of the balance sheet.

15. d　−$10,000 + $20,000 + $255,000 + $50,000 = $315,000

Dividends Payable would appear under Current Liabilities.

16. b　The category, share capital, consists of preferred and common shares.

17. d　The following are reported in the shareholders' equity section of the balance sheet: (1) contributed capital, (2) retained earnings, and (3) accumulated other comprehensive income.

18. a　($800,000 - $50,000) ÷ $3,000,000 = 25%

19. a　400,000 × $0.75 = $300,000 ÷ $800,000 = 37.5%

20. b　$0.75 ÷ $20 = 3.75%

21. d　($175,000 - $50,000) ÷ [80,000 + (40,000 × 6/12)] = $1.25

Problems

1. a.   Cash   90,000

            Common Shares   90,000

        (To record issue of shares—10,000
         shares at $9 per share)

    b.   Stock Dividends   558,000

            Common Stock Dividends Distributable   558,000

        (To record declaration of stock dividend)

         Common Stock Dividends Distributable   558,000

            Common Shares   558,000

        (To distribute stock dividend)

        310,000 shares × 15% = 46,500 new shares × $12 fair
        value per share = $558,000

    c.   Cash   120,000

            Common Shares   120,000

        (To record issue of shares—8,000 shares at $15 per share)

    d.   No entry required. The number of shares issued at this point, 364,500
         (300,000 + 10,000 + 46,500 + 8,000), doubles to 729,000. The fair value will be
         cut in half, $9.

    e.   Cash Dividends   72,900

            Dividends Payable   72,900

        (To declare a $0.10 per share cash dividend)

         Dividends Payable   72,900

            Cash   72,900

        (To pay the cash dividend)

        729,000 shares × $0.10 per share = $72,900

2. a.   Common Shares ($500,000 ÷ 100,000 × 70,000)   350,000

            Contributed Capital— Reacquisition of
            Common Shares   70,000

            Cash (70,000 × $4)   280,000

    b.   Common Shares ($500,000 ÷ 100,000 × 70,000)   350,000

         Contributed Capital—Reacquisition of Shares   20,000

         Retained Earnings   15,000

            Cash (70,000 × $5.50)   385,000

3.   a.

	Common Shares				
	Number of Shares	Legal Capital	Retained Earnings	Accumu-lated Other Compre-hensive Income	Total
AXWELL CORPORATION Statement of Shareholders' Equity Year Ended December 31, 2009					
Bal., Jan. 1, 2009	700,000	$6,610,000	$ 850,000	$188,000	$7,648,000
Issued common shares	20,000	200,000			200,000
Declared dividends			(72,000)		(72,000)
Comprehensive income					
Net earnings			360,000		360,000
Unrealized gain				45,000	45,000
Bal., Dec. 31, 2009	720,000	$6,810,000	$1,138,000	$233,000	$8,181,000

   b.

   Dividend payout = Cash dividends to common shareholders divided by net earnings = $72,000 ÷ $360,000 = 20%

   Dividend yield = Cash dividends to common shareholders divided by price per share = $0.10 ÷ $10.00 = 1%

   Return on common shareholders' equity = (Net earnings − Preferred dividends) divided by average common shareholders' equity, where
   Average common shareholders' equity = ($7,648,000 + $8,181,000) ÷ 2 = $7,914,500 = ($360,000 − $0) ÷ $7,914,500 = 4.5%

4.

   The formula for earnings per share (EPS) is:

   Earnings available to common shareholders ÷ Weighted average number of common shares

   Earnings available to common shareholders is:

   $549,600 − $40,000* = $509,600
   *Preferred dividend = 20,000 shares × $2 = $40,000

   The weighted average number of common shares for the year is:

Jan. 1	100,000 × 12/12 =	100,000
Mar. 1	(4,800) × 10/12 =	(4,000)

Jul. 1	$12,000 \times 6/12 =$	6,000
Nov. 1	$12,000 \times 2/12 =$	2,000
Weighted average number of common shares		104,000

EPS = $509,600 ÷ 104,000 = $4.90

5.

   a.   Balance sheet, statement of shareholders' equity, and cash flow statement (cash flow statement for Cascades only).

   b.   The payout ratio is calculated by dividing total cash dividends by net earnings as follows: *Note:* The cash dividend payment is obtained from the statement of shareholders' equity for both companies.

Domtar

Domtar did not pay any dividends in 2007.

Cascades ($ in millions):

2007: $16 ÷ $95 = 16.8%

   c.   The return on common shareholders' equity ratio is calculated by dividing net earnings available to common shareholders (net earnings minus preferred share dividends) by average common shareholders' equity. The common shareholders' equity is total shareholders' equity less preferred shares. Neither company had any preferred shares.

Domtar (U.S. $ in millions):

Common shareholders' equity for 2006 = $2,915

Common shareholders' equity for 2007 = $3,197

Average common shareholders' equity = ($2,915 + $3,197) ÷ 2 = $3,056

The return on common shareholders' equity for 2007 is:

$70 ÷ $3,056 = 2.3%

Cascades ($ in millions):

Common shareholders' equity for 2006 = $1,157

Common shareholders' equity for 2007 = $1,199

Average common shareholders' equity = ($1,157 + $1,199) ÷ 2 = $1,178

The return on common shareholders' equity for 2007 is:

$95 ÷ $1,178 = 8.1%

chapter 12

Reporting and Analyzing Investments

Chapter Overview

In this chapter, you will learn how to:

1. identify reasons to invest, and classify investments.
2. account for passive investments.
3. account for strategic investments.
4. indicate how investments are reported in the financial statements.
5. compare the accounting for a bond investment and a bond payable (Appendix 12A).

Review of Specific Study Objectives

- Corporations invest in debt or equity securities in one of two ways:

  1. as a **passive investment** to generate investment income, or
  2. as a **strategic investment** to influence or control the operations of another company in some way.

study objective 1

Identify reasons to invest, and classify investments.

While either debt or equity securities can be purchased as a passive investment, equity securities (normally common shares) are what a company purchases for strategic purposes. This is because only common shareholders have voting rights and therefore have influence or control.

- There are several reasons for a company to purchase debt or equity securities of another company as a passive investment.

   1. They have **excess cash** that they do not need for the purchase of operating assets until a future period. Excess cash may result from seasonal fluctuations in sales. When investing excess cash for short periods of time, corporations generally invest in debt securities, usually money-market instruments, which are low risk and high liquidity. Examples include money-market funds, bankers' acceptances, term deposits, and treasury bills. It is usually not wise to invest short-term excess cash in equity securities.

   2. Excess cash may also be invested for the longer term to **generate investment revenue**. Companies generate interest revenue from debt securities and dividend revenue from some equity securities.

   3. A company can also invest in debt and equity securities with the hope of later selling at a higher price than it originally paid for them. The company speculates that the investment will increase in value and result in a gain when sold.

- Passive investments can be further classified as either held-for-trading (HFT), available-for-sale (AFS), or held-to-maturity (HTM) investments. They can be a **short-term investment**, classified as a current asset on the balance sheet, or a **long-term investment**.

- HFT securities are always short-term and HTM securities are always long-term (unless they mature within the next year). The determination of whether an AFS security is short- or long-term depends on management's intent or purpose and whether the investment can be promptly liquidated.

- The classification of passive investments is discussed in the following sections. Strategic investments will be discussed in a later section.

study objective 2

Account for passive investments.

- The fair value of debt and equity investments can vary greatly during the time that they are held. The important question to be answered is: how should passive investments be valued on the balance sheet? Should they be valued at cost or fair value? The valuation of passive investments depends on the classification of the security. As mentioned earlier, there are three categories of securities:

   1. **Held-for-trading securities (HFT)** are securities held mainly to generate profits on short-term price differences.

   2. **Available-for-sale securities (AFS)** are securities that are not classified as HTM investments or HFT investments.

   3. **Held-to-maturity securities (HTM)** are debt securities that the investor has the intention and ability to hold to maturity.

HTM securities are valued at cost, while HFT and AFS securities are valued at fair value. The HFT and AFS classifications apply to passive equity investments. The AFS classification also applies to strategic equity investments where there is no significant influence or control. When there is significant influence or control, the accounting for strategic equity investments will differ, as we will learn later. When investments are valued at their fair value (whether they are HFT or AFS, as we will see in the next section), any increase or decrease in the market price of the investment will change the asset value reported on the balance sheet, with a corresponding unrealized gain or loss. The difference between cost and fair value while an investment is held is called an **unrealized gain or loss**. This is distinguished from a **realized gain or loss**, which is the real gain or loss that results when the investment is actually sold.

Assume that a company has the following **HFT** securities on December 31, 2009:

HFT Securities	Cost	Fair Value	Unrealized Gain (Loss)
Royal Bank bonds	$100,000	$120,000	$20,000
Fortis shares	48,000	45,000	(3,000)
Total	$148,000	$165,000	$17,000

On December 31, 2009, the $165,000 would be reported as a current asset on the balance sheet and the $17,000 would be reported as other revenue in the statement of earnings. Note that the unrealized gain or loss is reported the same way as a realized gain or loss for HFT securities.

The adjustment of the HFT securities to fair value and the recognition of any unrealized gain or loss is done through an adjusting entry as follows:

HFT Investments	17,000	
Unrealized Gain—HFT		17,000
(To record unrealized gain on HFT securities)		

Note that the entire portfolio of securities is adjusted above, but individual securities can be adjusted instead.

If, early in January, Plano sold its Fortis shares for $45,000, the following journal entry would be recorded:

Cash	45,000	
HFT Investments—Fortis Shares		45,000
(To record sale of Fortis shares)		

Although the Fortis shares originally cost $48,000, because they were written down to their fair value of $45,000 on December 31, the new carrying amount is $45,000. Consequently, the investment account is credited for that amount.

If the shares had been sold for $44,000 instead of $45,000, then a realized loss of $1,000 ($45,000 − $44,000) would have also been recorded. In other words, a loss of $3,000 ($48,000 − $45,000) would have been recorded in the last period when that loss occurred. A further loss of $1,000 would then be recorded in this period, again in the same period as when the loss occurs.

As indicated earlier, **AFS** securities are also valued at fair value at year end. The procedure for determining and recording any change in fair value and resulting unrealized gain or loss on these securities is the same as for HFT securities. However, there is a reporting difference because, while HFT securities will likely be sold in the near term, AFS securities may or may not be sold in the near term. Thus, before the actual sale of AFS securities, it is more likely that changes in fair value may reverse any unrealized gain or loss at a specific point in time. Consequently, an unrealized gain or loss on AFS securities is not reported as part of net earnings, contrary to the practice for HFT securities. Instead, unrealized gains and losses on AFS securities are separately reported as **other comprehensive income** (commonly abbreviated as OCI).

To illustrate, assume that a company has AFS securities as follows:

AFS Securities	Cost	Fair Value	Unrealized Gain (Loss)
Methanex shares	$ 70,000	$ 64,000	$ (6,000)
Royal Bank shares	125,000	116,000	(9,000)
Total	$195,000	$180,000	$(15,000)

As shown, there is an unrealized loss in the company's AFS investment portfolio of $15,000 because the total fair value ($180,000) is $15,000 less than the total cost ($195,000). The adjusting entry to record this loss would be as follows:

Unrealized Loss—AFS (OCI)	15,000	
AFS Investments		15,000

(To record unrealized loss on AFS securities)

The company would report its unrealized loss of $15,000 as other comprehensive income in the statement of comprehensive income.

- **Comprehensive income** includes all changes to shareholders' equity during a period, except changes resulting from investments by shareholders and dividends. Net earnings is a major component of comprehensive income, with OCI (such as unrealized gains and losses for AFS securities and other items) making up the remainder. Unrealized gains and losses on AFS securities are first recorded as increases or decreases to OCI. When an AFS security that changed OCI is later sold, the total of its changes to OCI must be reversed from OCI, and the AFS account adjusted for any previously recorded unrealized gains and losses. To be able to make such reversals, it is essential to know the original cost, and any adjustments, for the specific security. It is therefore important to keep individual subsidiary records that track each security's original cost and any adjustments.

  These individual subsidiary records are maintained as follows. At each year end, the carrying amount of each individual AFS security is compared with its fair value. Adjustments are then made to revalue the security to its fair value at that year end. Later, when the security is sold, any unrealized gains or losses must first be reversed from OCI before the actual realized gain or loss can be calculated and recorded.

- **HTM** investments are valued at their *amortized* cost, because any premiums or discounts included in the investment account must be amortized (similar to premiums and discounts on bonds payable). Rather, it is combined and recorded in the same account as the investment. Like many other long-term assets, HTM investments are evaluated at year end to determine if they are impaired. If the value falls below cost and the decline is considered permanent, then (and only then) will an HTM debt security be adjusted to its fair value. This value becomes the debt investment's new amortized cost base. Any writedown to fair value results in a debit to an impairment loss account and a credit to the investment (or contra allowance) account. International accounting standards allow the reversal of such a writedown in certain circumstances, although this rarely occurs.

- The **evaluation of financial performance** is important and is affected by the classification of the security—as HFT, AFS, or HTM. In addition, as HFT and AFS securities are valued at fair value, changing market prices can have a significant impact on the financial position and performance of the company. The statement on which realized and unrealized gains and losses are recorded can also affect the evaluation of a company's performance. Realized and unrealized gains and losses on HFT securities are reported in the statement of earnings, while only realized gains and losses are reported in this statement for AFS and HTM securities. This is important because ratio analyses use net earnings rather than comprehensive income in their formulas. As a result, companies are generally prohibited from reclassifying securities.

- Equity investments are investments in the share capital of other corporations. Accounting for equity investments is based on the extent of the investor's influence over the decisions of the issuing corporation (the investee).

study objective 3

Account for strategic investments.

Guidelines are as follows:

1. If the investor holds less than 20 percent of the investee's common shares, then there is an insignificant influence on the investee, and the cost method is used.
2. If the investor holds more than 20 percent of the investee's shares, then there is a presumption of significant influence on the investee, and the equity method is used.

- To determine an investor's influence, the following questions should be asked:

1. Does the investor have representation on the investee's board of directors?
2. Does the investor participate in the investee's policy-making process?
3. Are there material transactions between the investor and the investee?
4. Are the common shares held by other shareholders concentrated or dispersed?

Companies are required to use judgement instead of blindly following the guidelines.

- As mentioned earlier, the **cost method** is used to account for equity investments where there is no significant influence (normally holdings of less than 20 percent). Under the cost method, the investment is recorded at cost, and revenue is recognized only when cash dividends are received or declared. The accounting for equity investments using the cost method is identical regardless of whether the investment is short-term or long-term. Strategic equity investments that have no significant influence are normally classified as AFS investments. While the possibility exists for these investments to be classified as HFT, it would be an unlikely classification for a strategic investment.

- If a corporation acquires, on October 1, 2009, 2,000 common shares at $50 per share, then the journal entry is:

Oct. 1	AFS Investments	100,000	
	Cash		100,000
	(To record purchase of common shares)		

This investment would be reported as a current asset on the balance sheet if it is capable of prompt liquidation and management intends to sell it in the near term. This is unlikely in the case of a strategic investment. More often, it would be classified as a long-term investment on the balance sheet.

If on December 1, dividends of $3 per share are received, then the journal entry is:

Dec. 1	Cash	6,000	
	Dividend Revenue		6,000
	(To record receipt of dividends: 2,000 × $3 = $6,000)		

Dividend Revenue is reported separately, often as Other Revenues item in the statement of earnings.

If on December 15, the shares are sold for $105,000, then the journal entry is:

Dec. 15	Cash	105,000	
	AFS Investments		100,000
	Realized Gain on Sale of AFS Investments		5,000
	(To record sale of common shares)		

A loss account appears on the statement of earnings as an Other Expenses item. A gain appears on the statement of earnings as an Other Revenues item.

If the shares had not been sold on December 15 the cost (or carrying amount) would have been adjusted to the fair value at year end. Any difference between the fair value and the carrying amount would be recorded as an unrealized gain or loss. You will recall that unrealized gains and losses for AFS securities are reported as OCI in the statement of comprehensive income.

Because this investment was actually sold on December 15 in the same year it was purchased, there was no previously recorded unrealized gain or loss. If this investment had been sold subsequent to year end, in addition to recording the realized loss as shown above, any previously recorded OCI would also have to be reversed, as discussed earlier.

- For holdings of more than 20 percent, it is presumed that the investor has significant influence over the investee's financial and operating activities and plans to hold this investment for the long-term. In this case, the **equity method** is used. The investment is recorded initially at cost and is adjusted annually to show the investor's equity in the investee. The investor debits the investment account and increases revenue for its share of the investee's net earnings. The investor debits cash and credits the investment account for the amount of dividends received.

- Assume that on January 1, 2009, Reiher Corporation purchased 40 percent of the common shares of Ott Corporation for $250,000. The journal entry is:

Jan. 1	Equity Investment—Ott Corporation	250,000	
	Cash		250,000
	(To record purchase of Ott shares)		

For the year ended December 31, 2009, Ott reported $200,000 of net earnings and paid dividends of $50,000. The journal entries for Reiher are as follows:

Dec. 31	Equity Investment—Ott Corporation	80,000	
	Revenue from Investment in Ott Corporation		80,000
	(To record 40 percent equity in Ott's earnings: $200,000 \times 40\% = $80,000)		

Dec. 31	Cash	20,000	
	Equity Investment—Ott Corporation		20,000
	(To record dividends received: $50,000 \times 40\% = $20,000)		

After these entries, the balance in Equity Investment totals $310,000 ($250,000 + $80,000 − $20,000).

- Similar to HTM investments, equity investments must be assessed for impairment annually and written down if necessary. As discussed earlier, the writedown results in a debit to an impairment loss account and a credit to the equity investment account.

- The **statement of earnings** contains realized gains and losses and unrealized gains and losses from HFT securities. As well, other investment-related accounts, such as those for interest and dividend revenue, are reported as other revenue (expense) in the non-operating section of the statement of earnings.

study objective 4

Indicate how investments are reported in the financial statements.

- The statement of **comprehensive income** includes not only net earnings reported on the traditional statement of earnings but also "comprehensive income" transactions. Recall that comprehensive income is created when, among other things, unrealized gains and losses are recorded on AFS securities. Other sources of comprehensive income include certain translation gains and losses on foreign currency, unrealized gains and losses from effective cash flow hedges, and unrealized pension cost from a minimum pension liability adjustment. These are all topics for more advanced accounting courses.

- The **statement of shareholders' equity** includes changes in share capital, retained earnings, accumulated OCI (loss), and any other equity items that a company might report.

- The **balance sheet** contains investments that are classified as short- or long-term. Passive investments must be further categorized as HFT, AFS, or HTM.

- HFT investments are always classified as **current assets**, whereas AFS investments may be either current or long-term, depending on whether the investment is capable of reasonably prompt liquidation and when the management intends to sell the investment. HFT and short-term AFS investments are reported in the current assets section of the balance sheet at their fair value. No distinction is usually made between debt and equity securities for financial reporting purposes. These securities are usually combined and reported as one portfolio amount for each classification in the balance sheet.

- HTM securities are debt securities that are classified as **long-term investments** until they are about to mature. Any portion that is expected to mature within the year is classified as a current asset. HTM securities are reported at their amortized cost. Certain equity securities that are purchased to have significant influence or control are also classified as long-term investments, and supporting details are given in the notes to the financial statements.

- If a company owns between 20 percent and 50 percent of the common shares of another company, and does not have a controlling interest, the investment is simply reported as a long-term equity investment in the investor's financial statements. However, when a company owns more than 50 percent of the common shares of another company, it controls the company, and an additional set of financial statements is then required. When one company (known as the **parent company**) controls another company (known as the **subsidiary company**), **consolidated financial statements** must be prepared for financial reporting purposes. Consolidated financial statements present the assets and liabilities that are controlled by the parent company and the total revenues and expenses of the subsidiary companies. They indicate the size and scope of operations of the companies under common control. Most publicly traded Canadian companies present consolidated financial statements.

study objective 5

Compare the accounting for a bond investment and a bond payable (Appendix 12A).

- Short-term investments in bonds can be classified as HFT securities or AFS securities, depending on the intent to sell. Long-term investments in bonds are classified as AFS or HTM. When a bond is purchased, the investment account is debited for the purchase cost of the bond (i.e., for the face value net of any premium or discount).

- You will recall from Chapter 10 that premiums or discounts on long-term bonds payable must be amortized using the effective-interest method of amortization. Similarly, premiums or discounts on bond investments must be amortized using the effective-interest method. This is true for all bond investments except those that are held for trading. Because HFT bond investments are expected to be held only for a short time, there is no requirement to amortize any premium or discount.

- For long-term bonds payable, the amortization of a bond investment is recorded in an Interest Revenue account. If there is a bond premium on a long-term bond investment, the Interest Revenue account is *reduced* by the amortized amount. If there is a bond discount, the Interest Revenue account is *increased* by the amortized amount.

Chapter Self-Test

As you work through the questions and problems, remember to use the **Decision Toolkit** discussed and used in the text:

1. *Decision Checkpoints*: At this point, you ask a question.
2. *Info Needed for Decision*: You make a choice regarding the information needed to answer the question.
3. *Tool to Use for Decision*: At this point, you review just what the information chosen in step 2 does for the decision-making process.
4. *How to Evaluate Results*: You conduct an evaluation of information for answering the question.

Note: The notation (SO1) means that the question was drawn from study objective number one.

Multiple Choice

Please circle the correct answer.

(SO1)   1. Corporations invest in other companies for all of the following reasons *except* to
   a.   use excess cash that it does not immediately need.
   b.   generate investment revenue.
   c.   meet strategic goals.
   d.   increase trading of the other companies' shares.

(SO1)   2. Passive investments include:
   a.   HTM investments only.
   b.   HFT investments only.

    c.   AFS investments only.

    d.   all of the above.

3. On January 1, 2009, Meyers Corporation acquired as an HFT investment, 20   (SO2)
of Sayer Corporation five-year, 6 percent, $1,000 bonds for $22,000. Meyers
Corporation's year end is December 31. The entry to record the acquisition of
the bonds includes a debit to:

    a.   HFT Investment—Sayer Bonds $20,000.

    b.   Bonds Payable for $22,000.

    c.   HFT Investment—Sayer Bonds $22,000.

    d.   Cash for $22,000.

4. Refer to 3 above. On December 31, 2009, the fair value of the Sayer bonds is   (SO2)
$19,000. Meyers' adjusting entry on December 31, 2009 would include:

    a.   debit Unrealized Loss—HFT for $3,000

    b.   debit Unrealized Loss—HFT for $1,000

    c.   credit Cash for $3,000

    d.   Credit HFT Investment for $3,000

5. HTM securities are valued at their: (SO2)

    a.   acquisition cost.

    b.   fair value.

    c.   amortized cost.

    d.   equity value.

6. Mack Corporation owns 10 percent of the common shares of Knife Corporation.   (SO3)
When Mack receives $5,000 in cash dividends, the journal entry is:

    a.   Cash   5,000

                  Dividend Revenue   5,000

    b.   Cash   5,000

                  Equity Investment—Knife   5,000

    c.   Equity Investment—Knife   5,000

                  Dividend Revenue   5,000

    d.   Equity Investment—Knife   5,000

                  Cash   5,000

7. Mack Corporation owns 40 percent of the common shares of Knife Corporation.   (SO3)
When Mack receives $5,000 in cash dividends, the journal entry is:

    a.   Cash   5,000

                  Dividend Revenue   5,000

    b.   Cash   5,000

                  Equity Investment—Knife   5,000

    c.   Equity Investment—Knife   5,000

                  Dividend Revenue   5,000

    d.   Equity Investment—Knife   5,000

                  Cash   5,000

(SO3)   8.   Ross Corporation owns 40 percent of the common shares of Searcy Corporation. When Searcy reports net earnings of $200,000, the journal entry on Ross's books is:

a.   Cash   80,000
          Revenue from Equity Investment   80,000

b.   Equity Investment—Searcy   80,000
          Revenue from Equity Investment   80,000

c.   Equity Investment—Searcy   200,000
          Revenue from Equity Investment   200,000

d.   Equity Investment—Searcy   200,000
          Cash   200,000

(SO4)   9.   Trice Corporation purchased 80 percent of the common shares of Waters Corporation. Trice is the _____ company, and Waters is the _____ company.
a.   subsidiary, controlling
b.   controlling, subsidiary
c.   subsidiary, parent
d.   parent, subsidiary

(SO4)   10.   With respect to the Trice purchase of Waters Corporation shares in number 9 above, which of the following is true?
a.   Only consolidated financial statements are prepared.
b.   Trice and Waters each prepare their own financial statements. Trice uses the equity method to account for its investment in Waters in its own financial statements. Consolidated financial statements are also prepared.
c.   Trice and Waters each prepare their own financial statements, and consolidated financial statements are not prepared.
d.   Since Trice is the purchaser, it prepares its own financial statements; Waters does not, and consolidated financial statements are also prepared.

(SO2)   11.   An unrealized gain on AFS securities would be shown:
a.   in the "other revenues" section in the statement of earnings.
b.   in the cash flow statement.
c.   in the statement of comprehensive income.
d.   as a contra account to AFS investment account on the balance sheet.

(SO2)   12.   Caissie Corporation has a portfolio of HFT securities with a total cost of $75,000. On the date of the financial statement, the fair value of the portfolio is $78,000. The adjusting entry is:

a.   HFT Investment   3,000
          Unrealized Gain—HFT   3,000

b.   Unrealized Gain—HFT   3,000
          HFT Investment   3,000

c.   Cash   3,000
          Unrealized Gain—HFT   3,000

d.   No adjusting journal entry is required.

13. A portfolio of HFT investments that is intended to be sold in two years is (SO4)
reported:
    a. in the shareholders' equity section of the balance sheet.
    b. in the current assets section of the balance sheet.
    c. in the long-term assets section of the balance sheet.
    d. in the statement of comprehensive income.

14. Shares of another corporation purchased to gain some influence are reported: (SO4)
    a. in the shareholders' equity section of the balance sheet.
    b. in the current assets section of the balance sheet.
    c. in long-term investments on the balance.
    d. in the statement of shareholders' equity.

Use the following information for questions 15–17. (SO2, 5)

Pujol acquired 100 Smeac 5-year, 7 percent, $1,000 bonds on January 1, 2009 for
$95,948. The price of the bond is based on a market interest rate of 8 percent.
The bonds pay interest on July 1 and January 1. Assume that Pujol is holding
these bonds as an AFS security.

*15. Pujol's accounting entry to record the investment on January 1 is:

    a. AFS Investment—Smeac Bond   95,948
          Cash   95,948

    b. AFS Investment—Smeac   95,948
       Unrealized Loss   4,052
          Cash   100,000

    c. Cash   95,948
          Bonds Payable   95,948

    d. AFS Investment—Smeac   100,000
          Cash   100,000

*16. On July 1, Pujol receives the interest from the Smeac bonds. The accounting
entry for the receipt of interest by Pujol is:

    a. Interest Expense (4% × $95,948)   3,838
          Bonds Payable ($3,838 – $3,500)   338
          Cash   3,500

    b. Cash ($100,000 × 7% × 6/12)   3,500
       AFS Investment—Smeac ($3,838 – $3,500)   338
          Interest Revenue ($95,948 × 8% × 6/12)   3,838

    c. Cash ($100,000 × 7% × 6/12)   3,500
       Bond Payable ($3,838 – $3,500)   338
          Interest Revenue ($95,948 × 8% × 6/12)   3,838

    d. Cash ($100,000 × 7% × 6/12)   3,500
          Interest Revenue   3,500

*17. The accounting entry for Smeac for the issue of the bonds on January 1 is:

a.   Cash   95,948

            AFS Investment   95,948

b.   Cash   95,948

        Unrealized Loss   4,052

            Bonds Payable   100,000

c.   Cash   95,948

            Bonds Payable   95,948

d.   Cash   100,000

            Bonds Payable   100,000

Problems

(SO2)   1. Assume that on December 31, 2009, Scott Corporation has the following costs
              and fair values for its HFT securities:

HFT Securities	Cost	Fair Value	Unrealized Gain (Loss)
Royal Bank bonds	$125,000	$128,000	$3,000
Rogers shares	75,000	70,000	(5,000)
Total	$200,000	$198,000	$(2,000)

a. Prepare the required adjusting entry on December 31, 2009.
b. Assume that on January 30, 2010, Scott sells its Rogers shares for $72,000.
    Prepare the journal entry to record the sale.

Date	Account Titles	Debit	Credit
	HFT Investment A	2,00	
	Unrealized loss		
	Rogers Shar Cash	7 000	
	realized Gain		
	cash HFT In PA		

2. On February 1, 2009, Floss Corporation acquired 10 percent of the common shares   (SO3)
of Georgia Corporation to hold as an AFS investment for $50,000. On March
31, 2009, Georgia reported $300,000 of net earnings and paid cash dividends of
$80,000. On July 1, 2009, Floss sells the Georgia shares for $55,000.

    a.   Record Floss Corporation's purchase of the shares and any other necessary
journal entries.

Date	Account Titles	Debit	Credit
	Investment	50 000	
	Cash		50 000
	Cash	8 000	
	Dividends Rev		8000

    b.   Assume the same data as shown above, but the shares purchased represents
30 percent of the common shares of Georgia Corporation. Record the
purchase of the investment and any other necessary journal entries. Assume
that on July 1, 2009, the Georgia shares are sold for $115,000.

Date	Account Titles	Debit	Credit
	Equity Investment		
	Cash		
	Equity Investment		
	Revenue from Investment		
	Divids		
	Equity invest		

(SO4) 3. The following selected general ledger account balances are provided for Rebus Corporation as of December 31, 2009. This is the corporation's first year of operations.

Accounts payable	$ 15,000
Accounts receivable	64,000
Accumulated depreciation—building	10,000
Accumulated OCI	14,000
Advertising expense	1,000
Allowance for doubtful accounts	20,000
AFS securities (long-term)	10,000
AFS securities (short-term)	7,000
Bad debt expense	2,000
Bonds payable	98,000
Building	350,000
Cash	140,000
Common shares, no par value, 40,000 shares issued	271,000
Depreciation expense	5,000
Dividends	10,000
Equity investments	20,000
Realized gain—HFT	15,000
HTM securities	15,000
HFT securities	20,000
Income tax expense	13,000
Interest expense	8,000
Interest payable	13,000
Land	100,000
Mortgage payable	175,000
Notes payable, 6-month	40,000
Payroll tax expense	1,000
Provincial sales tax payable	13,000
Retained earnings, January 1	15,000
Service revenue	75,000
Wages expense	10,000
Wages payable	2,000

Prepare a balance sheet for Rebus Corporation for 2009, assuming $30,000 of the mortgage is payable next year.

4. On January 1, 2009, Burber Corporation acquired, as an AFS investment,   (SO5)
    $650,000 of 7 percent, 5-year bonds of Highlife Corporation for $698,354. The
    price of the bond is based on a market interest rate of 6 percent. The bonds pay
    interest on July 1 and January 1.
    a.   Prepare the entry for January 1, 2009.
    b.   Record the semi-annual interest received on July 1, 2009.
    c.   The bonds are sold on September 1, 2009, at 97. Prepare the entry required
         to record the sale.

Date	Account Titles	Debit	Credit

5. Please refer to the Domtar and Cascades financial statements found in the   (SO4)
    appendices at the end of this study guide. What information is provided regard-
    ing investments?

Solutions to Self-Test

Multiple Choice

1. d   Answers a, b, and c are all reasons why a corporation may invest in other
       companies.

2. d   Passive investments can be classified as either HFT, AFS, or HTM invest-
       ments.

3. c   The journal entry is:

       HFT Investment—Sayer Bonds   22,000

           Cash   22,000

4. a   The journal entry is:

Unrealized Loss—HFT	3,000	
HFT Investment		3,000

5. c   HTM investments are valued at their amortized cost, because any premiums or discounts included in the investment account must be amortized.

6. a   The cost method is used.

7. b   The equity method is used.

8. b   The equity method is used. ($200,000 × 40% = $80,000)

9. d   "Controlling" refers to the interest the parent has in the subsidiary.

10. b   Consolidated financial statements are prepared as an addition to the financial statements for the parent company and each subsidiary company.

11. c   An unrealized gain or loss on AFS securities is not reported as part of net earnings, contrary to the practice for HFT securities. Instead, unrealized gains and losses on AFS securities are separately reported as other comprehensive income (OCI) in the statement of comprehensive income.

12. a   When investments are valued at their fair value (whether they are HFT or AFS), any increase or decrease in the market price will change the asset value reported on the balance sheet, with a corresponding gain or loss. The difference between cost and fair value while an investment is held is called an unrealized gain. In this case, the gain is $78,000 − $75,000 = $3,000.

13. c   HFT investments are reported in the current assets section of the balance sheet at their fair value, regardless of when they are intended to be sold.

14. c   Equity securities that are purchased to have significant influence or control are classified as long-term investments. Note also that supporting details are given in the notes to the financial statements.

15. a   The bonds are recorded at their acquisition cost of $95,948. The $4,052 discount on the bonds is not separately recorded but is netted with the cost in the investment account.

16. b   Interest to be received is calculated by multiplying the face value of the bond investment by the contractual or stated interest rate per semi-annual period. Pujol will collect interest of $3,500 ($100,000 × 7% × 6/12) semi-annually on July 1 and January 1.

    Interest revenue is calculated by multiplying the carrying amount of the bond investment by the market rate of interest per semi-annual interest period. Pujol's interest revenue is $3,838 ($95,948 × 8% × 6/12, rounded) for the first interest period. Interest revenue is then compared with the interest received to determine the amount to amortize the discount (i.e., the portion of the $4,042 discount that is amortized this 6-month period). The amortization is $338 ($3,838 − $3,500), in this case, and is debited to the bond investment account.

17. c   The bond discount is netted in the bonds payable account. ($100,000 − $4,052)

Problems

1.   a.   Dec. 31, 2009   Unrealized Loss—HFT   2,000
                            HFT Investments   2,000
                         (To record unrealized loss on HFT securities)

     b.   Jan. 30, 2010   Cash   72,000
                            Realized Gain—Rogers Shares   2,000
                            HFT Investments—Rogers Shares   70,000
                         (To record sale of HFT Rogers shares)

2.   a.   The cost method is used because the purchase is 10 percent of the shares of
          Georgia Corporation. Only dividends are recognized.

          Feb. 1, 2009   AFS Investment—Georgia   50,000
                            Cash   50,000
                         (To record purchase of 10 percent of Georgia Corporation
                         shares)

          Mar. 31, 2009   Cash   8,000
                            Dividend Revenue   8,000
                         (To record dividends: 10% × $80,000 = $8,000)

          July 1, 2009   Cash   55,000
                            Realized Gain—AFS   5,000
                            AFS Investment—Georgia   50,000
                         (To record sale of Georgia Corporation shares)

     b.   The equity method is used because the purchase is 30 percent of the shares
          of Georgia Corporation.

          Feb. 1, 2009   Equity Investment—Georgia   50,000
                            Cash   50,000
                         (To record purchase of 30 percent of Georgia Corporation
                         shares)

          Mar. 31, 2009   Equity Investment—Georgia   90,000
                            Revenue from Investment in
                            Georgia   90,000
                         (To record 30 percent equity in Georgia's net earnings:
                         $300,000 × 30% = $90,000)

                          Cash   24,000
                            Equity Investment—Georgia   24,000
                         (To record dividends received: 30% × $80,000 =
                         $24,000)

July 1, 2009	Cash	115,000	
	Realized Loss—AFS	1,000	
	AFS Investment—Georgia		116,000
	(To record sale of Equity Investment—Georgia: $50,000 + $90,000 − $24,000 = $116,000)		

3.

REBUS CORPORATION
Balance Sheet
December 31, 2009

Assets

Current assets

Cash			$140,000
Held-for-trading securities			20,000
AFS securities			7,000
Accounts receivable		$64,000	
Less: Allowance for doubtful accounts		20,000	44,000
Total current assets			211,000

Long-term investments

AFS securities		$10,000	
HTM securities		15,000	
Equity investments		20,000	
Total long-term investments			45,000

Property, plant, and equipment

Land		$100,000	
Building	$350,000		
Accumulated depreciation—building	10,000	340,000	
Total property, plant, and equipment			440,000
Total assets			$696,000

Liabilities and Shareholders' Equity

Current liabilities

Accounts payable			$ 15,000
Wages payable			2,000
Interest payable			13,000
Provincial sales tax payable			13,000
Notes payable, 6-month			40,000
Current portion of mortgage payable			30,000
Total current liabilities			113,000

Long-term liabilities

Bonds payable	$ 98,000	
Mortgage payable	145,000	
Total long-term liabilities		243,000
Total liabilities		356,000

Shareholders' equity

Common shares, no par value, 40,000 shares issued	$271,000	
Retained earnings	55,000	
Accumulated OCI	14,000	
Total shareholders' equity		340,000
Total liabilities and shareholders' equity		$696,000

Note: Retained Earnings = Opening retained earnings balance + all revenues − all expenses − dividends. ($15,000 + $75,000 + $15,000 − $10,000 − $1,000 − $5,000 − $1,000 − $2,000 − $8,000 − $13,000 − $10,000 = $55,000)

4. a. Jan. 1, 2009   AFS Investment—Highlife   698,354

            Cash   698,354

            (To record purchase of Highlife bonds)

The bonds are recorded at their acquisition cost of $698,354. These bonds are issued at a premium ($698,354 − $650,000), which is netted with the cost in the investment account.

   b. July 1, 2009   Cash ($650,000 × 7% × 6/12)   22,750

            AFS Investment—Highlife ($22,750 − $20,951)   1,799

            Interest Revenue
            ($698,354 × 6% × 6/12, rounded)   20,951

            (To record receipt of interest on Highlife bonds)

Interest revenue is compared with the interest received to determine the amount to amortize the bond premium that is, the portion of the $48,354 premium that is amortized this 6-month period. The amortization is $1,799 ($22,750 − $20,951) and is credited to the AFS investment account.

   c. Sep. 1, 2009   Cash ($650,000 × 7% × 2/12, rounded)   7,583

            AFS Investment—Highlife ($7,583 − $7,002)   581

            Interest Revenue
            ($700,153 × 6% × 2/12, rounded)   7,002

            (To record receipt of interest on Highlife bonds)

The carrying amount of the bonds must be adjusted for the amortization of the premium on July 1, 2009: $698,354 + $1,799 = $700,153

The carrying amount of the investment is now $695,136, as shown here:

AFS Investment—Highlife Bonds

Jan. 1	698,354		
		July 1	1,799
		Sep. 1	581
Bal. Sep. 1	695,974		

Sep. 1, 2009	Cash ($650,000 × 97%)	630,500	
	Realized Loss on Sale of AFS Investment	65,474	
	AFS Investment—Highlife		695,974
	(To record sale of Highlife bonds)		

5. Neither Domtar nor Cascades separately reports information about investments (other than cash equivalents) on their balance sheet.

Domtar does not report any information on its statement of earnings but Cascades reports earnings from significantly influenced companies on its statement of earnings.

Both companies report business acquisitions in the investing activities sections of their cash flow statements.

Further detail about the companies' investments can be found in the notes to the financial statements found in the Study Tools section of the textbook website.

chapter 13

Cash Flow Statement

Chapter Overview

In this chapter, you will learn about the purpose and format of the cash flow statement; preparing the statement using either the direct or the indirect method; and using the cash flow statement to evaluate a company's liquidity and solvency.

- The main purpose of the cash flow statement is to provide information about cash receipts; cash payments; and the net change in cash resulting from the operating, investing, and financing activities of a company during a specific period.

- The information in a cash flow statement should help investors, creditors, and others assess the following aspects of a company's financial position:

  1. The reasons for the difference between net earnings and cash provided (used) by operating activities.
  2. The investing and financing transactions during the period.
  3. The company's ability to generate future cash flows.

- The cash flow statement is often prepared using **cash and cash equivalents** as its basis. Cash equivalents are short-term, highly liquid investments that are readily convertible to cash within a very short period of time. Generally, only money market instruments due within three months qualify with this definition. Examples include treasury bills, commercial paper, and money market funds.

The International Accounting Standards Board and the Financial Accounting Standards Board are currently working on a project to improve the presentation of information in certain financial statements, including the cash flow statement. While this project is still in its early stages, preliminary views have been issued and discussed. One of the recommendations is to exclude "cash equivalents" from the definition of cash. In other words, the cash flow statement would present information about the changes in cash only, and not cash and cash equivalents. You will note that the cash flow statements in this chapter have been prepared using cash only.

- The general format of the cash flow statement is organized around the following activities:

  - **Operating activities** include the cash effects of transactions that create revenues and expenses. They affect net earnings. The operating activities category is the most important because it shows the cash provided or used by company operations. Ultimately, a company must generate cash from its operating activities in order to continue as a going concern and to expand.

  - **Investing activities** include purchasing and disposing of investments and productive long-lived assets using cash and lending money and collecting the loans.

  - **Financing activities** include obtaining cash from issuing debt and repaying the borrowed amounts and obtaining cash from shareholders and paying them dividends.

- In general:

  - **Operating activities** involve statement of earnings items and current assets and current liabilities.

  - **Investing activities** involve investments and other long-term asset items.

  - **Financing activities** involve long-term liabilities and shareholders' equity items.

- **A company may also have significant noncash activities**, such as issues of common shares to purchase assets, conversions of debt into equity, issues of debt to purchase assets, and exchanges of property, plant, and equipment. These are not reported in the body of the cash flow statement but, instead, are reported in a separate note to the financial statements. Reporting of such activities satisfies the full disclosure principle.

study objective 2
Prepare a cash flow statement using one of two approaches: (a) the indirect method or (b) the direct method.

- With respect to the **format of the statement**, the section reporting cash flows from operating activities always appears first. It is followed by the investing section and then the financing activities section. Individual inflows and outflows from investing and financing activities are reported separately, not netted against each other. The reported operating, investing, and financing activities result in net cash either provided or used by the activity. The amounts of net cash either provided or used by the activity are then totalled to show the net increase or decrease in cash for the period. The net increase or decrease is then added to or subtracted from the beginning-of-period cash balance to obtain the end-of-period cash balance. The end-of-period cash balance should agree with the cash balance reported on the balance sheet.

Significant noncash investing and financing activities are shown separately in a note to the financial statements.

- The cash flow **statement** is not prepared from the adjusted trial balance. The accrual concept is not used in its preparation.

- **Information for preparation of the statement** comes from three sources: the comparative balance sheet, the statement of earnings, and selected additional information.

- The four steps used in the preparation of the statement are as follows:

  1. Determine the net cash provided (used) by operating activities by converting net earnings from an accrual basis to a cash basis.
  2. Determine the net cash provided (used) by investing activities by analyzing changes in short-term investments and long-term asset accounts.
  3. Determine the net cash provided (used) by financing activities by analyzing changes in short-term notes payable and long-term liability and equity accounts.
  4. Determine the net increase (decrease) in cash. Compare the net change in cash reported on the cash flow statement with the change in cash reported on the balance sheet to make sure the amounts agree.

- In order to perform step one and determine the cash provided (used) by operating activities, **net earnings must be converted from an accrual basis to a cash basis**. This conversion may be done by either the **indirect or the direct method**. Both methods arrive at the same number, just in different manners. Note that the two different methods affect only the operating activities section.

- The direct method is preferred by standard setters. It is considered to be more informative to users and is easier to compare with other financial statements. Despite this preference, the **indirect method is used by a majority of companies** because it is easier to prepare, focuses on the differences between net earnings and net cash flow from operating activities, and tends to reveal less company information to competitors.

Indirect Method

- Under the indirect method, net earnings is converted from the accrual to cash for items that affect reported net earnings but not cash. There are various expenses and losses that reduce net earnings but do not involve cash, and various revenues and gains that increase net earnings but do not involve cash. The expenses and losses are added back to net earnings, and the revenues and gains are subtracted from net earnings to convert them to net cash provided by operating activities.

- Depreciation expense is one of those expenses added back to net earnings. This is often the first adjustment to net earnings. It is important to understand that depreciation expense is not added to operating activities as if it was a source of cash. It is added to cancel the deduction created by the depreciation expense in the determination of net earnings.

- The textbook's discussion of the individual mechanics is solid and clear, and the following is a **summary of conversion to net cash provided by operating activities with respect to current assets and current liabilities**:

Change in	Add to Net Earnings	Deduct from Net Earnings
Accounts receivable	Decrease	Increase
Inventory	Decrease	Increase
Prepaid expenses	Decrease	Increase
Accounts payable	Increase	Decrease
Accrued expenses payable	Increase	Decrease

In other words, if the balance in the Accounts Receivable account decreases during the period, this amount is added to accrual-based net earnings in order to calculate cash provided (used) by operating activities. If the balance increases, the amount is deducted from accrual-based net earnings and so on, as explained in the table above.

- **Noncash charges that must be added back to accrual basis net earnings** include depreciation expense and loss on sale of assets. These items all reduce net earnings but have nothing to do with cash flow, and they must be added back to produce net cash flows from operating activities.

- **Noncash credits that must be deducted from accrual basis net earnings** include gain on sale of assets. This item increases net earnings but has nothing to do with cash flow, and it must be deducted to produce net cash flows from operating activities.

Direct Method

- As stated earlier, use of the **direct method** affects only the operating activities section of the statement. Under the direct method, **net cash provided by operating activities** is calculated by adjusting each item in the statement of earnings from the accrual basis to the cash basis. Only major classes of operating cash receipts and cash payments are reported. An **efficient way to apply the direct method** is to analyze the revenues and expenses reported in the statement of earnings in the order in which they are listed.

- The textbook's discussion of the individual mechanics is solid and clear, and the following is a **summary of the formulas for calculating the various cash inflows and outflows in order to arrive at net cash provided by operating activities:**

To calculate **Cash Receipts from Customers**, do the following:

Revenues from sales
Deduct: Increase in accounts receivable OR
Add: Decrease in accounts receivable
Equals: Cash receipts from customers

To calculate **Cash Payments to Suppliers**, do the following:

Purchases*
Deduct: Increase in accounts payable OR
Add: Decrease in accounts payable
Equals: Cash payments to suppliers

*To solve for purchases:

Cost of goods sold
Deduct: Decrease in inventory OR

Add: Increase in inventory
Equals: <u>Purchases</u>

To calculate **Cash Payments for Operating Expenses**, do the following:

Operating expenses
Deduct: Decrease in prepaid expenses OR
Add: Increase in prepaid expenses AND
Deduct: Increase in accrued expenses payable OR
Add: Decrease in accrued expenses payable
Equals: <u>Cash payments for operating expenses</u>

To calculate **Cash Payments to Employees**, do the following:

Wages expense
Deduct: Increase in wages payable OR
Add: Decrease in wages payable
Equals: <u>Cash payments to employees</u>

To calculate **Cash Payments for Income Taxes**, do the following:

Income tax expense
Deduct: Increase in income taxes payable OR
Add: Decrease in income taxes payable
Equals: <u>Cash payments for income taxes</u>

- The **following do not appear on a cash flow statement under the direct method because they are noncash charges**: depreciation expense and loss on sale of assets. A gain on sale of assets likewise will not appear because it is a noncash credit.

- **Net earnings is not reported on the cash flow statement under the direct method.** In the operating activities section, cash payments are subtracted from cash receipts to arrive at net cash provided by operating activities.

- The investing and financing activities sections are prepared in the same way under both methods. The **investing activities section** deals with short-term investments and long-term assets, and the **financing** activities section deals with short-term notes payable, long-term debt, and shareholders' equity items.

- All items are to be listed separately, not netted against one another. For example, if a company purchases one asset for $80,000 and sells another asset for $20,000, each cash flow must be listed, not just the net outflow of $60,000.

- **Liquidity** is the ability of a company to meet its immediate obligations. In Chapter 2, you learned that one measure of liquidity is the current ratio calculated by dividing current assets by current liabilities. A cash-based measure of liquidity is the **cash current debt coverage ratio** calculated by dividing cash provided or used by operating activities by average current liabilities.

> **study objective 3**
>
> Use the cash flow statement to evaluate a company's liquidity and solvency.

- Solvency is the ability of a company to survive over the long term. In Chapter 2, you learned that one cash-based measure of solvency is **free cash flow**. It is calculated by subtracting net capital expenditures and dividends paid from cash provided by operating activities. It is a measure of a company's ability to generate sufficient cash to finance the purchase of new assets. Another cash-based measure of solvency is the **cash total debt coverage ratio** calculated by dividing cash provided or used by operating activities by average total liabilities.

Chapter Self-Test

As you work through the questions and problems, remember to use the **Decision Toolkit** discussed and used in the text:

1. *Decision Checkpoints*: At this point, you ask a question.
2. *Info Needed for Decision*: You make a choice regarding the information needed to answer the question.
3. *Tool to Use for Decision*: At this point, you review just what the information chosen in step two does for the decision-making process.
4. *How to Evaluate Results*: You conduct an evaluation of information for answering the question.

Note: The notation (SO1) means that the question was drawn from study objective number one.

Multiple Choice

Please circle the correct answer.

(SO1)   1. What type of activity is the purchase of a piece of equipment?
     a.   Operating activity
     b.   Investing activity
     c.   Financing activity
     d.   Balance sheet activity

(SO1)   2. Which of the following is listed first on the cash flow statement?
     a.   Operating activities
     b.   Investing activities
     c.   Financing activities
     d.   Manufacturing activities

(SO1)   3. Which of the following statements is correct?
     a.   Significant noncash activities are never reported in a company's annual report.
     b.   Significant noncash activities are reported in the body of the cash flow statement.
     c.   Significant noncash activities are reported in a separate note to the financial statements.
     d.   Significant noncash activities are always reported on the company's balance sheet.

(SO1)   4. The primary purpose of the cash flow statement is to:
     a.   prove that net cash flow provided by operating activities equals the amount shown for cash on the balance sheet.
     b.   prove that revenues exceed expenses if there are net earnings.
     c.   provide information about the cash receipts and cash payments during a period.
     d.   facilitate banking relationships.

5. If a company reports a net loss, it: (SO2)
   a.   may still have a net increase in cash.
   b.   will not be able to pay cash dividends.
   c.   will not be able to get a loan.
   d.   will not be able to make capital expenditures.

6. Which of the following is a source of information for preparation of the cash   (SO1)
   flow statement?
   a.   Comparative balance sheet
   b.   Current period statement of earnings
   c.   Selected additional information
   d.   All of the above are needed.

7. If the indirect method is used for preparation of the cash flow statement, then a   (SO2)
   decrease in accounts receivable is accounted for as a(n):
   a.   cash inflow in the investing activities section.
   b.   cash inflow in the financing activities section.
   c.   addition to net earnings in the operating activities section.
   d.   deduction from net earnings in the operating activities section.

8. If the indirect method is used for preparation of the cash flow statement, then an   (SO2)
   increase in prepaid expenses is accounted for as a(n):
   a.   cash inflow in the investing activities section.
   b.   cash inflow in the financing activities section.
   c.   addition to net earnings in the operating activities section.
   d.   deduction from net earnings in the operating activities section.

9. If a company purchases land through the issue of long-term bonds, then this is   (SO2)
   accounted for as a(n):
   a.   operating activity.
   b.   investing inflow.
   c.   financing outflow.
   d.   significant noncash investing and financing activity that merits disclosure.

10. A company has $200,000 of net earnings, $500,000 of revenues from sales, and an   (SO2)
    increase in accounts receivable of $50,000. If the company uses the direct method
    of preparing the cash flow statement, then cash receipts from customers total:
    a. $500,000.
    b. $450,000.
    c. $300,000.
    d. $150,000.

11. A company has a cost of goods sold of $300,000, an increase in inventory of   (SO2)
    $100,000, and an increase in accounts payable of $30,000. If it uses the direct
    method of preparing the cash flow statement, then purchases total:
    a. $400,000.
    b. $370,000.
    c. $300,000.
    d. $200,000.

(SO2)   12. A company has a cost of goods sold of $300,000, an increase in inventory of
              $100,000, and an increase in accounts payable of $30,000. If it uses the direct
              method of preparing the cash flow statement, then cash payments to suppliers total:
              a. $400,000.
              b. $370,000.
              c. $300,000.
              d. $200,000.

(SO2)   13. Starting with net earnings and adjusting it for items that affected reported net
              earnings but not cash is called the:
              a.   direct method.
              b.   indirect method.
              c.   allowance method.
              d.   cost-benefit method.

(SO2)   14. Which of the following adjustments to convert net earnings to net cash provided
              by operating activities is not added to net earnings?
              a.   Gain on Sale of Equipment
              b.   Depreciation Expense
              c.   Realized Loss from Sale of Investment
              d.   Loss on Sale of Equipment

(SO3)   15. Firth Corporation shows the following:

              Cash provided by operating activities $500,000
              Capital expenditures   125,000
              Dividends   40,000

              What is the company's free cash flow?
              a. $335,000
              b. $375,000
              c. $415,000
              d. $500,000

(SO3)   16. Which of the following ratios is a measure of liquidity?
              a.   Cash total debt coverage
              b.   Free cash flow
              c.   Cash current debt coverage
              d.   Debt to total assets

(SO3)   17. The cash current debt coverage ratio demonstrates:
              a.   the company's ability to repay its liabilities from cash generated from all
                    sources without having to liquidate assets.
              b.   the company's ability to repay its short-term liabilities from cash generated
                    from operating activities without having to liquidate assets.
              c.   how fast the company collects cash.
              d.   the company's ability to meet interest payments.

(SO2)   18. The indirect and direct methods of preparing the statement of cash flows are
              identical except for the
              a.   significant noncash activity section.
              b.   operating activities section.

c.   investing activities section.
d.   financing activities section.

Problems

1. The following are comparative balance sheet data for Panther Corporation for years 2009 and 2008:

PANTHER CORPORATION
Comparative Balance Sheet Data
December 31

	2009	2008
Cash	$ 3,600	$ 2,300
Accounts receivable	3,500	2,600
Inventory	3,200	3,800
Equipment	3,800	3,400
Accumulated depreciation	(2,400)	(2,340)
Held-to-maturity investments	2,600	2,840
	$14,300	$12,600
Accounts payable	$ 2,400	$ 1,800
Accrued liabilities	400	500
Bonds payable	2,800	3,100
Common shares	3,800	3,400
Retained earnings	4,900	3,800
	$14,300	$12,600

Selected data from the statement of earnings include net earnings of $2,140 and depreciation expense of $60. Cash dividends paid totalled $1,040.

Using the indirect method, prepare a cash flow statement for Panther Corporation for the year ended December 31, 2009. Make assumptions as appropriate.

2. The statement of earnings for the Warnon Corporation is shown below: (SO2)

WARNON CORPORATION
Statement of Earnings
Year Ended December 31, 2009

Sales		$12,300,000
Cost of goods sold		8,100,000
Gross profit		4,200,000
Operating expenses	$1,800,000	
Depreciation expense	180,000	1,980,000
Net earnings		$2,220,000

Additional information:
1. Accounts receivable increased $600,000 during the year.
2. Inventory increased $375,000 during the year.

3. Prepaid expenses increased $300,000 during the year.
4. Accounts payable to merchandise suppliers increased $150,000 during the year.
5. Accrued expenses payable increased $270,000 during the year.

Using the direct method, prepare the operating activities section of the cash flow statement for the year ended December 31, 2009, for the Warnon Corporation.

(SO2)   3. A company has the following selected account balances related to property, plant, and equipment.

	2009	2008
Equipment	$200,000	$175,000
Accumulated depreciation—equipment	88,000	95,000

Additional information:
1. During 2009, the company sold equipment for cash. The equipment had a cost of $38,000, a carrying amount of $7,000, and a gain on sale of $2,500.
2. During 2009, the company recorded $24,000 of depreciation expense on the equipment.
3. During 2009, the company purchased equipment for cash.

Calculate the cash received from the sale of equipment and the cash paid for equipment for 2009.

(SO2)   4. The Axel Corporation has the following selected general ledger account balances as of December 31, 2009.

Accounts payable	$ 25,000
Bonds payable, due July 1, 2020	87,500
Common shares	270,000
Retained earnings	15,000
Dividends	10,000
Interest payable	11,000
Mortgage payable	150,000
Notes payable, due April 1, 2010	20,000
Provincial sales tax payable	8,000
Wages payable	2,000

The following additional information is provided:

1. $20,000 of the mortgage is payable next year.
2. Cash provided by operating activities for 2009 was $139,750.
3. Current liabilities totalled $90,000 on December 31, 2008.
4. Long-term liabilities totalled $212,500 on December 31, 2008.
5. Net capital expenditures for 2009 are $70,000.

Calculate the following for 2009:
a. cash current debt coverage ratio
b. free cash flow
c. cash total debt coverage ratio

5. Please refer to the Domtar and Cascades financial statements found in the appendices at the end of this study guide for information for answering the following questions. Do not forget to use the **Decision Toolkit** approach to help in the problem solving.

   (SO2, 3)

   a.   What method—indirect or direct—do Domtar and Cascades use in their preparation of their cash flow statements?

   b.   In 2007, did Cascades have a net increase or decrease in cash?

   c.   In 2007, what is Cascades' largest use of cash?

   d.   Calculate and compare the cash current and total debt coverage ratios for 2007 for Domtar and Cascades.

Solutions to Self-Test

Multiple Choice

1. b   Operating activities deal with statement of earnings items and with current assets and current liabilities. Financing activities deal with short-term notes and long-term liabilities and with shareholders' equity items.

2. a   It is critical that a company generate its cash flow from operating activities, not from investing and financing activities.

3. c   Significant noncash activities are reported but not in the body of the cash flow statement. They do not appear on the statement of earnings.

4. c   The main purpose of the cash flow statement is to provide information that enables its users to assess a company's ability to generate cash, and the needs of the company in using these cash flows.

5. a   Noncash items, such as depreciation expense, may be greater than a reported net loss and thus create a net increase in cash.

6. d   The information to prepare the cash flow statement usually comes from three sources:

        1.   The comparative balance sheet.

        2.   The statement of earnings.

        3.   Additional information.

7. c   A change in a current asset is an operating activity, not an investing or a financing activity. The decrease in receivables is not a deduction from net earnings.

8. d   A change in a current asset is an operating activity, not an investing or a financing activity. The increase in prepaid expenses is not an addition to net earnings.

9. d   Cash is not involved in this transaction; therefore it is not an operating, investing, or financing activity. It is a noncash transaction.

10. b $500,000 - $50,000 = $450,000

11. a $300,000 + $100,000 = $400,000

12. b $300,000 + $100,000 - $30,000 = $370,000

13. b   To determine the net cash provided (or used) by operating activities under the indirect method, net earnings is adjusted for items that did not affect cash.

14. a   A gain is deducted from net earnings (not added) to determine cash provided by operating activities.

15. a $500,000 – $125,000 – $40,000 = $335,000

16. c   Measures of liquidity include the current ratio and the cash current debt coverage ratio.

17. b   The cash current debt coverage ratio measures a company's ability to generate sufficient cash from operating activities to meet its current obligations.

18. b   Use of the indirect method affects only the operating activities section of the statement but it is important to note that both methods arrive at the same total amount for "Net cash provided (used) by operating activities." The investing and financing activities sections are prepared in the same way under both methods.

Problems

1.

PANTHER CORPORATION
Cash Flow Statement
Year Ended December 31, 2009

Operating activities		
Net earnings		$2,140
Adjustments to reconcile net earnings to net cash provided by operating activities:		
Depreciation expense	$ 60	
Decrease in inventory	600	
Increase in accounts payable	600	
Increase in accounts receivable	(900)	
Decrease in accrued liabilities	(100)	260
Net cash provided by operating activities		2,400
Investing activities		
Sale of long-term investments	$ 240	
Purchase of equipment	(400)	
Net cash used by investing activities		(160)
Financing activities		
Issue of common shares	$ 400	
Retirement of bonds payable	(300)	
Payment of cash dividends	(1,040)	
Net cash used by financing activities		(940)
Net increase in cash		1,300
Cash, January 1		2,300
Cash, December 31		$3,600

Without other information available, the assumption is that the increase in Equipment is due to a cash purchase. The decrease in Long-Term Investments is attributed to a sale of these. The decrease in Bonds Payable is attributed to a retirement of some bonds, and the increase in Common Shares is assumed to be from a sale of shares for cash. The increase of $1,100 in Retained Earnings is due to net earnings of $2,140 less dividends declared and paid of $1,040.

2.

WARNON CORPORATION
Cash Flow Statement (partial)
Year Ended December 31, 2009

Operating activities

Cash receipts from customers		$11,700,000 (1)
Cash payments:		
To suppliers	$8,325,000 (2)	
For operating expenses	1,830,000 (3)	10,155,000
Net cash provided by operating activities		1,545,000

Schedules:

(1) Sales	$12,300,000
Deduct: Increase in accounts receivable	600,000
Cash receipts from customers	$11,700,000
(2) Cost of goods sold	$8,100,000
Add: Increase in inventory	375,000
Purchases	8,475,000
Deduct: Increase in accounts payable	150,000
Cash payments to suppliers	$8,325,000
(3) Operating expenses	$1,800,000
Add: Increase in prepaid expenses	300,000
	2,100,000
Deduct: Increase in accrued expenses payable	270,000
Cash payments for operating expenses	$1,830,000

3.   To calculate the cash received from the sale of equipment, the accumulated depreciation for the equipment that was sold is determined as follows: Original cost $38,000 – Carrying amount $7,000 = $31,000.

The cash received from sale of equipment is derived from the following journal entry:

Cash	9,500	
Accumulated Depreciation—Equipment	31,000	
Gain on Sale of Equipment		2,500
Equipment		38,000

The cash paid for purchase of equipment is obtained from an analysis of the following T-account:

Equipment			
Opening bal.	175,000		
Purchase of equipment	63,000	Sale of equipment	38,000
Ending balance	200,000		

The following T-account would be balanced as indicated:

Accumulated Depreciation—Equipment			
		Opening balance	95,000
Sale of equipment	31,000	Depreciation expense	24,000
		Ending balance	88,000

4. To calculate the ratios, the following needs to be calculated:

Current liabilities, December 31, 2009:

Accounts payable	$ 25,000
Interest payable	11,000
Notes payable, due April 1, 2010	20,000
Provincial sales tax payable	8,000
Wages payable	2,000
Current portion of mortgage payable	20,000
Total current liabilities	86,000

Long-term liabilities, December 31, 2009:

Bonds payable due July 1, 2020		87,500
Mortgage payable	$150,000	
Less: current portion	20,000	130,000
Total long-term liabilities		217,500
Total liabilities		$303,500

a. Current debt coverage ratio = cash provided by operating activities divided by average current liabilities
Cash provided by operating activities = $139,750
Average current liabilities: ($90,000 + $86,000) ÷2 = $88,000
Cash current debt coverage ratio: $139,750 ÷ $88,000 = 1.6 times

b. Cash flow = cash provided by operating activities – net capital expenditures – dividends = $139,750 – $70,000 – $10,000 = $59,750

c. Total debt coverage ratio = cash provided by operating activities divided by average total liabilities
Cash provided by operating activities = $139,750
Total liabilities, December 31, 2008: $90,000 + $212,500 = $302,500
Average total liabilities: ($302,500 + $303,500) ÷ 2 = $303,000
Cash total debt coverage ratio: $139,750 ÷ $303,000 = 0.5 times

5.   (Domtar $ in USD millions; Cascades $ in CAD millions)

a.   In order to answer this question, you need to look at the operating activities section of the cash flow statement. Both companies report net earnings and add noncash items and changes in working capital items. This would indicate the use of the indirect method. The direct method does not include net earnings (loss). Net cash provided by operating activities is calculated by adjusting each item on the statement of earnings from an accrual to a cash basis.

b.   Cascades had a net decrease in cash of $9, as shown near the end of the cash flow statement. This increase explains the change from $34 in 2006 to $25 in 2007 in the cash and cash equivalents account shown on the balance sheet.

c.   Cascades' largest use of cash was the additions to property, plant, and equipment of $167, as shown in the investing activities section.

d.

Domtar:

Cash current debt coverage ratio:

$$\frac{\$606}{(\$895 + \$268) \div 2} = 1.0 \text{ times}$$

Cash total debt coverage ratio:

$$\frac{\$606}{(* \$4,551 + \$1,083) \div 2} = 0.2 \text{ times}$$

*Total liabilities (2007) = $895 + $2,213 + $1,003 + $440 = $4,551
             (2006) = $268 + $32 + $758 + $25 = $1,083

Cascades:

Cash current debt coverage ratio:

$$\frac{\$89}{(\$623 + \$658) \div 2} = 0.1 \text{ times}$$

Cash total debt coverage ratio:

$$\frac{\$89}{(\$2,570 + \$2,754) \div 2} = 0.0 \text{ times}$$

Domtar's cash coverage ratios are far stronger than those of Cascades for 2007.

chapter 14

Performance Measurement

Chapter Overview

The purpose of this chapter is to explain the importance of performance measurement in serving the interests of users. In this chapter, you will learn about sustainable earnings, comparative analysis, and the limitations of financial analysis.

Review of Specific Study Objectives

- **Sustainable earnings** are the levels of earnings that are most likely to be obtained in the future. They differ from actual net earnings by the amount of irregular (i.e., non-typical) revenues, expenses, gains, and losses that are included in net earnings. There are two types of irregular items in this chapter—discontinued operations and changes in accounting principle.

study objective 1

Understand the concept of sustainable earnings and indicate how irregular items are presented.

- **Discontinued operations** refers to the disposal or availability for sale, of an identifiable operating segment of a business, such as the elimination of a separate subsidiary company or an operating division of a company. The effect on the balance sheet and statement of earnings is as follows. Assets (net of any related liabilities) that are held for sale as discontinued operations are valued and reported on the balance sheet at the lower of their carrying amount and fair value (less any anticipated costs of selling). They retain their original classification as assets or liabilities, and are reported as current or noncurrent. Once an asset has been classified as held for sale, no additional depreciation is recognized. When a company disposes of, or plans to dispose, one of its operating segments, the disposal is reported separately on the statement of earnings as an irregular item called discontinued operations. The discontinued operations item can consist of two parts: the earnings (loss) from the discontinued operations and the gain (loss) on the disposal of the segment. The gain (loss) on disposal, of course, only exists if the operating segment has been actually disposed of. Both the operating earnings or loss and the disposal gain or loss are reported net of income taxes.

- Another type of irregular item, one that affects prior-period earnings, is a **change in accounting principle**. A change in accounting principle occurs when the principle used in the current year is different from the one used in the preceding year. When a change is made, it is classified as either voluntary or mandatory. A voluntary change in accounting principle is allowed when management can show that the new accounting principle results in a more reliable and relevant presentation of events or transactions in the financial statements. Examples of voluntary changes include changes in the method used for depreciation and in the cost formula used for inventory. A mandatory change in accounting principle is one that is required by **standard setters**. We can expect to see more of these in the next few years as Canadian standards move closer to international financial reporting standards.

  Changes in accounting principles affect financial reporting in four ways:

  1. The cumulative effect of the change in accounting principle should be reported (net of income tax) as an adjustment to opening retained earnings. Since prior-period earnings are affected, a change in accounting principle must be reported in the retained earnings section of the statement of shareholders' equity (or in the statement of retained earnings), rather than on the current period's statement of earnings.
  2. The new principle should be used for reporting the results of operations in the current year.
  3. All prior-period financial statements should be restated to make comparisons easier.
  4. The effects of the change should be detailed and disclosed in a note.

- **For data to be meaningful, it must be compared with something**. Comparisons may be as follows:

  1. Intracompany comparisons. Comparisons may be made within a company on a year-to-year basis to detect changes in financial relationships and significant trends.
  2. Intercompany comparisons. Comparisons with other companies provide insight into a company's competitive position.
  3. Industry comparisons. Comparisons with industry averages provide information about a company's relative position within the industry.

- **Three basic tools** are used in financial statement analysis: horizontal analysis, vertical analysis, and ratio analysis.

study objective 2

Explain and apply horizontal analysis.

- **Horizontal analysis,** also called **trend analysis**, is a technique for evaluating a series of financial statement data over a period of time. Its purpose is to determine the increase or decrease that has taken place, expressed as either an amount or a percentage.

- Horizontal analysis can be calculated as a percentage of a base-period amount or as a percentage change for the period.

- A company has net sales of $100,000 in 2007, $110,000 in 2008, and $116,000 in 2009. Assume that 2007 is the base year. The formula for calculating the percentage of the base-period amount is:

$$\frac{\text{Analysis-Period Amount}}{\text{Base-Period Amount}}$$

In our example, net sales in 2008 are 110% of the base year:

$$\frac{\$110,000}{\$100,000} = 110\%$$

For 2009, net sales are 116% of the base year:

$$\frac{\$116,000}{\$100,000} = 116\%$$

Note that the base-period amount is always the first year, or $100,000 in this case.

If, instead, we wanted to calculate the changes for each period, rather than from a base period, the formula for calculating the percentage change for the period is:

$$\frac{\text{Dollar Amount of Change Since Base Period}}{\text{Base-Period Amount}}$$

In our example, net sales in 2008 increased $10,000, or 10 percent, over 2007.

$$\frac{\$110,000 - \$100,000}{\$100,000} = 10\%$$

For the year 2009, net sales increased 5 percent, over 2008.

$$\frac{\$116,000 - \$110,000}{\$110,000} = 5\%$$

- An **advantage of using horizontal analysis** is that it helps highlight the significance of a change by reducing the change to a percentage. Sometimes, it is difficult to see the magnitude of a change when only the dollar amount is examined.

- **Several complications can arise while using horizontal analysis.** If an item has no value in a base year or preceding year and a value in the next year, then no percentage change can be calculated. If a negative number appears in the base year or preceding year and a positive amount exists the next year, or vice versa, then no percentage change can be calculated.

- **Vertical analysis**, also called **common size analysis**, is a technique for evaluating financial statement data, which expresses each item in a financial statement as a percentage of a base amount. On the balance sheet, assets are usually expressed as percentages of total assets and liability, and shareholders' equity items are usually expressed as percentages of total liabilities and shareholders' equity. On the statement of earnings, items are usually expressed as percentages of net sales.

> study objective 3
>
> Explain and apply vertical analysis.

- When comparative balance sheets and statements of earnings are presented, vertical analysis shows not only the relative size of each category in each year on the balance sheet and on the statement of earnings, but also the percentage change in the individual items on the two financial statements.

- If current assets are $2,200 and total assets are $9,000, then current assets are 24.4 percent of total assets ($2,200 ÷ $9,000).

- Just as is true with horizontal analysis, an **advantage of vertical analysis** is that it helps highlight the significance of a change by reducing the change to a percentage. It also helps when making comparisons between companies of different sizes.

study objective 4

Identify and calculate ratios used to analyze liquidity, solvency, and profitability.

- Ratios can be classified into three types: **liquidity**, which measures the short-term ability of the company to pay its maturing obligations and to meet unexpected needs for cash; **solvency**, which measures a company's ability to survive in the long term; and **profitability**, which measures the earnings or operating success of a company for a specific period of time.

- The following are **liquidity ratios**:

  1. **Current ratio** is calculated by dividing current assets by current liabilities. If the current ratio is 1.25:1, then the company has $1.25 of current assets for every $1 of current liabilities. This ratio can also be expressed as an equation. The difference between current assets and current liabilities is called **working capital**.
  2. **Inventory turnover** is calculated by dividing cost of goods sold by average inventory. If the ratio is eight times, then the company sold its inventory eight times during the accounting period. Since the business of a merchandiser is to sell inventory, this ratio is very closely monitored. If it shows significant change in either direction, then action is taken. This ratio varies widely among industries.
  3. **Days in inventory** is calculated by dividing 365 by the inventory turnover. Using the eight times from the previous ratio, the average days in inventory number is 46.5 days. The company takes approximately 46 days to sell its inventory.
  4. **Receivables turnover** is calculated by dividing net credit sales by average gross accounts receivable. Companies seldom disclose their net credit sales, and so total sales are often used as a substitute. This ratio measures the number of times, on an average, receivables are collected during this period. If the ratio is 12.5 times, then the company collects its receivables 12.5 times during the accounting period.
  5. **Average collection period** is calculated by dividing 365 by the receivables turnover. Using the 12.5 times from the previous ratio, the average collection period for this company is 29.2 days (365 ÷ 12.5). The general rule is that the collection period should not greatly exceed the credit term period (the time allowed for payment).
  6. **Cash current debt coverage ratio** is calculated by dividing cash provided (used) by operating activities by average current liabilities. Instead of using the numerator and denominator balances from just one point in time, this ratio uses numbers covering a period of time and thus may provide a better representation of liquidity. If the ratio is 0.5 times, then the company has $0.50 of cash provided by operating activities for every $1 of current liabilities. This ratio is cash based, not accrual based.

In the case of the current ratio, inventory turnover, receivables turnover, and cash current debt coverage ratio, the higher the ratio, the better the result. In some cases, a high current ratio may not be good, as it may be artificially inflated by slow moving inventory and receivables. It is always wise to check that the inventory and receivables turnover ratios are improving and not deteriorating before evaluating the current ratio. In the case of the days in inventory and average collection period ratios, lower is better (fewer days to sell inventory or collect receivables). This is the case because these ratios are the inverse of the turnover ratios.

- The following are **solvency ratios**:

  1. **Debt to total assets** is calculated by dividing total liabilities by total assets. It measures the percentage of the total assets provided by creditors and provides some indication of the company's ability to withstand losses without impairing the interests of its creditors. If the ratio is 65 percent, then creditors have provided financing sufficient to cover 65 percent of the company's total assets. The higher the percentage of liabilities to total assets, the greater the risk that the company may be unable to pay its debts; therefore, creditors usually like to see a low ratio. The debt to equity ratio shows the relative use of borrowed funds compared with resources invested by the owners.

  2. **Free cash flow** is calculated by subtracting the sum of capital expenditures and dividends paid from cash provided (used) by operating activities. It indicates the cash available for paying dividends or expanding operations.

  3. **Times interest earned** is calculated by dividing earnings before interest expense and income tax expense (EBIT) by interest expense. EBIT can also be calculated by adding back interest expense and income tax expense to net earnings (net earnings + interest expense + income tax expense). This ratio indicates the company's ability to meet interest payments as they come due. If the ratio is 13 times, then the company has earnings before interest and taxes that is 13 times the amount needed for interest expense.

  4. **Cash total debt coverage** is calculated by dividing cash provided (used) by operating activities by average total liabilities. It indicates a company's ability to repay its debts from cash generated from operating activities without having to liquidate the assets used in its operations. If the ratio is 0.24 times, then net cash generated from one year of operations is sufficient to pay off 24 percent of the company's total liabilities. This ratio is cash based, not accrual based.

Except for the debt to total assets ratio, where lower is better, the higher the ratio or measure, the better the result is for all the other solvency ratios.

- The following are **profitability ratios**, divided into corporate measures and investor measures (profitability is used frequently as the ultimate test of management's operating effectiveness):

Corporate Measures

1. **Gross profit margin** is calculated by dividing gross profit by net sales. It indicates a company's ability to maintain an adequate selling price above its costs. The more competition there is in an industry, the lower will be the gross profit margin. If the gross profit margin is 58 percent, then each dollar of net sales generates a gross profit of $0.58.

2. **Profit margin** is calculated by dividing net earnings by net sales. This is a measure of the percentage of each dollar of sales that results in net earnings. If the ratio is 12 percent, then each dollar of sales results in $0.12 of net earnings. High-volume enterprises (grocery stores) generally have low profit margins, whereas low-volume enterprises (jewellery stores) usually have high profit margins. Two factors strongly influence this ratio: the gross profit margin and the control of operating expenses.

3. **Return on assets** is calculated by dividing net earnings by average total assets. It measures the rate earned on each dollar invested in assets.

4. **Asset turnover** is calculated by dividing net sales by average total assets. It measures how efficiently a company uses its assets to generate sales. This ratio varies widely among industries.

5. **Return on common shareholders' equity** is calculated by dividing earnings available to common shareholders (net earnings less preferred dividends) by average common shareholders' equity. The numerator is the difference between net earnings and preferred dividends declared for the period, if any. The denominator is total shareholders' equity less the amount (if any) in the preferred shares account. This ratio shows how many dollars of net earnings were earned for each dollar invested by the shareholders.

Investor Measures

1. **Earnings per share** is calculated by taking net earnings available to common shareholders (net earnings less preferred dividends) and dividing that sum by the weighted average number of common shares (where the shares are weighted based on the time they have been outstanding). It is a measure of the net earnings earned on common shares. If earnings per share is $2.05, then $2.05 of net earnings was earned on each common share. Earnings per share are generally not comparable between companies because of differing capital structures.

2. **Price-earnings ratio** is calculated by dividing the market price per common share by earnings per share. It measures the ratio of the market price of each share to the earnings per share. If the price-earnings ratio is 23, then each share sold for 23 times the amount that was earned on each share.

3. **Payout ratio** is calculated by dividing cash dividends declared on common shares by net earnings. It measures the percentage of earnings distributed in the form of cash dividends. Growth companies have low payout ratios because they reinvest earnings in the business.

4. **Dividend yield** is calculated by dividing earnings per share by market price per share. It measures earnings generated by each share, based on the share price.

For all profitability ratios, the higher the ratio, the better the result.

- **Availability of information** is not a problem in financial statement analysis. The goal is to perform relevant analysis and select pertinent comparative data, as well as to know what ratio will give the answer to the question being asked.

study objective 5

Understand the limitations of financial analysis.

- Before relying on the information you have gathered through your horizontal, vertical, and ratio analyses, you must understand the limitations of these tools and of the financial statements they are based on. Some of the factors that can limit the usefulness of your analysis include alternative accounting principles, professional judgement, inflation, and diversification.

- Variations among companies in the application of **generally accepted accounting principles** (GAAP) may lessen comparability of their statements. Companies may choose from a large number of acceptable accounting policies, such as different inventory cost flow assumptions or depreciation methods. Different choices result in differing financial positions, which affect comparability. Also, in an increasing number of industries, competition is global, which means that investors must make comparisons with companies from other countries.

Even if we are able to adequately compare different accounting principles, we must accept that management has to use **professional judgement** in choosing the most appropriate principle for the circumstances. In addition, numerous estimates are required in preparing financial information. To the extent that these estimates are inaccurate or biased, ratios and percentages that are based on such information will also be inaccurate or biased. Fortunately, the chief executive officer and chief financial officer of publicly traded companies must ensure and personally declare that the reported financial information is accurate, relevant, and understandable. In addition, audit committees are held responsible for questioning management on the degree of aggressiveness or conservatism that has been applied, and the quality of the underlying accounting principles, key estimates, and judgements.

- Our accounting information system does not adjust data for price-level changes. In Canada, inflation is not very significant right now.

- Diversification in Canadian industries also can limit the usefulness of financial analysis. Many firms today are so diversified that they cannot be classified by industry. Because of this diversification, analysts must be careful in interpreting consolidated financial statements. When companies have significant operations in different lines of business, they are required to report additional disclosures in a segment information note to their financial statements. Many analysts say that segment information is the most important data in the financial statements, especially when comparing diversified companies.

Chapter Self-Test

As you work through the questions and problems, remember to use the **Decision Toolkit** discussed and used in the text:

1. *Decision Checkpoints*: At this point, you ask a question.
2. *Info Needed for Decision*: You make a choice regarding the information needed to answer the question.
3. *Tool to Use for Decision*: At this point, you review just what the information chosen in step two does for the decision-making process.
4. *How to Evaluate Results*: You conduct an evaluation of information for answering the question.

Note: The notation (SO1) means that the question was drawn from study objective number one.

Multiple Choice

Please circle the correct answer.

1. The discontinued operations section of the statement of earnings refers to   (SO1)
   a.   discontinuance of a product line.
   b.   the earnings or loss on products that have been completed and sold.
   c.   obsolete equipment and discontinued inventory items.
   d.   the disposal of an identifiable operating segment of a business.

2. Sustainable earnings   (SO1)
   a.   refer to earnings that were obtained in the past.
   b.   include a once-in-a-lifetime gain.
   c.   are the level of earnings that are most likely to be obtained in the future.
   d.   include irregular items such as discontinued operations.

(SO3)   3. A change in accounting principle appears on the
         a.   statement of earnings net of income taxes, below Earnings from Continuing
              Operations.
         b.   statement of shareholders' equity in the retained earnings section.
         c.   statement of comprehensive income.
         d.   cash flow statement.

(SO1)   4. Which of the following is a type of comparison that provides decision usefulness
             of financial information?
         a.   Industry averages
         b.   Intercompany basis
         c.   Intracompany basis
         d.   All of the above provide decision usefulness.

(SO2)   5. Total current liabilities are $10,000 in 2007, $18,000 in 2008, and $22,000 in 2009.
             What is the percentage of a base-period amount in 2009, assuming 2007 is the
             base year?
         a.   22 percent
         b.   120 percent
         c.   122 percent
         d.   220 percent

(SO3)   6. Consider the following data for Elizabeth Corporation:

         Net sales $100,000
         – Cost of goods sold   30,000
         Gross profit   70,000
         – Operating expenses   50,000
         Net earnings $ 20,000

             Performing vertical analysis and using net sales as the base, what percentage
             of net sales is cost of goods sold?
         a.   20 percent
         b.   30 percent
         c.   70 percent
         d.   333 percent (rounded)

(SO4)   7. Measures of a company's ability to survive over a long period of time
             are called
         a.   liquidity ratios.
         b.   solvency ratios.
         c.   profitability ratios.
         d.   vertical analysis.

(SO4)   8. _____ is frequently used as the ultimate test of management's operating
             effectiveness.
         a.   Net earnings
         b.   Liquidity

c.   Solvency
d.   Profitability

Please use the following data for questions 9 through 11.

Current assets	$150,000
Total assets	500,000
Current liabilities	125,000
Total liabilities	200,000
Net credit sales	600,000
Cost of goods sold	160,000
Average accounts receivable	50,000
Average inventory	40,000

9.   What is the receivables turnover?   (SO4)
   a.   3.2 times
   b.   4 times
   c.   12 times
   d.   15 times

10.   What is the inventory turnover?   (SO4)
   a.   3.2 times
   b.   4 times
   c.   12 times
   d.   15 times

11.   What is the debt to total assets ratio?   (SO4)
   a.   25.0 percent
   b.   40.0 percent
   c.   62.5 percent
   d.   83.3 percent

12.   Net sales are $6,000,000, net earnings are $800,000, earnings available to com-   (SO4)
      mon shareholders are $700,000, and the weighted average number of common
      shares issued is 300,000. What is the profit margin?
   a.   13.3 percent
   b.   11.7 percent
   c. $2.67
   d. $2.33

13.   Net sales are $6,000,000, net earnings are $800,000, earnings available to com-   (SO4)
      mon shareholders are $700,000, and the weighted average number of common
      shares issued is 300,000. What is the earnings per share?
   a.   13.3 percent
   b.   11.7 percent
   c. $2.67
   d. $2.33

(SO4)   14. Which of the following is considered a profitability ratio?
a.   Price-earnings ratio
b.   Times interest earned
c.   Average collection period
d.   Cash current debt coverage

(SO4)   15. Which of the following is considered a solvency ratio?
a.   Price-earnings ratio
b.   Times interest earned
c.   Average collection period
d.   Cash current debt coverage

(SO5)   16. A factor that affects the usefulness of financial analysis is
a.   management style of corporate executives.
b.   professional judgement.
c.   extraordinary items.
d.   sustainable earnings.

(SO1)   17. Comparisons of financial data made within a company are called
a.   intracompany comparisons.
b.   interior comparisons.
c.   intercompany comparisons.
d.   intramural comparisons.

Problems

Note: See Illustrations 14–7 through 14–9 in the textbook for a description of each ratio.

(SO4)   1. Selected information from the comparative financial statements of Fallis Ltd. for the year ended December 31, appears below:

	2009	2008
Accounts receivable	$ 150,000	$170,000
Inventory	110,000	130,000
Total assets	1,170,000	770,000
Current liabilities	110,000	80,000
Long-term debt	370,000	270,000
Total liabilities	480,000	350,000
Net credit sales	1,470,000	670,000
Cost of goods sold	570,000	500,000
Depreciation expense	25,000	1,000
Interest expense	20,000	5,000
Income tax expense	30,000	9,000
Net earnings	120,000	55,000
Net cash provided by operating activities	210,000	105,000

Preferred dividends paid	8,000	7,500
Common dividends paid	12,000	11,000
Net capital expenditures	115,000	108,000
Market price per share	28	25
Weighted average number of common shares	30,000	30,000

Calculate the following for the year ended December 31, 2009:
  a. Liquidity ratios
  b. Solvency ratios
  c. Profitability ratios

2. State the effect of the following transactions on a current ratio of 1.5 to 1. (SO4)
    Use increase, decrease, or no effect for your answer.
    a. Collection of an accounts receivable.
    b. Declaration of cash dividends.
    c. Additional shares are sold for cash.
    d. Accounts payable are paid.
    e. Equipment is purchased for cash.
    f. Inventory purchases are made for cash.
    g. Short-term investments are purchased for cash.

3. The following selected profitability ratios are available for two companies, Pace (SO4)
    Corporation and Moly Corporation, and their industry, for a recent fiscal year:

Ratio	Pace	Moly	Industry
Gross profit margin	36.5%	42.2%	35.9%
Profit margin	4.2%	3.9%	3.8%
Return on common shareholders' equity	18.3%	12.4%	12.0%
Return on assets	6.6%	6.2%	5.8%
Asset turnover	1.6 times	1.6 times	1.5 times
Payout ratio	18.9%	57.1%	36.5%
Earnings per share	$1.28	$1.56	$1.19
Price-earnings ratio	14.1 times	15.0 times	N/A

    a. Which company is more profitable? Explain.
    b. Which company do investors favour? Is your answer consistent with your
        findings in (a)?

4. The following selected solvency ratios are available for two companies, Olama
    Corporation and Yomanda Corporation, and their industry, for a recent fiscal year:

Ratio	Olama	Yomanda	Industry
Debt to total assets	45.5%	37.2%	45.3%
Times interest earned	3.7 times	7.6 times	7.2 times

Which company is more solvent? Explain.

5.   Please refer to the Domtar and Cascades financial statements found in the appendices at the end of this study guide for information for answering the following questions. Do not forget to use the **Decision Toolkit** approach for help in the problem solving.

(SO3)   a.   In Chapter 5, the profit margin was calculated as 1.2 percent of net sales for Domtar and 2.4 percent for Cascades for 2007. Using vertical analysis, explain the difference between the two companies' profit margins.

(SO3)   b.   Comment on your results obtained in (a) above.

(SO3)   c.   Using horizontal analysis with 2005 as the base year, determine the direction in net sales and cost of sales since 2005 for both companies?

(SO5)   d.   Using your results obtained in (a) and (d) above, what further conclusions can you make regarding the profitability of the companies?

(SO1)   e.   Are there any discontinued operations from Domtar and/or Cascades?

Solutions to Self-Test

Multiple Choice

1. d   When a company disposes of one of its operating segments, the disposal is reported separately on the statement of earnings as an irregular item called discontinued operations.

2. c   Sustainable earnings are the levels of earnings that are most likely to be obtained in the future. They differ from actual net earnings by the amount of irregular (i.e., non-typical) revenues, expenses, gains, and losses that are included in net earnings.

3. b   Changes in accounting principle are reported net of tax as an adjustment to opening retained earnings in the statement of retained earnings.

4. d

5. d $22,000 \div $10,000 = 220\%$

6. b $30,000 \div $100,000 = 30\%$

7. b   Liquidity refers to a company's short-term ability to pay obligations as they arise, and profitability measures the operating success of a business for a given period of time. Vertical analysis relates to a given period of time as well.

8. d   Net earnings is simply the difference between revenues and expenses, and liquidity and solvency refer to the company's ability to survive on short-term and long-term bases, respectively.

9. c $600,000 \div $50,000 = 12$ times

10. b $160,000 \div $40,000 = 4$ times

11. b $200,000 \div $500,000 = 40.0\%$

12. a $800,000 \div $6,000,000 = 13.3\%$

13. d $700,000 \div 300,000$ shares $= 2.33

14. a   Times interest earned is a solvency ratio, and average collection
         period and the cash current debt coverage are liquidity measures.

15. b   The price-earnings ratio is a profitability ratio and the average
         collection period and cash current debt coverage ratios are liquidity
         measures.

16. b   Some of the factors that can limit the usefulness of financial analysis
         include alternative accounting principles, professional judgement,
         inflation, and diversification.

17. a   Intracompany analysis compares an item or financial relationship
         inside a company within the current year or with one or more prior
         years.

Problems

1. a.   **Liquidity ratios are:**
         Current ratio:

$$\frac{\$150,000 + \$110,000}{\$110,000} = 2.4:1$$

Inventory turnover:

$$\frac{\$570,000}{(\$110,000 + \$130,000) \div 2} = 4.8 \text{ times}$$

Days in inventory:

$$\frac{365}{4.8} = 76.0 \text{ days}$$

Receivables turnover:

$$\frac{\$1,470,000}{(\$150,000 + \$170,000) \div 2} = 9.2 \text{ times}$$

Average collection period:

$$\frac{365}{9.2} = 40 \text{ days}$$

Cash current debt coverage:

$$\frac{\$210,000}{(\$110,000 + \$80,000) \div 2} = 2.2 \text{ times}$$

b.   **Solvency ratios are:**

Debt to total assets:

$$\frac{\$110,000 + \$370,000}{\$1,170,000} = 41.0\%$$

Free cash flow:

$$\$210,000 - \$115,000 - \$8,000 - \$12,000 = \$75,000$$

Times interest earned:

$$\frac{\$120,000 + \$30,000 + \$20,000}{\$20,000} = 8.5 \text{ times}$$

Cash total debt coverage:

$$\frac{\$210,000}{(\$480,000 + \$350,000) \div 2} = 0.5 \text{ times}$$

c.   **Profitability ratios are:**

Earnings per share:

$$\frac{\$120,000 - \$8,000}{30,000 \text{ common shares}} = \$3.73 \text{ per share}$$

Price-earnings ratio:

$$\frac{\$28.00}{\$3.73} = 7.5 \text{ times}$$

Gross profit margin:

$$\frac{\$1,470,000 - \$570,000}{\$1,470,000} = 61.2\%$$

Profit margin:

$$\frac{\$120,000}{\$1,470,000} = 8.2\%$$

Return on assets:

$$\frac{\$120,000}{(\$1,170,000 + \$770,000) \div 2} = 12.4\%$$

Asset turnover:

$$\frac{\$1,470,000}{(\$1,170,000 + \$770,000) \div 2} = 1.5 \text{ times}$$

Payout ratio on preferred shares:

$$\frac{\$8,000}{\$120,000} = 6.7\%$$

Payout ratio on common shares:

$$\frac{\$12,000}{\$120,000} = 10.0\%$$

Dividend yield on common shares:

$$\frac{\$12,000 \div 30,000 \text{ shares}}{\$28 \text{ per share}} = 1.4\%$$

Return on common shareholders' equity:

$$\frac{\$120,000 - \$8,000}{(\$690,000 + \$420,000) \div 2^*} = 20.2\%$$

(*Shareholders' equity = Total assets – Total liabilities:
$1,170,000 – $480,000 = $690,000 for 2009: $770,000 – $350,000 = $420,000
for 2008)

2.

a. no effect (no effect on current assets: cash increases and accounts receivable decreases)
b. decrease (current liabilities increase: retained earnings decreases and dividends payable increases)
c. increase (current assets increase: cash increases, share capital increases)
d. increase (current liabilities decrease and current assets decrease by the same amount but the proportionate impact is likely higher for the denominator: accounts payable decrease and cash decreases. Assume current assets were $150 and current liabilities $100 before the payment and $125 and $75 after the payment. The current ratio increases from 1.5:1 to 1.7:1.)
e. decrease (current assets decrease: equipment increases and cash decreases)
f. no effect (no effect on current assets: inventory increases and cash decreases)
g. no effect (no effect on current assets: short-term investments increase and cash decreases)

3. a.   Both companies appear to be profitable. The Moly Corporation has a higher gross profit margin than the Pace Corporation, but both companies have a profit margin that is higher than that of the industry. It would appear that Moly does not do as good a job as Pace at controlling its operating expenses, as Pace has the higher profit margin.

Pace appears to be more profitable than Moly as well when comparing return ratios (return on common shareholders' equity and return on assets), most likely because of its higher net earnings. Pace's profit margin and return ratios are also above those of the industry. All of this would indicate that Pace is the more profitable company.

   b.   Despite the findings in (a) that Pace is the more profitable company, investors seem to favour Moly because it has the higher price-earnings ratio. This is not consistent with the above analysis, as you would expect investors to favour the more profitable company. Investors are likely favouring Moly because of the larger payout ratio. Alternatively, investors may be anticipating better future profitability from Moly.

4.   Yomanda appears to be the more solvent of the two companies. Yomanda has a lower debt to total assets ratio, indicating that it has a lower percentage of its assets financed by debt. As well, Yomanda has a higher times interest earned ratio indicating that it has a better ability to service its debt as interest payments become due. When looking at the debt to total assets, Olama appears to be on par with the average company in the industry. However, when assessing Olama's ability to service its debt (as indicated by the times interest earned ratio) it can be seen that Olama is not as solvent as the average firm in the industry.

5. a.

| | Year 2007 | | | |
	Domtar (U.S. $ millions)	%	Cascades ($ millions)	%
Sales	$5,947	100.0	$3,929	100.0
Cost of sales	4,757	80.0	3,201	81.5
Gross profit	1,190	20.0	728	18.5
Less operating expenses:				
Selling, general, administrative	408	6.9	390	9.9
Depreciation and amortization	471	7.9	208	5.3
Other costs (gains)	41	0.7	(14)	(0.4)
Total operating expenses	920	15.5	584	14.8
Earnings from operations	270	4.5	144	3.7
Interest expenses	171	2.8	102	2.6
Gain on foreign exchange	0	0	(59)	(1.5)
Earnings before income taxes	99	1.7	101	2.6
Income tax expense	29	0.5	11	0.3
Earnings before other items	70	1.2	90	2.3
Share of earnings from companies	0	0	24	0.6

Net earnings from continuing operations	70	1.2	114	2.9
Net gain (loss) from discontinued operations	0	0	(19)	(0.5)
Net earnings	$ 70	1.2	$ 95	2.4

b. Cascades' ratio of net earnings to sales (its profit margin) of 2.4 percent is higher than Domtar's 1.2 percent, primarily because of Cascades' lower total operating expenses and because of Cascades' gain on foreign exchange and revenue obtained from earnings of other companies. These factors more than compensated for Cascades' higher cost of sales (81.5 percent versus 80 percent). You should note that Cascades' net earnings were minimally affected (by 0.5 percent) from a net loss from discontinued operations.

c. To answer this question, you must perform a horizontal analysis where year 2005 is established as the base year and the percentage increase or decrease for each subsequent year is calculated as a percentage of the base year. The calculations are as follows:

(U.S. $ millions) Domtar:	2007	2006	2005
Sales	$5,947	$3,306	$3,267
	182%	101%	100%
Cost of sales	$4,757	$2,676	$2,784
	171%	96%	100%
($ millions) Cascades:			
Sales	$3,929	$3,278	$3,201
	123%	102%	100%
Cost of sales	$3,201	$2,657	$2,632
	122%	101%	100%

The horizontal analysis shows that for Domtar, sales have increased more rapidly over the period 2005 to 2007 than its cost of sales—182 percent compared with 171 percent. For Cascades, its sales increased slightly more from 2005 to 2007 than its cost of sales over the same period—123 percent compared with 122 percent in 2007.

d. The vertical analysis in (a) shows that cost of sales is a major expense category for both companies—80 percent for Domtar and 81.5 percent for Cascades. The horizontal analysis in (c) shows that for Domtar, sales and cost of sales increased from 2005 to 2007 but sales increased at a faster rate than cost of sales, thereby boosting net earnings.

For Cascades, the same thing happened. Sales increased from 2005 to 2007, and at a rate marginally faster than cost of sales, thereby also boosting net earnings.

e. Cascades shows a net loss from discontinued operations of $19 million.

Appendices

In this appendix and the next, we illustrate current financial reporting using the financial statements for two competitors in the forest products industry headquartered in Quebec: Domtar Corporation and Cascades Inc.

Domtar presents its financial statements in accordance with U.S. generally accepted accounting principles. Cascades presents its financial statements in accordance with Canadian generally accepted accounting principles.

Use the financial statements given in the appendices to complete the problems about Domtar and Cascades at the end of each chapter. A link to the complete financial statements of the two companies, including the notes, can be found in the Study Tools section of the companion website of the book <wiley.com/canada/kimmel>.

Appendix A: Financial Statements of Domtar Corporation

DOMTAR CORPORATION
CONSOLIDATED STATEMENT OF EARNINGS (LOSS)
(IN MILLIONS OF US DOLLARS, UNLESS OTHERWISE NOTED)

	Year ended December 30, 2007	Year ended December 31, 2006	Year ended December 25, 2005
Sales	$5,947	$3,306	$3,267
Operating expenses			
Cost of sales, excluding depreciation and amortization	4,757	2,676	2,784
Depreciation and amortization	471	311	357
Selling, general and administrative	408	174	174
Impairment of property, plant and equipment (NOTE 16)	92	—	499
Impairment of goodwill (NOTE 12)	4	749	1
Closure and restructuring costs (NOTE 16)	14	15	38
Other operating income (NOTE 7)	(69)	(63)	(8)
	5,677	3,862	3,845
Operating income (loss)	270	(556)	(578)
Interest expense (NOTE 8)	171	—	—
Earnings (loss) before income taxes	99	(556)	(578)
Income tax expense (benefit) (NOTE 9)	29	53	(100)
Net earnings (loss)	70	(609)	(478)
Per common share (in dollars) (NOTE 5)			
Net earnings (loss)			
Basic	0.15	(2.14)	(1.68)
Diluted	0.15	(2.14)	(1.68)
Weighted average number of common and exchangeable shares outstanding (millions)			
Basic	474.1	284.1	284.1
Diluted	475.9	284.1	284.1

DOMTAR CORPORATION
CONSOLIDATED BALANCE SHEETS
(IN MILLIONS OF US DOLLARS, UNLESS OTHERWISE NOTED)

	December 30, 2007	December 31, 2006
Assets		
Current assets		
Cash and cash equivalents	$ 71	$ 1
Receivables, less allowances of $9 and $2 (NOTE 10)	542	340
Inventories (NOTE 11)	936	520
Prepaid expenses	14	6
Income and other taxes receivable	53	—
Deferred income taxes (NOTE 9)	182	22
Total current assets	1,798	889
Property, plant and equipment, at cost (NOTE 13)	9,685	6,696
Accumulated depreciation (NOTE 13)	(4,323)	(3,631)
Net property, plant and equipment (NOTE 13)	5,362	3,065
Goodwill (NOTE 12)	372	14
Intangible assets, net of amortization (NOTE 14)	111	—
Other assets (NOTE 15)	105	30
Total assets	7,748	3,998
Liabilities and shareholders' equity		
Current liabilities		
Bank indebtedness	63	—
Trade and other payables (NOTE 17)	765	250
Income and other taxes payable	50	6
Long-term debt due within one year (NOTE 18)	17	12
Total current liabilities	895	268
Long-term debt (NOTE 18)	2,213	32
Deferred income taxes (NOTE 9)	1,003	758
Other liabilities and deferred credits (NOTE 19)	440	25
Commitments and contingencies (NOTE 21)		
Shareholders' equity		
Business Unit equity	—	2,852
Common stock (NOTE 20)		
$0.01 par value; authorized 2,000,000,000 shares; issued and outstanding: 471,169,959 and 1,000 shares	5	—
Exchangeable shares (NOTE 20)		
No par value; unlimited shares authorized; issued and held by nonaffiliates: 44,252,831 shares	293	—
Additional paid-in capital	2,573	—
Retained earnings	47	—
Accumulated other comprehensive income	279	63
Total shareholders' equity	3,197	2,915
Total liabilities and shareholders' equity	7,748	3,998

DOMTAR CORPORATION
CONSOLIDATED STATEMENT OF SHAREHOLDERS' EQUITY
(IN MILLIONS OF US DOLLARS, UNLESS OTHERWISE NOTED)

CONSOLIDATED STATEMENT OF SHAREHOLDERS' EQUITY	Issued and outstanding common and exchangeable stock (millions of shares)	Common stock, at par	Exchangeable shares	Business Unit equity	Additional paid-in capital	Retained earnings	Accumulated other comprehensive income	Total shareholders' equity
Balance at December 26, 2004	—	$ —	$ —	$ 4,148	$ —	$ —	$113	$ 4,261
Net loss	—	—	—	(478)	—	—	—	(478)
Foreign currency translation adjustments	—	—	—	—	—	—	(50)	(50)
Additional minimum pension liability adjustments, net of tax	—	—	—	—	—	—	(6)	(6)
Contribution from Weyerhaeuser Co	—	—	—	37	—	—	—	37
Cash flow hedge fair value adjustment, net of tax	—	—	—	—	—	—	9	9
Balance as at December 25, 2005	—	—	—	3,707	—	—	66	3,773
Net loss	—	—	—	(609)	—	—	—	(609)
Foreign currency translation adjustments	—	—	—	—	—	—	19	19
Additional minimum pension liability adjustments, net of tax	—	—	—	—	—	—	6	6
Adjustment to initially adopt SFAS 158	—	—	—	—	—	—	(12)	(12)
Distribution to Weyerhaeuser Co	—	—	—	(246)	—	—	—	(246)
Cash flow hedge fair value adjustment, net of tax	—	—	—	—	—	—	(16)	(16)
Balance at December 31, 2006	—	—	—	2,852	—	—	63	2,915
Contribution of Weyerhaeuser fine paper business to Domtar Corporation	284.1	3	—	—	—	—	—	3
Net earnings to March 6, 2007	—	—	—	23	—	—	—	23
Distribution to Weyerhaeuser Co prior to March 7, 2007	—	—	—	(1,431)	—	—	—	(1,431)
Acquisition of Domtar Inc. (NOTE 3)	231.0	2	500	—	1,032	—	—	1,534
Post closing adjustments (NOTE 1)	—	—	—	(112)	—	—	5	(107)
Transfer of business unit equity	—	—	—	(1,332)	1,332	—	—	—
Conversion of exchangeable shares	—	—	(207)	—	207	—	—	—
Issuance of common shares	0.3	—	—	—	2	—	—	2
Net earnings from March 7 to December 30, 2007 (NOTE 1)	—	—	—	—	—	47	—	47
Foreign currency translation adjustments, net of tax	—	—	—	—	—	—	250	250
Change in unrecognized losses and prior service cost related to pension and post retirement benefit plans, net of tax	—	—	—	—	—	—	(39)	(39)
Balance at December 30, 2007	515.4	5	293	—	2,573	47	279	3,197

DOMTAR CORPORATION
CONSOLIDATED STATEMENT OF COMPREHENSIVE INCOME (LOSS)
(IN MILLIONS OF US DOLLARS)

	Year ended December 30, 2007	Year ended December 31, 2006	Year ended December 25, 2005
Net earnings (loss)	$ 70	$(609)	$(478)
Other comprehensive income (loss)			
Foreign currency translation adjustments, net of tax	250	19	(50)
Additional minimum pension liability adjustment, net of tax	—	6	(6)
Change in unrecognized losses and prior service cost related to pension and post retirement benefit plans, net of tax	(39)	—	—
Net change in cash flow fair value adjustments, net of tax	—	(16)	9
Comprehensive income (loss)	281	(600)	(525)

DOMTAR CORPORATION
CONSOLIDATED STATEMENT OF CASH FLOWS
(IN MILLIONS OF US DOLLARS)

	Year ended December 30, 2007	Year ended December 31, 2006	Year ended December 25, 2005
Operating activities			
Net earnings (loss)	$ 70	$(609)	$(478)
Adjustments to reconcile net earnings (loss) to cash flows from operating activities			
Depreciation and amortization	471	311	357
Deferred income taxes (NOTE 9)	(73)	(52)	(135)
Closure and restructuring costs (NOTE 16)	14	15	38
Impairment of property, plant and equipment (NOTE 16)	92	—	499
Impairment of goodwill (NOTE 12)	4	749	1
Debt restructuring costs	25	—	—
Other	(2)	4	—
Changes in assets and liabilities, net of effects of acquisition			
Receivables	(75)	(19)	(40)
Inventories	38	43	(25)
Prepaid expenses	6	(2)	(4)
Trade and other payables	54	(79)	(9)
Income and other taxes	49	—	—
Other assets and other liabilities	(67)	(4)	(14)
Cash flows provided from operating activities	606	357	190
Investing activities			
Additions to property, plant and equipment	(116)	(64)	(113)
Proceeds from disposals of property, plant and equipment	29	1	4
Business acquisitions—cash acquired	573	—	—
Other	(1)	—	—
Cash flows provided from (used for) investing activities	485	(63)	(109)
Financing activities			
Net change in bank indebtedness	(21)	—	—
Drawdown of revolving bank credit facility	50	—	—
Issuance of short-term debt	1,350	—	—
Issuance of long-term debt	800	—	—
Repayment of short-term debt	(1,350)	—	—
Repayment of long-term debt	(311)	(7)	(6)
Debt issue costs	(39)	—	—
Premium on redemption of long-term debt	(40)	—	—
Repurchase of minority interest	(28)	—	—
Distribution to Weyerhaeuser prior to March 7, 2007	(1,431)	(287)	(76)
Other	(5)	—	—
Cash flows used for financing activities	(1,025)	(294)	(82)
Net increase (decrease) in cash and cash equivalents	66	—	(1)
Translation adjustments related to cash and cash equivalents	4	—	—
Cash and cash equivalents at beginning of year	1	1	2
Cash and cash equivalents at end of year	71	1	1

Consolidated Balance Sheets

As at December 31, 2007 and 2006 (in millions of Canadian dollars)	Note	2007	2006
Assets			
Current assets			
Cash and cash equivalents		25	34
Accounts receivable	9 a)	624	650
Inventories	6, 9 a)	555	548
		1,204	1,232
Property, plant and equipment	3, 7, 9 a)	1,886	2,063
Intangible assets	8 a)	130	91
Other assets	8 a)	237	212
Goodwill	8 b)	312	313
		3,769	3,911
Liabilities and Shareholders' Equity			
Current liabilities			
Bank loans and advances		47	42
Accounts payable and accrued liabilities		572	607
Current portion of long-term debt	9	4	9
		623	658
Long-term debt	9	1,570	1,657
Other liabilities	10	377	439
		2,570	2,754
Shareholders' equity			
Capital stock	11	517	517
Retained earnings		725	649
Accumulated other comprehensive income (loss)	20	(43)	(9)
		1,199	1,157
		3,769	3,911

Consolidated Statements of Shareholders' Equity

For each of the years in the three-year period ended December 31, 2007
(in millions of Canadian dollars)

	Note	Capital stock	Retained Earnings[3]	Accumulated other comprehensive income (loss)[3]	Shareholders' equity
					2007
Balance–Beginning of year		517	649	(9)	1,157
Cumulative impact of accounting changes	2 c), h)	–	–	1	1
Restated balance–Beginning of year		517	649	(8)	1,158
Comprehensive income:					
Net earnings for the year		–	95	–	95
Change in foreign currency translation of self-sustaining foreign subsidiaries, net of related hedging activities		–	–	(41)	(41)
Change in fair value of foreign exchange forward contracts designated as cash flow hedges[1]		–	–	4	4
Change in fair value of commodity derivative financial instruments designated as cash flow hedges[2]		–	–	2	2
Comprehensive income for the year					60
Dividends		–	(16)	–	(16)
Adjustment related to stock options		2	–	–	2
Redemption of common shares	11 e)	(2)	(3)	–	(5)
Balance–End of year		517	725	(43)	1,199

	Note	Capital stock	Retained Earnings	Accumulated other comprehensive income (loss)	Shareholders' equity
					2006
Balance–Beginning of year		264	669	(36)	897
Comprehensive income:					
Net earnings for the year		–	3	–	3
Change in foreign currency translation of self-sustaining foreign subsidiaries, net of related hedging activities		–	–	27	27
Comprehensive income for the year					30
Dividends		–	(13)	–	(13)
Net proceeds from issuance of common shares	11 c)	250	(7)	–	243
Adjustment related to stock options		4	–	–	4
Redemption of common shares		(1)	(3)	–	(4)
Balance–End of year		517	649	(9)	1,157

	Note	Capital stock	Retained Earnings	Accumulated other comprehensive income (loss)	Shareholders' equity
					2005
Balance–Beginning of year		265	783	11	1,059
Comprehensive loss:					
Net loss for the year		–	(97)	–	(97)
Change in foreign currency translation of self-sustaining foreign subsidiaries, net of related hedging activities		–	–	(47)	(47)
Comprehensive loss for the year					(144)
Dividends		–	(13)	–	(13)
Adjustment related to stock options		1	–	–	1
Redemption of common shares		(2)	(4)	–	(6)
Balance–End of year		264	669	(36)	897

1. The change in fair value of foreign exchange forward contracts designated as cash flow hedges is presented net of income taxes of $2 million and reclassification adjustments to the consolidated statement of earnings. The portion to be realized within the next twelve month is $4 million.
2. The change in fair value of commodity derivative financial instruments designated as cash flow hedges is presented net of income taxes of $1 million and reclassification adjustments to the consolidated statement of earnings. The portion to be realized within the next twelve month is $1 million.
3. The sum of retained earnings and accumulated other comprehensive income (loss) amounted to $682 million as of December 31, 2007 (2006–$640 million, 2005–$633 million).

Consolidated Statements of Earnings (Loss)

For each of the years in the three-year period ended December 31, 2007 (in millions of Canadian dollars, except per share amounts)	Note	2007	2006	2005
Sales		3,929	3,278	3,201
Cost of sales and expenses				
Cost of sales (exclusive of depreciation and amortization shown below)		3,201	2,657	2,632
Depreciation and amortization		208	161	170
Selling and administrative expenses		390	304	305
Gains on disposal and other	12	(17)	(4)	(10)
Impairment and other restructuring costs	13 a)	9	67	65
Loss (gain) on financial instruments	14 a)	(6)	(3)	10
		3,785	3,182	3,172
Operating income from continuing operations		144	96	29
Interest expense		102	79	76
Gain on derivative financial instruments	14 b)	–	–	(2)
Foreign exchange gain on long-term debt		(59)	–	(10)
		101	17	(35)
Provision for (recovery of) income taxes	15	11	6	(8)
Share of results of significantly influenced companies and dilution gain	8 a)	(27)	(8)	(7)
Non-controlling interest		3	–	–
Net earnings (loss) from continuing operations		114	19	(20)
Net loss from discontinued operations	4	(19)	(16)	(77)
Net earnings (loss) for the year		95	3	(97)
Basic net earnings (loss) from continuing operations per common share		1.14	0.23	(0.24)
Basic and diluted net earnings (loss) per common share	11 f)	0.95	0.04	(1.19)
Weighted average number of common shares outstanding during the year		99,329,472	80,941,603	81,136,576

Consolidated Statements of Cash Flows

For each of the years in the three-year period ended December 31, 2007
(in millions of Canadian dollars)

	Note	2007	2006	2005
Operating activities from continuing operations				
Net earnings (loss) from continuing operations		114	19	(20)
Adjustments for				
Depreciation and amortization		208	161	170
Gains on disposal and other	12	(29)	(4)	(10)
Impairment and other restructuring costs	13 a)	3	50	52
Unrealized loss (gain) on financial instruments	14 a)	–	(5)	9
Amortization of transitional deferred unrealized gain	14 a)	–	–	(1)
Foreign exchange gain on long-term debt		(59)	–	(10)
Future income taxes	15 a)	(22)	(28)	(29)
Share of results of significantly influenced companies and dilution gain		(27)	(8)	(7)
Non-controlling interest		3	–	–
Others		(13)	(2)	5
		178	183	159
Changes in non-cash working capital components	16 a)	(89)	35	(17)
		89	218	142
Investing activities from continuing operations				
Purchases of property, plant and equipment		(167)	(110)	(121)
Proceeds from disposal of property, plant and equipment	12 b), f)	7	–	19
Increase in other assets		(3)	(10)	(12)
Business acquisitions, net of cash acquired	5 a), b), c)	(10)	(572)	(52)
Business disposals, net of cash disposed	5 d), e)	37	8	–
		(136)	(684)	(166)
Financing activities from continuing operations				
Bank loans and advances		7	(4)	(1)
Change in revolving credit facilities, net of related expenses		100	186	159
Increase in other long-term debt		–	2	3
Payments of other long-term debt		(8)	(9)	(69)
Net proceeds from issuances of common shares	11 c)	1	242	–
Redemption of common shares	11 e)	(5)	(4)	(6)
Dividends		(16)	(13)	(13)
		79	400	73
Change in cash and cash equivalents during the year from continuing operations		32	(66)	49
Change in cash and cash equivalents from discontinued operations, including proceeds on disposal	4	(40)	56	(33)
Net change in cash and cash equivalents during the year		(8)	(10)	16
Translation adjustments on cash and cash equivalents		(1)	1	(3)
Cash and cash equivalents–Beginning of year		34	43	30
Cash and cash equivalents–End of year		25	34	43

General Journal				
Date	Account Titles and Explanation	Ref.	Debit	Credit

	Debit	Credit
